V&R Academic

NATIONAL TAIWAN
UNIVERSITY PRESS

Global East Asia

Volume 5

Edited by
Chun-chieh Huang

The volumes of this series are peer-reviewed.

Henry Rosemont Jr. / Roger T. Ames

Confucian Role Ethics

A Moral Vision for the 21st Century?

V&R unipress

National Taiwan University Press

This book series is subsidized in part by, and published in cooperation with, the Institute for Advanced Studies in Humanities and Social Sciences, National Taiwan University.

MIX
Papier aus verantwortungsvollen Quellen
FSC® C083411

Bibliographic information published by the Deutsche Nationalbibliothek

The Deutsche Nationalbibliothek lists this publication in the Deutsche Nationalbibliografie; detailed bibliographic data are available online: http://dnb.d-nb.de.

ISSN 2365-7871
ISBN 978-3-8471-0605-0 (Print, without Asia Pacific)
ISBN 978-986-350-164-0 (Print, Asia Pacific only)

You can find alternative editions of this book and additional material on our website: www.v-r.de

Printed in Germany.
Cover image: Roger Ames (left) and Henry Rosemont Jr. crossing over the Concord River on the "Rude bridge that arched the flood," to the place where "The shot heard 'round the world" was fired that began the Revolutionary War. Photo courtesy of Dona Cady, Dean of Global Education, Middlesex Community College.

Printed and bound by CPI buchbuecher.de GmbH, Zum Alten Berg 24, D-96158 Birkach, Germany.

Printed on aging-resistant paper.

Contents

Introduction

It is indisputable that there is much wrong with the world today. Many people of good will think the problems are basically political and economic, but both of us believe that the politics and economics are embedded in a conceptual framework of moralities grounded in one type of foundational individualism or another, none of which are even capable of addressing those problems any longer, much less contribute to their solutions. Thus we believe that new moralities are needed (containing some very old elements), with intellectual and psychological resources that more closely resemble the hopes, fears, dreams and aspirations of actual people than the deracinated individuals who currently populate our patterns of moral thinking. For us, a role ethics largely inspired by the canons of classical Confucian philosophy, suitably modified for our modern sensibilities, presents one such conceptual framework for grounding a morality appropriate for the present day. And more than that, such a role ethic can appeal to what are referred to as liberals and conservatives alike, with room as well for both the faithful and the skeptics, proffering as it does a vision of the good life for human beings that can provide useful guidelines for addressing our political, economic, environmental – and perhaps even spiritual – problems, in a more cooperative manner, without any necessary theological grounding.

That we are all social creatures, strongly influenced by the others with whom we interact, has been acknowledged broadly by philosophers of all persuasions. But within our classical and modern discourse, there are reasons why this social dimension has been marginalized and rarely seen as being of the essence of our humanity at the moral and political (and ontological) level. On this view, our social selves cannot be of compelling worth because our concrete circumstances are in an important sense accidental in that we have exercised no control over them – that is, we are not responsible for who our parents are, the native languages we speak, our ethnicity, and so forth. Consequently, what does give human beings their primary worth, their dignity, their integrity, and their value – and what must command the respect of all – is their ability to act purposively and to exercise their capacity for self-determination, that is, their *autonomy*. And of course, in order for human beings to be truly autonomous, they must neither be coerced nor governed by instinct or passion. That is, they must be *free* and *rational* in the choices that they make. But this view of human beings is not the only one that can accord dignity and respect to everyone.

The Genesis of Confucian Role Ethics

We both came to Confucian role ethics as an alternative to autonomous individualism through our study of classical Confucian texts, and then later when we worked closely together over a number of years on Confucian translation and interpretation projects. The concept of role ethics had its genesis in a paper Rosemont wrote in 1991 for a *Festschrift* in honor of Herbert Fingarette wherein he suggested that seeing the Chinese as flesh and blood role-bearers rather than potential candidates to be abstract rights-holders might give Western-trained philosophers a better background for reading early Confucian texts. Ames then began to work with the idea for developing an ethics of roles in some depth, contextualizing it within the centrality of family as the governing metaphor in Chinese culture. Rosemont then picked up on Ames's discussions of family in his search for an appropriate English vocabulary to describe such a morality since it was without counterpart in the history of Western ethics. And Rosemont further addressed his cudgel to retrofit the Chinese lexicon and thereby allow the early Confucians to speak more clearly and faithfully in their own voices while at the same time expressing views applicable to our present conditions. Ames developed the notion of paranomasia to explain how the Chinese lexicon makes its meaning, and Rosemont moved from thinking of concepts and words to think more of concept-clusters, especially, but not confined to terms central for philosophers, especially as they are seen as definitive of ethics, politics and religion. It is largely against this background of the three shared interrelated themes – role ethics, family, and language/translation – that our collaborative efforts are best understood: two textual translations (the *Analects of Confucius* and the *Chinese Classic of Family Reverence)*, our joint articles, and two separately authored books, Ames's *Confucian Role Ethics: A Vocabulary* (2011) and Rosemont's *Against Individualism: A Confucian Rethinking of the Foundations of Morality, Politics, Family and Religion* (2015).

At first we attempted to articulate Confucian role ethics somewhat unreflectively in terms that could conceivably be descriptive of free, autonomous individual selves as well as role-bearers – even though we became increasingly suspicious of the former – especially as we embarked upon our translation of the *Analects*. Our suspicions were confirmed fairly quickly after we began the work, encountering two major difficulties: (1) while passages in the text pertaining to the conduct of human beings as role-bearers abound, we could find none that describe the activities of these role-bearing persons in terms of freedom or autonomy, and very few in which any of the participants are not discussed in terms of close relationships to others; and (2) as we continued to think about and develop the notion of role ethics, and began to speak of human "beings" as always "*becoming*," we found less work for the concept of the free, autonomous, and rationally choosing individual self to do, or even to *be*. Instead, it increasingly seemed to us that describing the proper performances of persons in their various roles and the appropriate attitude expressed in such roles in their relationship to others with whom they are engaged, sufficed to articulate an ethics that seemed both to give the greatest consistency and coherence to the text, and also to conform to our own everyday experience much better than those abstract accounts reflected in the writings of the heroes of Western moral philosophy, past and present.

By the time we came to translate the *Chinese Classic of Family Reverence,* we were willing to jettison the concept of the free and autonomous individual altogether for several reasons. First, we became increasingly puzzled when trying to make clear sense of what it would mean to be a free and autonomous individual self – apart from the habits of an old psychology – supported in our growing doubts by much recent work in the neurosciences and social psychology, as well as in philosophy. Second, we were able to begin work with both the Chinese and English languages to try to capture the vision of Confucius as we saw it without doing violence to the text, and to explicate more generally what an ethics of roles might be like.

Third, we came to the philosophical position, and began arguing for the idea that an insistence on the paramouncy of individual freedom in ethical and political theories – and instantiated in democratic societies – was purchased at the expense of equality and social justice, as libertarians have been (unintentionally) making increasingly clear, especially in the U.S. Consequently, we found that all moral arguments for equality and social justice grounded in the concept of individual freedom could be met by counter arguments equally moral. Moreover, although our interpreting the *Analects* as a role ethics met with some initial skepticism, we have not been persuaded by any of the critiques of what might be wrong with our translations of the text or our interpretations of it, and that has held for our *Chinese Classic of Family Reverence* efforts as well. Further, if we are correct in our claim that championing the freedom and autonomy of individuals has come at the expense of social justice, then clearly we would not be doing the early Confucians any favors by attributing a concept of autonomous individualism to them.

And finally, a fourth reason for abandoning the fiction of the autonomous individual is that it seemed increasingly to be the case that all of the important *good* work done by deontological, consequentialist, or virtue ethics based on individualism could also be captured by an ethics of roles, and hence Confucius did not have to be seen as a marginal, second-class moral philosopher. The concept of human beings as free, autonomous individuals could thus be dispensed with by one pass of Ockham's razor.

Believing that every society worth living in must be characterized by a robust sense of social justice and a fair measure of economic equality, we have thus been led in recent work to abandon altogether *every* ethical theory grounded in what we have come to call a default "foundational individualism" that would include care ethics, Marxism, and the communal anarchism of Peter Kropotkin no less than the strictly individualist version of Max Stirner, and almost all other philosophers in between, otherwise as disparate as Rousseau, Rawls, Sandel, MacIntyre, Susan Okin, and Charles Taylor. If we are correct that all ethics and politics grounded in the freedom and autonomy of individuals hinders significantly the achievement of social justice in a society, and if many of the horrors confronting the world today have the social injustices of poverty and inequality as their root cause, then, to repeat, it becomes clear to us that we do no favors to the early Confucians to ascribe to them an individualist foundation to their thinking, for they then can have little to say about solving contemporary world problems, and we would be reduced to reading the *Analects* for its antiquarian interest.

We may be wrong in some or all of these beliefs. It may be the case that there is an ethics and politics grounded in individualism that can indeed claim the moral high ground for social justice and wealth redistribution, and we would urge those colleagues so persuaded to continue to attempt to develop their ideas. But because we believe that foundational individualism is a major *cause* of our contemporary malaise we are not optimistic that any theory accepting it can contribute to its cure; thus far we have not seen any plausible candidates, and until we do, we will continue to push the envelope for an ethics and politics grounded in the roles lived by interrelated persons, whose sole constant is change.

Why not Autonomous Individualism?

The need for us to pursue what we might alternatively call a narrative notion of person arises from the fact that the concept of the autonomous individual underlying modern moral and political philosophy has come to have at least four pernicious effects. First, it enables libertarian capitalists, growing in their numbers in the U.S., Europe, and Asia, to claim moral purchase in justifying an unfettered human freedom as the basis and ultimate source of political justice, and on that basis, to then reject any conception of justice that retards such freedom as fundamentally immoral. The notion of the individual so defined thus continues to provide a moral basis for a more or less *laissez-faire* global free market capitalist economy that is compounding exponentially the gross inequities in human well-being within, between, and beyond modern nation states. And as long as the conservatives, liberals, communitarians, and socialists alike all continue to ground their objections to libertarianism in their own version of the same autonomous individual, the libertarian will always be able to counter their challenges and remain above moral reproach.

The second related reason that the concept of the autonomous individual is pernicious is its monopoly on the consciousness of Western intellectuals. The foundational individual is entrenched at a depth that makes it almost impossible for us to see any alternative to an individualism so defined except that of a more or less faceless collectivism in a decidedly post-Marxist era. It has become extraordinarily difficult within our political and ethical discourse to view human beings (including ourselves, of course) in any way other than as free, autonomous, and rational (and usually self-interested) individuals, making it equally difficult to act on any other basis. Indeed, the assumption that the essential characteristics and actions of human beings are best understood by regarding them as fundamentally free, autonomous, and rational individuals has in the sense of brooking no alternatives, become a default, uncritical ideology. And from this ideological perspective, social relations and actions will be seen as justifiable – that is, as being just – only to the extent that they are agreed to by individuals so described.

Thus, within this ideology, community is not the natural state of and for human beings, but only the artificial construct of otherwise discrete individuals. And again within this contractarian ideology, while procedure and retribution play a dominant if not definitive role in our regnant conceptions of justice, any effort to pursue social justice that challenges personal autonomy becomes contentiously dismissed as European "socialism," and any gesture made in the direction of restorative justice will likely be perceived as undeserving of such a description. And so long as this ideology of the individual holds us in its orbit, it will be impossible to be objective or impartial in evaluating any conception of justice or of any notion of the human being that underlies such a concept of justice that has the temerity to take issue with autonomous individualism.

A third corollary of foundational individualism is that ironically, it does not make good on its promises. Stated simply, acting to advance one's own self-interest at the expense of others seldom serves those same interests, and acting altruistically to serve the interests of others at one's own expense in the end gives the other very little. Drinking a fine bottle of wine by oneself is not as enjoyable as sharing it with good friends, and to the extent the self-abnegation is entailed by altruism, the "other" receives only diminishing returns. We will see in a Confucian conception of the relationally constituted conception of a person, a good teacher and a good student can only emerge together, and your welfare and the welfare of you neighbor are coterminous and mutually entailing.

The fourth pernicious effect of an entrenched individualism and perhaps its most visible detriment is that there is an aura of the self-fulfilling prophecy that haloes this ideology: The more we have come to see ourselves as autonomous individuals contracting with others in service to our own self-interests, the more we have come to act as, and ultimately, to become just such individuals. The degree of angst, alienation, and violence that has become characteristic of contemporary urban living is a direct consequence of our dysfunctional families and our failure to transform mere associated living into communities of shared values and interests.

Why Confucian Role Ethics?

The starting point is simple. In Confucian role ethics, association is a fact. We do not live our lives inside our skins. Everything we do – physically, psychologically, socially – is resolutely transactional and collaborative. And the roles we live are simply the way in which this fact of association is further stipulated and specified. Confucian role ethics appeals to specific roles for stipulating the forms that association take within lives lived in family and community – that is, the various roles we live as sons and teachers, grandmothers and neighbors. For Confucianism, not only are these roles descriptive of our associations, but once stipulated, they are also prescriptive in the sense that roles in family and community are themselves normative, guiding us in the direction of appropriate conduct. One is a good or bad spouse, and a good or bad teacher. Whereas mere association is a given, flourishing families and communities are what we are able to make of this associative condition as the highest human achievement.

Confucian role ethics has a holistic and compelling vision of the moral life that is grounded in and is responsible to our empirical experience. First, Confucian role ethics would insist on the primacy of vital relationships, and would preclude any notion of final individuality. Personal discreteness is a conceptual abstraction and strict autonomy a misleading fiction; association is a fact. And giving up the notion of a superordinate "self," far from surrendering one's personal uniqueness, in fact, enhances it. That is, the "natural kinds" talk that usually stands behind claims about a shared human nature and a concomitant essential self mitigates the degree of difference we find in a Confucian notion of person where person is constituted by a dynamic manifold of always specific relations.

Secondly, Confucian role ethics resists the uncritical substance ontology underlying a conception of agency that requires a separation between the agent of conduct and the conduct itself. The notion of *ren* 仁 that is central to Confucian role ethics entails no such agency/action dichotomy. *Ren* requires a narrative rather than an analytic understanding of person. And *ren* is cultivated by correlating one's own conduct with those models close at hand rather than by acting in concert with some abstract moral principles. It is for this reason that it is often unclear whether *ren* denotes a consummate person or the conduct of such a person, or like its cognate *ren* 人, whether the referent is singular or plural. *Ren* is an open-ended generalization made off of particular historical accomplishments of consummate conduct rather than referencing some innate and essential element that is characteristic of all members of the set called human "beings." Indeed, *ren* is a gerundive notion – a verbal noun – that is descriptive of consummate "person-ing."

Thirdly, Confucian role ethicists appreciate the dramatic role that body has as integral to achieving personal identity and consummate conduct – the body as the root or trunk through which human conduct, being nourished and grown, becomes refulgent. It is no coincidence that the simplified graph for body 體 is 体 – that is, quite literally, the graphic denotation of the root and stem of a person. The body – always a collaboration between person and world, between organism and environment – is at once carnal and vital, seen and lived, receptive and responsive. Not only does the world shape the body, but through our bodily sensorium we structure, conceptualize, and theorize our world of experience. Indeed, it is because the body is the medium through which our ancestors and their culture live on in us that keeping one's body intact has been the first among the several precepts of family reverence (*xiao* 孝).

Fourthly, Confucian role ethics emphasizes the vital role that the process of moral imagination plays in consummate thinking and living. In Confucian role ethics, it is our educated imagination that, drawing upon all of our human resources, defers action until we can conjure forth the full range of possibilities that allows for optimal growth in our relationships. And said plainly, it is this growth in relationships that is the very substance of morality.

And finally, Confucian role ethics does not compete with virtue ethics or any other ethical *theory* but is rather a vision of the moral life that resists the theoretical/practical divide. When we read the Confucian canons, the expectation is that while we certainly can appropriate a cluster of terms that enable a critical reflection on our conduct, we ought, more fundamentally, to be inspired by the exhortations and the models of the cultural heroes to become better people.

Documenting the Genesis of Confucian Role Ethics

The eight essays gathered here represent the evolution of our joint efforts to simultaneously develop our two basic theses: first, that classical Confucianism is best interpreted as being fundamentally an ethics of roles rather than principles or character traits, and that it is *sui generis* with no close Western counterpart. And second, that this role ethics, appropriately modified, can encompass all of the good work done by the standard ethical theories while avoiding their shortcomings, and for this reason, is perhaps singularly suited to attract our allegiance today. That is, while individualism of any sort has in our opinion exhausted its usefulness, the standard proffered alternative of a Marxist, Stalinist, or Fascist collectivism is certainly not a worthy candidate to succeed it.

All of the following essays were originally invited, some to appear in anthologies, others to be read at conferences and later to be published as proceedings volumes. They span a quarter of a century in terms of when they were first written, with the bulk of them composed between 2008 and 2013. These essays appear here in only rough chronological order because we thought it better as much as possible to group them by major theme.

The first essay, "Translation and Interpretation" was first given by us jointly at a conference organized by Frank Kraushaar on the topic of Western approaches to East Asian cultures held at the University of Riga, Latvia, in 2008. We wanted to begin the present volume with this essay because it is a fairly clear statement of our methodological assumptions and our approach to comparative philosophy in general, and to the parsing of Chinese materials in particular.

The second essay, "Rights-bearing Individuals and Role-bearing Persons" was originally written by Rosemont as a contribution to a *Festschrift* for Herbert Fingarette, *Rules, Rituals and Responsibility,* edited by Mary Bockover. Written in 1990 and published a year later, it turned out to be the first in a series of works we did both together and separately, developing the idea of viewing the early Confucian thinkers as concerned much more with an ethics of roles than of principles.

The third essay, published in a special issue of *Dao: A Journal of Comparative Philosophy* devoted to the dispute then going on in China about the relation of "family reverence" (*xiao* 孝) to "consummate person/conduct" (*ren* 仁) was the first appearance of "family reverence" instead of "filial piety" as translation for *xiao* in our work, and "consummatory person/conduct" for *ren* instead of "authoritative person/conduct," or something similar. This paper, modified and expanded significantly, became the motive force for what was to be published a year later as *The Chinese Classic of Family Reverence: A Philosophical Translation of the* Xiaojing. And a follow-up to the third essay is the fourth, a more recent discussion of *xiao*, "Family Reverence (*xiao*) in the *Analects:* Confucian Role

Ethics and the Dynamics of Intergenerational Transmission." It is one of a collection of articles on Confucius and the *Analects* gathered and edited by Amy Olberding.

The fifth essay, still dealing largely with the family and family reverence, is Rosemont's contribution to the 2012 Conference at Alet-les-Bains on the topic of "Landscape and Traveling East and West: A Philosophical Journey." Rosemont focused on the family and travel through time rather than space, and his presentation was followed immediately by Ames, whose presentation on that same occasion is the final work in this present volume.

Interpreting Confucianism as a role ethics remains a controversial claim among many of our comparativist colleages. The next two essays are devoted to arguing not only for our claim, but also *against* other interpretations. Essay six: "Were the Early Confucians Virtuous?" – argues that Western interpretations of Chinese ethics follows the Anscombe turn from rule-based ethics to virtue ethics in our own academy, and is not the best reading of the early Confucian texts, however *au courant* virtue ethics may be in contemporary Western moral philosophy.

Essay seven is our contribution to another *Festschrift*, this one for our dear friend Joel Kupperman that was edited by two of his students, Chenyang Li and Peimin Ni. The thrust of our contribution is evident in the title: "From Kupperman's Character Ethics to Confucian Role Ethics: Putting Humpty Dumpty Together Again."

The final and concluding article in this collection is the paper Ames presented at the Alet conference in 2012 immediately after Rosemont: "Travelling with *Gravitas:* The Intergenerational Transmission of Chinese Culture." In this essay, Ames moves from treating the family and family memory through time to the intergenerational project of acquiring, enhancing and transmitting culture through time. At the outset Ames suggests that our collaborative efforts to interpret Confucianism for a Western audience – namely, the nature of our work, and the fact of doing much of it together – is at the heart of the Confucian persuasion as we believe it is best interpreted. This is, to say the least, a rather unusual sort of philosophical claim, but Rosemont stands by Ames in proffering it, for we both believe we are better people for having worked with each other while exploring and writing about Confucian role ethics, forging our Way in the world together.

Several of our claims are made in more than one of the articles in this volume because the papers were originally presented to different audiences at different times, and we believed it best not to alter them for this reprinting.

Henry Rosemont, Jr. / Roger T. Ames

On Translation & Interpretation (With Special Reference to Classical Chinese)

The Italian statement *Tradduttore, traditore* is unusual in that it serves as its own proof. Not even in other Indo-European languages can the succinct expressiveness of the sentence come through well: "translators are traducers" is probably the best that can be done in English, but it is nowhere as clear in meaning as the original, nor as straightforward.[1]

It is our opinion this little example is not an isolated curiosity. Very few sentences in any language can be precisely rendered in any other, in part due to the fact that if our sole concern is with truth conditions there are many different ways to express exactly the same fact even in a single language ("John broke the window; the window was broken by John; what John broke was the window; what John did was break the window; it was the window that John broke; what was broken by John was the window; what John did to the window was break it; it was the window that was broken by John;" and so on). Which of the varied ways of expressing a singular fact a writer or speaker employs will depend on context and intent, and translators must thus be sensitive to both when electing a specific syntactic form to employ in the target language. Unfortunately, neither context nor intent are often clear, and hence translators cannot but engage in interpretation on a significant scale, whether they wish to admit it or not (we will have more to say on this point below).

Semantic issues in translation are in all probability even more numerous than syntactic ones. Even within the same family of languages we seldom find precise equivalents for individual lexical items between the object and target languages (Although sharing similar roots, modern English and German nevertheless differ in their epistemological vocabulary, for example, with the *kennen/wissen* distinction in German having no English counterpart).

Both syntactic and semantic problems loom especially large when the languages under consideration are as different as the classical Chinese language of

1 Some of the material in this essay is taken from the introduction and appendices to our *The Analects of Confucius; A Philosophical Translation.* New York, Ballantine Books, 1998.

roughly the sixth to the second centuries BCE[2] and modern English. Different translators may well have different views about the nature of the differences between the two languages, and in our opinion it is thus incumbent upon all translators to inform their readers of what they believe the nature of the languages to be.[3] In addition, we believe it important for translators to proffer their basic notions of the nature of human languages in general; a behaviorist view differs significantly from a generativist one, both of them from a structural approach, and all three from a deconstructionist orientation toward languages. We begin with a brief overview of the latter, and then will turn specifically to Chinese, warning readers at the outset that our views are not uncontroversial; there are translators whose work we respect who would disagree with our philosophical approach to matters of translation (and, as we shall also argue, interpretation).

It is essential first to point out some differences between speech and writing that we believe are important, and must always be kept in mind when engaged in translation efforts. In the first place, there is the obvious fact that all cultures have spoken languages, but relatively few – until very recently – have had a writing system. Not unrelatedly, there is a sense in which writing is artificial in a way that speech is not. We learn to speak and understand the language of our birth simply by being exposed to it; we do not have to be taught our native tongue unless we have an impediment of some sort. Reading and writing, on the other hand, are not natural; we must learn to master different senses (visual and tactile as opposed to aural and oral) and we must be taught that mastery. Without specific and detailed instruction we remain illiterate.

Moreover, we believe all human languages share many features at an abstract – but substantive – level, most importantly syntactic structures, that constrain the way words may be strung together while yet enabling speakers to be able to creatively express their thoughts. We are thus in the generativist camp of linguists, and an example may illustrate wherein our views are grounded.

Let us take a sentence such as:

The boy walked up the hill.

2 We specify these dates because there is no general agreement on when and/or where to use the term "classical" as opposed to "archaic," or "ancient" when referring to the language in which the classical texts were written, often referred to by the Chinese as "literary Chinese." 文言 *wen yan)*

3 Christoph Harbsmeier – who disagrees with our position – has written a lengthy essay outlining the several views prevalent among sinologists on the nature of the Chinese language(s). The essay is in Volume 7, Part 1, of *Science and Civilisation in China,* by Joseph Needham and Christoph Harbsmeier. Cambridge UK: Cambridge University Press, 1998.

Now if we are asked to add the adverb *slowly* to the sentence, there are seven positions in which we might place it: at the beginning or end of the sentence, or in any of the five spaces between the words.

But not all of these placements will retain the grammaticality of the sentence:

1) *Slowly the boy walked up the hill*
2) *The slowly boy walked up the hill*
3) *The boy slowly walked up the hill*
4) *The boy walked slowly up the hill*
5) *The boy walked up slowly the hill*
6) *The boy walked up the slowly hill*
7) *The boy walked up the hill slowly*

Sentences 1, 3, 4 and 7 are grammatical, but 2, 5 and 6 are not; how do we account for this fact?

(The short answer is that grammatical structures – (in English, noun phrase, verb phrase, prepositional phrase – must maintain their integrity, and the offending sentences violate it, whereas in 1, 3, 4, and 7 the adverb is placed before, after, or between those phrase structures).[4]

Moreover, it is necessary to note that writing is not solely – and at times, not even mainly – a transcription of speech. No indirect discourse is speech transcribed, nor are newspaper headlines, many advertisements, and much else. This feature of language is particularly important with respect to classical Chinese, especially Confucianism, because of the ubiquity, in the *Analects*, of 子曰, "The Master said." In the first place, one feature of all natural (spoken) languages is their capacity to unambiguously express grammatical relations; without this feature of languages the *slowly* example above would be inexplicable. But classical Chinese does not have this feature; absent a specific context, grammatical relations are not unambiguously expressed.

An equally important reason for not seeing classical Chinese as a transcription of speech is phonetic. There is very little direct evidence to suggest that basic *verbal* communication took place through this medium. Nor could there be such, in our view, because the extraordinarily large number of homonyms in the language makes it virtually uninterpretable by ear alone (without the use of binomes). A great many semantically unrelated lexical items have exactly the same phonological realization to be understood aurally, even when tonal distinctions are taken into account.

4 For a more complete analysis of these points see Henry Rosemont, Jr. & Huston Smith, *Is There a Universal Grammar of Religion?* Chicago & LaSalle, IL: Open Court Publishing Co., 2008, especially the second chapter.

This is not to suggest a complete disconnect between the spoken and written Chinese languages at the various times that the classical texts were being written and edited. The *Book of Poetry* obviously was a recording of sounds, and phonetic loan words are found early on in the written record. And *perhaps* one or two of the disciples of Confucius did place a *verbatim* quote from the Master into the text that has come down to us. But it remains that *wenyan* should not be seen as fundamentally a transcription of speech. Originally the classical language had a number of syllabic consonantal endings which are no longer present in the modern language, but even then the number of homonyms was high, with anywhere from two to seven different graphs – with different meanings – pronounced identically.[5] No one will understand a passage from a classical text unless they have read it earlier, and can contextualize it. Thus the language of the classical texts was fundamentally like the good little boy: primarily to be seen and not heard.

A moment's reflection on the nature of written English will suggest that it, too, has a visual component above and beyond its being a pronunciation indicator. We must all be pleased that G.B. Shaw's demand for a purely phonetic alphabet for the spelling of English has never been met. Admittedly we have difficulty initially seeing that his made-up word *ghoti* should be pronounced "fish," (enouGH, wOmen, attenTIon), but English spelling often provides semantic no less than – and often more than – phonetic information. If we know what "nation" means, for example, we can make a good guess about what "national" might mean too the first time we come across it because of the orthographic parallels between the terms. Yet they are pronounced differently. The same may be said for a whole host of common words in English: *photograph/photography; anxious/anxiety, child/children,* and so forth.

We also believe that classical Chinese differs from all other languages in another, philosophically important way that other translators have neglected or ignored: It is more an event-based than a "thing"-based language, more akin to Hebrew than to most members of the Indo-European language groupings. We have argued for this claim elsewhere, and will not rehearse it herein, save to make the related claim that the nature of early Chinese metaphysics reflects the structural nature of the Chinese language. There is little by way of substance ontology – "*being*" – to be found in early Chinese thought, but much in the way of events, processes – "*becoming.*" Many English nouns can be "verbed," to be sure, but in classical Chinese, virtually every graph can function as noun and verb, and usually as an adjective or adverb as well, which is no more than to say that apart from context the grammatical function of a Chinese term cannot be ascertained.

5 See, for example, Bernhard Karlgren, *Grammata Serica.* Taipei, Ch'eng-Wen Publishing Co., 1966 (reprint).

The resultant linguistic dynamism of classical Chinese will thus only be captured at all well in English if verbs take pride of place in translation. Thus instead of "Zizhang asked about government" for 子張問政, we make it "Zizhang asked about governing effectively."

There are several implications of our several views on the unique nature of the classical Chinese language that go beyond issues of translation. If they can be sustained, for example, it will follow that the written texts that have come down to us will not always reflect well the grammatical patterns of the spoken language of the time; our guess would be that the use of binomes has a very long history, even though both graphs in any uttered binomial expression would seldom be transcribed together. Another implication is that it would be folly to replace the Chinese written graphs with an alphabetic system more geared to representing sounds, for the number of distinct sounds in modern Chinese is relatively small, and there is no easy way to represent the tonal inflections of each morpheme. But this latter problem is of relatively little moment, for many sounds have over thirty different graphs associated with them even when the tones are taken into account: *yi* has 41, for example, *shi* has 32, *zhi* 31, and so on.

Still a third implication of our views on the contrasting nature of English and classical Chinese may be generalized for all translation work: it is not possible to translate a text from one language to another without an interpretation of it. In our own case we link the de-emphasis on nouns in classical Chinese with the absence of the concept of *substance* or *essence* in classical Chinese thought. In the same way, if events are linguistically center stage, then relational persons rather than individual selves will make up the *dramatis personae* in ethics. Aesthetic expressiveness (not alone in literature) may place a higher value on nuance and ambiguity than on precision.[6]

Turning now to issues of semantics facing translators, it has long been lamented that many terms of import in one language have no close lexical equivalent in others, necessitating the use of lengthier locutions in the target language that can either multiply or eliminate a nuance or ambiguity intended in the original. Here it becomes clear that interpretation affects translation right from the beginning.

In classical Chinese, to take an important philosophical illustration, there is no single lexical equivalent for the English word "moral." Most translators from the Chinese have not attended to this fact – or stretched some graph or another to make it come out as "*moral*" in parts of the translation – and the consequence has been that most Western philosophers have refused to take Chinese thinkers

6 On the importance of the term "aesthetic" as we employ it for understanding Chinese thought, see David L. Hall and Roger T. Ames, *Thinking Through Confucius.* Albany NY: State University of New York Press, 1987.

seriously *as philosophers*, for if, say, Confucius was indeed concerned with morals, why doesn't he take up problems of *choice?* Apart from the negative golden rule perhaps, where are moral *principles* to be found in the *Analects?* Why is he seemingly unaware of the issues surrounding *freedom* in moral deliberations? Does he not see how *dilemmas* arise when principles conflict? Why is he constantly blurring the distinction between the *public* and the *private* realms of our behavior?

These are serious questions, for it would be very difficult to think of *moral* issues apart from the related concepts here placed in italics. But *none* of those terms has a lexical equivalent in classical Chinese, nor for the other terms necessary to engage in moral discourse in contemporary English:

liberty, right/wrong, rational, objective/subjective, even *ought.*

But rather than attribute simple-mindedness or extreme naïveté to Confucius, we might posit that he has a different vocabulary for describing, analyzing and evaluating human conduct, conceptually grounded in different presuppositions about the world and the place of human beings in it than have been standard in Western thought for many centuries. The 15+ English terms listed above constitute what we call a "concept-cluster," centered on the concept *moral.* Early Confucian writings deployed a different concept-cluster for describing, analyzing and evaluating human conduct, centered on the concept of 仁 *ren,* and including such concepts as 心 *xin,* 孝 *xiao,* 德 *de,* 信 *xin,* 君子 *junzi,* 知 *zhi,* 小人 *xiaoren,* 義 *yi,* 誠 *cheng,* and 礼 *li,* plus a few others. All of these terms are polysemous in English, and hence when translating them we must not look solely at each Chinese graph in isolation, but rather see it in relation to the other terms in the cluster. None of them fit neatly or easily into the concept-cluster for *morals*, but they do mesh with each other, a meshing which all translators should be sensitive to while engaged in their work.

Our notion of concept-clusters, and the importance of the notion for translation, can be seen more clearly by considering other examples. In Chaucerian England the concept-cluster employed in the description, analysis and evaluation of human conduct centered in *honour,* which was discussed using terms like *villein, shent, liegeful, sake, varlet, boon, soke, sooth, chivalric, gentil,* and *sinne.* Some of these terms are still vaguely familiar to English speakers, but their meanings have shifted, (*gentil*/gentle, *sinne*/sin), or we use them without knowing what they mean (*sake*), still others we skip over quickly when reading Robin Hood or King Arthur (*varlet, boon*), and still others have no meaning at all for us (*soke, shent*).

We find another concept-cluster in ancient Greece, wherein moral philosophy dealt largely with the cultivation of virtues (*aretai*), especially in the philosophy of Aristotle, who used related terms in his account like *eidos, dike, logos, akrasia, phronesis, eudemonia, agathos, nous, psuche, eros,* and related terms.

In ancient India the concept-cluster employed in the several strands of Hindu thought and in Buddhism revolved around the concept of *dharma*, and included *varna*, *moksha*, *samadhi*, *samsara*, *skhandas*, *nirvana*, *dukkha*, *bodhi*, *(an)atman*, *yog*, and of course *karma*.

What all of these examples illustrate, we believe – and they could be multiplied tenfold – is that the idea of concept-clusters is a great aid to translating and understanding texts written against conceptual backgrounds that differ from our own, and can provide a means of giving the "other" their otherness without making them either *wholly* other, or, equally mischievous, more simple-minded versions of ourselves.

The careful reader will probably have noted that we have used "term" and "concept" almost interchangeably herein. Of course the two morphemes have different meanings, but it is fundamental to our position as philosopher-translators that a concept not be imputed to the authors and editors of foreign texts unless there is a specific lexical entry denoting that concept in the text itself. To do otherwise – assuming Confucius had the concept of "morals" in anything like the sense that contemporary speakers of English do – is to either rob the Master of his distinctiveness, or make him appear simple-minded, guaranteeing that the translators will not capture well the lessons he has to teach us today.

But that is not the end of it. It is methodologically dangerous to assume that writers in foreign languages had ideas just like us when they don't have words just like us to express them. What purely textual evidence could be adduced to suggest that Confucius had the concept of "morals?" (Or of "karma", for that matter). Did the author(s) of the *Daodejing* have a concept of "*freedom*"? What might count as evidence that the authors of the *Bhagavad-Gita* had a concept of 仁 *ren?*

Philosophers have drawn linguistic and epistemological swords on this issue for some time. To some, our position will seem to be "unfair to babies," making the point that we are willing to attribute concepts to infants before they have the words to express them. And it must be allowed that at times it is legitimate to assume that a single concept might indeed have been held by the author of a text if the translation runs more coherently. But it is the idea of concept-clusters that can stop the morphemes of other languages from becoming Rorschach blots to the translator: the significance of our insistence on pointing out the lack of a lexical equivalent for "morals" in classical Chinese lies in the fact that none of the other terms associated with "morals" in contemporary English will be found in the texts either.

It has been this problem of translation as interpretation and the importance of thinking in terms of concept-clusters that has driven our happy collaboration in retranslating the Chinese classics. Our starting point has been that, without sufficient concern for the parameter of the interpretive context set by concept-clusters, translators in the process of introducing Confucianism into the Western academy have willy-nilly overwritten its key philosophical vocabulary and terms of art with the values of an Abrahamic religiousness not its own, thereby reducing Confucianism in the eyes of many to a necessarily anemic, second rate form of Christianity. Witness the standard formula of translations: *tian* 天 is "Heaven," *li* 禮 is "ritual," *yi* 義 is "righteousness," *dao* 道 is "*the* Way," *ren* 仁 is "benevolence," *de* 德 is "virtue," *xiao* 孝 is "filial piety," *li* 理 is "principle,"and so on. In sum, such a vocabulary cluster conjures forth a pre-established, single-ordered and divinely sanctioned cosmos guided by the hand of a righteous God that ought to inspire human faith and compliance.

There have been subsequent efforts by some scholars to rescue an uprooted and transplanted Confucianism from this Christian soil. But the result has often been to reconstruct its ideas and values through the prism of an Orientalism that would ostensibly save the integrity of Confucianism by dismissing its profoundly religious dimensions, and in so doing, reduce it to a kind of secular humanism. Or perhaps worse, in interpreting Confucianism's inclusive and provisional approach to philosophical understanding as unstructured and indeterminate, reduce its holistic sensibilities to mysticism and the occult.

The consequence, then, of this overtly Christianized and then Orientalized reading of the Confucian vocabulary has located the study of this tradition within Western seats of higher learning in religion and area studies departments rather than as a proper part of the philosophy curriculum, and has relegated translations of the Confucian texts to the new age and suspect "Eastern Religions" corners of our bookstores and libraries.

In attempting to provide a more nuanced explanation of these same Confucian terms, the twentieth century Confucian scholar Qian Mu 錢穆 is adamant that this vocabulary expressing the unique and complex Confucianism vision of a moral life simply has no counterpart in other languages.[7] Qian Mu's point in making this claim is not to argue for cultural purism and incommensurability; on the contrary, he would allow that with sufficient exposition, the Confucian world can be "appreciated" in important degree by those from without. Qian Mu's claim is on behalf of the uniqueness and the value of a tradition that has defined its terms of art through the lived experience of its people over millennia, and anticipates the real difficulty we must face in attempting to capture its complex and organically related vocabulary in other languages without substantial qualification and explanation.

Some earnest interpreters of this Confucian tradition who are as committed to the enduring value of Confucian philosophy as Qian Mu was, disagree funda-

7 Jerry Dennerline, *Qian Mu and the World of Seven Mansions*. New Haven: Yale University Press,1988, p. 9.

mentally with his claims about the difficulty of translation. The erudite scholar Zhang Longxi 張隆溪, for example, states with confidence that while we will never find strict identity among cultures, we can find "equivalency:"

> Linguistic and cultural differences between China and the West are obvious, that is, in the etymological sense of "standing in the way" (*ob viam*) like obstacles, and it is the task of translation to clear the way for understanding and communication by discovering equivalent formulations underneath the changing surface of differences.[8]

What makes the formulation of such equivalents possible is an acknowledged sameness in thinking among cultures:

> Against such an overemphasis on difference and cultural uniqueness ... I would like to argue for the basic translatability of languages and cultures. ... Only when we acknowledge different peoples and nations as equal in their ability to think, to express, to communicate, and to create values, we may then rid ourselves of ethnocentric biases ...[9]

We would insist that respect for interpretive context is integral to the project of translation, and would contest the resistance among such scholars to sanction the thick cultural generalizations being made by Qian Mu that we believe are necessary if we are to respect the rich differences that obtain among traditions and if we are to avoid as best we can an impoverishing cultural reductionism. We would argue that the canopy of an always emerging cultural vocabulary is itself rooted in and grows out of a deep and relatively stable soil of unannounced assumptions sedimented over generations into the language, the customs, and the life forms of a living tradition. And further, we would argue that to fail to acknowledge the fundamental character of cultural difference as an erstwhile safeguard against the sins of either "essentialism" or "relativism" is not itself innocent. Indeed, ironically, this antagonism to cultural generalizations leads to the uncritical essentializing of one's own contingent cultural assumptions and to the insinuating of them into one's interpretations of the ways of thinking and living of other traditions.

What separates we self-confessed cultural pluralists (rather than "purists") from Zhang are what we take to be several troubling implications of his basic assumptions about how the translation between and among cultural traditions is to be carried out. To begin with, one might argue that the bugbear of "essentialism" that properly worries Zhang is itself, like any strict philosophical notion of "universalism," largely a culturally specific deformation. Indeed, universalism is closely associated with "the transcendental pretense" described above as a fallacy

8 Zhang Longxi, "Translating Cultures: China and the West." *Chinese Thought in a Global Context: A Dialogue Between Chinese and Western Philosophical Approaches.* Edited by Karl-Heinz Pohl. Leiden: Brill, 1999, p. 43.

9 Zhang Longxi (1999), p. 46.

pervasive in the pre-Darwinian Western philosophical narrative that is immediately aligned with what John Dewey has called "*the* philosophical fallacy." After all, we can only "essentialize" (rather than analogize) if we are predisposed to believe there are such things as "essences," a way of thinking about things that did not recommend itself to the formative thinkers of classical China. Essentialism itself arises from familiar classical Greek assumptions about ontology as "the science of being," and from the application of strict identity as the principle of individuation. It is this notion of "essences" that grounds Platonic idealism and the Aristotelian doctrine of species (*eidos*) as natural kinds.

Again, Zhang's claim about peoples and cultures being "equal" in their ability to think is intended to be inclusive and liberating and respectful, and while such assurances might be so for some, such an assertion is anything but innocuous. Why to allow that other traditions have culturally specific modalities of thinking is to claim that such traditions do not know how to think, unless we ourselves believe that in fact there is only one way of thinking, and that this way of thinking – that is, *our* way of thinking, is the only way? The uncritical assumption that other cultures must think the same way as we do is for us the very definition of essentialism and ethnocentrism. We would argue that it is precisely the recognition and appreciation of the degree of difference obtaining among cultures in living and thinking that properly motivates cultural translation in the first place, and that ultimately rewards the effort. Surely arguing that there are culturally contingent modalities of thinking can be pluralistic rather than relativistic, and can be accommodating rather than condescending. At the very least, if comparative studies is to provide us with the mutual enrichment that it promises, we must strive with imagination to take other cultures on their own terms and appreciate fully the differences that obtain among them. It is to this end that we have suggested above that different cultures have fundmentally different concept-clusters and ways of thinking about becoming consummate as a human being.

And acknowledging what Whitehead has described as "the perils of abstraction," we would argue that the kind of rich aesthetic harmony achieved when we are able to find the proper balance between concreteness and abstraction, between unique detail and a productive coherence, requires that we exercise our imagination in identifying and respecting the differences among cultures; without the possibilities made available to us by these protean differences, we are left with a lifeless and insipid sameness.[10]

10 In making its case for the importance of difference to an achieved harmony, the *Zuo Commentary to the Spring and Autumn Annals* Duke Zhao 20 uses the examples of cooking, music, and an evolving cultural genealogy:
The Marquis of Qi had returned from the hunt, and was being attended by Master Yan at the

Thirdly, much of Zhang's exasperation seems to arise from interpreters such as Arthur Wright and Jacque Gernet (and us too) who in allowing for "fundamentally distinct ways of thinking and speaking" would claim (using Zhang's language) that the difference between the Chinese and Western cultures is "the ability, or lack of it, to express abstract ideas."[11] For Zhang, those who would

Chuan pavilion when Ju of Liangqiu galloped up to them. The Marquis said, "Only Ju is in harmony with me!"
"All that Ju does is agree with you." said Master Yan. "Wherein is the harmony?"
"Is there a difference between harmony and commonality?" asked the Marquis.
"There is indeed." replied Master Yan. "Harmony is like making congee. One uses water, fire, vinegar, sauce, salt, and plum to cook fish and meat, and burns firewood and stalks as fuel for the cooking process. The cook blends these ingredients harmoniously to achieve the appropriate flavor. Where it is too bland, he adds flavoring, and where it is too concentrated, he dilutes it with water. When you partake of this congee, Sir, it lifts your spirits.
The relationship between ruler and minister is another case in point. Where the ruler considers something right and yet there is something wrong about it, the minister should point out what is wrong as a way of achieving what is right. Where the ruler considers something wrong and yet there is something right about it, the minister should point out what is right as a way of setting aside what is wrong. In such a way governing will be equitable without violating ritual propriety and the common people will not be contentious. Thus the *Book of Songs* says:
'There is indeed harmoniously blended congee;
The kitchen has already been cautioned to bring out a balanced and even taste.
The spirits will come to partake of it without finding cause for blame,
And those above and below will be free of contention.'
The Former Kings blended the five flavors and harmonized the five notes to lift their spirits and to achieve success in their governing. Music functions similarly to flavoring. There is one field of sound; the two kinds of music: martial and civil; the three kinds of songs: airs of the states, odes, and hymns; the four quarters from which materials are gathered for making instruments; the five note pentatonic scale; the six pitch pipes; the seven sounds, the winds of the eight directions, and the nine ballads – all of which complement each other. There are the distinctions between clear and turbid, small and great, short and long, quick and slow, plaintive and joyous, hard and soft, delayed and rapid, high and low, beginning and ending, and intimate and distant – all of which augment each other. You listen to these, Sir, and it lifts your spirits, which in turn enables you to excel harmoniously. Hence the *Book of Songs* says, 'There are no imperfections in the sound of excellence.'
Now Ju is not acting in this way. Whatever you say is right, Ju also says is right; whatever you say is wrong, Ju also says is wrong. If you season water with water, who would want to partake of it? If you keep playing the same note on your lutes, who would want to listen to it? The inadequacy of 'commonality' lies in this."
They were drinking wine and enjoying themselves when the Marquis observed, "If from ancient times there had been no death, what then would be the extent of our joy!"
"If from ancient times there had been no death," ventured Master Yan, "there would be the joy of the ancients, and what would you, Sir, get out of that! In ancient times, the Shuangjiu clan first settled this territory, then came the Jice clan, followed by Youfeng Boling, the Pugu clan and finally by your first ancestor. If from ancient times there had been no death, there would be the joy of the Shuangjiu clan, and I doubt that you would want that!"

11 Zhang Longxi (1999), p. 44. Actually, in Ames and Rosemont (1998) pp. 39–43 and Appendix II, an argument is made that the written literary language is uniquely abstract in the sense

allow for alternative modalities of thinking that place a different degree of emphasis on the functional value of abstraction are guilty of a clear debasement of the Chinese language and culture:

> The Chinese language, as seen in this formulation, appears to be a language of concrete things and specific objects, a language bogged down in matter and unable to rise above the ground of materiality and literality toward any spiritual height. The judgment is thus not on Chinese translation of particular foreign words and concepts, but on the very nature and ability of the Chinese language as a whole.[12]

Here on our reading of Zhang, he is buying into two dualistic assumptions common to a tradition grounded in Greek ontology. First, in disallowing "distinct ways of thinking and speaking" he is locating cultural differences in the "content" and "objects" of thought rather than in its subjective instrument, as though thinking and what is thought about are somehow distinct, and that some definition of the human "mind" is not only an inclusive universal, but is also what is most distinctively and most valuably human. The implication of this distinction is that modes of thinking are essentially separable from the content of thinking by virtue of some pre-cultural faculties of the human mind and some *a priori* categories that structure it. Such mind/body and theory/praxis dualism has never been a distraction in a Chinese correlative *yinyang* cosmology in which mind/body (*shenxin*身心) and theory/praxis (*zhixing* 知行) have been taken to be collaborative, coterminous, and mutually entailing aspects of experience. Indeed, the continuity and wholeness of experience is defined in terms of "forming" and "functioning" (*tiyong* 體用), and "flux" and "persistence" (*biantong* 變通) – cosmological assumptions that preclude any strictly dualistic categories.

A corollary assumption implicit in Zhang's critique, again itself profoundly dualistic, is that the theoretical and spiritual idealities entertained by this essentialized conception of mind are superior to practical efficacy in our everyday experience, and that entertaining these abstractions elevates us closer to the mind of God. Such abstraction as the work of intellection is somehow more real and refined than embodied concrete experience, providing us with a quality of knowledge uncontaminated by the changing world whence these abstractions arise, and from a Confucian perspective, to which they perhaps ought to owe their allegiance. Indeed Zhang is endorsing the superiority and the arrogance of a theo-ontological tradition that has defined itself as being preoccupied by abstractions – a tradition that assumes its interpretation of the human experience is

that semantic overload contributes to a kind of productive vagueness requiring disambiguation on the part of the reader.

12 Zhang Longxi (1999), p. 45.

more noble and spiritual than one that pursues practical wisdom and the alternative spiritual and religiousness sensibilities produced therefrom.

At the end of the day, the irony is that Zhang is affirming for Confucian philosophy precisely the long-lived and hobbling fallacy that many twentieth and twenty-first century Western philosophers have been struggling to put to rest within our own narrative. As players in the internal critique raging within Western philosophy today, contemporary philosophers are attempting to reverse the gravity of theoretical ascent, and to reinstate what had been left behind. Indeed, the recent compensatory turn in Western philosophy toward applied ethics, virtue ethics, particularism, care ethics, pragmatic ethics, and so on, not to mention fresh attention being paid to somaticity and the emotions, is directed at rehabilitating the wholeness of the lived experience and at reestablishing an appropriate balance between the abstract and the concrete by reinstating the singular value of practical wisdom.[13]

But we are not done. Fourthly, Zhang Longxi is eliding an important distinction we might borrow from Saussure between *langu*e (language) and *parole* (speech), between the evolved, theoretical and conceptual structure of a language system that is shaped by an aggregating intelligence over millennia and that makes speech possible, and the application of any natural language in the individual utterances we make.[14] We pluralists need this distinction to galvanize our claim that the Chinese language has not developed and does not have available to

13 For examples of care ethics, see the work of Carol Gilligan, *In a Different Voice.* Cambridge MA: Harvard University Press, 1982, Nel Noddings, *Caring.* Second edition. Berkeley and Los Angeles: University of California Press, 2003, Margaret Walker (editor), *Mother Time.* Lanham, MD: Rowman and Littlefield, 2000, Virginia Held, *The Ethics of Care.* Oxford: Oxford University Press, 2006, and the works mentioned in Joan C. Tronto, "Care Ethics: Moving Forward." *Hypatia,* Volume 14, Number 1 Winter (1999), among others. Similarly, there is also an attempt to reinstate the fundamental importance of context in recent work in Pragmatist ethics: for example Todd Lekan, *Making Morality: Pragmatist Reconstruction in Ethical Theory.* Nashville: Vanderbilt University Press, 2003 and Steven Fesmire, *John Dewey and Moral Imagination: Pragmatism in Ethics.* Bloomington: Indiana University Press, 2003. For moral particularism, see Brad Hooker and Margaret Little (editors), *Moral Particularism.* Oxford UK: Oxford University Press, 2000. Most recently Richard Shusterman in *Body Consciousness: A Philosophy of Mindfulness and Somaesthetics.* Cambridge: Cambridge University Press, 2008 and *Practicing Philosophy: Pragmatism and the Philosophical Life.* New York: Routledge, 1997, and in many of his other books has argued for an educated and elegant somaticity as integral to the cultivation of the consummate life. Robert C. Solomon over a distinguished career led the discipline in arguing for and promoting literacy in the philosophy of the emotions.

14 We are "borrowing" this distinction from Saussure because we do not want to endorse the kind of structuralism that would allow for any severe separation between *langue* and *parole*, instead siding with the sentiments of Mikhail Bakhtin who would see these two dimensions of language as mutually shaping and evolving in their always dialectical relationship. Utterances gradually change the structure of language, and the changing structure orients and influences the utterances that it makes possible.

it either a concept or a term that can be used to capture the Abrahamic notion of "God," while at the same time allowing us to insist that the same Chinese language has all of the semantic and syntactic resources necessary to give a fair account of such an idea. What we are saying about this absence in the *langue* of the Chinese language is precisely what Qian Mu is quite properly saying about the want of a Western vocabulary to adequately speak Confucianism: you cannot say "*li* 禮" in English or German although you can say lots about it.

Finally, Zhang in disqualifying our claim of disparity in the relative value that different cultures invest in abstract conceptualizations inadvertently saves Confucianism from what we would take to be an entirely appropriate critique. It precludes what we would accept as a salutary criticism of the limits of Confucianism made by many scholars late and soon, Western and Chinese alike, the philosopher Bertrand Russell and the sociologist Jin Yaoji 金耀基 (Ambrose King) being prominent among them. In these pages we want to join these scholars in advocating for a revitalized Confucian moral philosophy adequate to the complexities of the modern world that complements its traditional emphasis upon family feeling as both the entry point and the substance of moral competence with a more robust framework of regulative ideals directed at preempting the all too frequent misuse of intimate relationships that gives rise to nepotism, cronyism, and other forms of social and political corruption. Just as intimacy needs the restraining complement of integrity, concrete family feelings require the guiding complement of some form of more general ideals.

This same argument against Zhang Longxi in favor of articulating an interpretive context might be summarized this way. We would contend that the only thing more dangerous than striving to make the responsible cultural generalizations that provide interpretive context is failing to make them. Generalizations do not have to preclude appreciating the richness and complexity of always evolving cultural traditions; in fact, it is generalizations that locate and inform specific cultural details and provide otherwise sketchy historical developments with the thickness of their content. There is no alternative in making cultural comparisons to an open, hermeneutical approach that is ready to modify always provisional generalizations with the new information that additional detail yields as it is interpreted within the grid of generalizations.

Recently, and specifically in reference to the classical Chinese language, the distinguished sinologist Angus Graham concludes that in reporting on the eventful flow of *qi* cosmology, the sentence structure of Classical Chinese places us in a world of process about which we ask … "Whence?" and also, since it is moving, "At what time?"[15] It is for this reason that we have consistently advocated

15 Angus Graham, *Studies in Chinese Philosophy and Philosophical Literature.* Albany NY: State University of New York Press, 1990, p. 408.

a holistic, narrative understanding as being more revealing of underlying cultural assumptions than merely an atemporal and essentializing analytical approach.

How can we address this gap between our languages and their implicit worldviews? If Ludwig Wittgenstein is insightful in suggesting that "the limits of our language are the limits of our world," then perhaps we need more language. By developing a nuanced understanding of a classical Greek vocabulary – *logos, nous, phusis, kosmos, eidos, alethea*, and so on – we are able to get behind Descartes and in degree, read classical Greek texts on their own terms, and in a more sophisticated way. By generating and appropriating a glossary of key philosophical terms around which the Chinese texts are woven, we will be better able to locate these seminal texts in their own intellectual landscape.

Philosophical interpreters must sensitize the student of Chinese philosophy to the ambient uncommon assumptions reflected in concept clusters that have made the Chinese philosophical narrative so different from our own. It is these assumptions that inform the philosophical vocabulary and set parameters on their meanings. Are these generic assumptions essential and unchanging? Of course not, but that is not to say that we can venture to make cultural comparisons without a hermeneutical sensibility that guards against the perils of cultural reductionism. A failure of interpreters to be self-conscious and to take fair account of their own Gadamerian "prejudices" with the excuse that they are relying on some "objective" lexicon that, were the truth be known, is itself heavily colored with cultural biases, is to betray their readers not once, but twice. Just as each generation selects and carries over earlier thinkers to reshape them in their own image, each generation reconfigures the classical canons of world philosophy to its own needs. We too are inescapably people of a time and place. This self-consciousness is not to distort the Chinese philosophical tradition, but to endorse its fundamental premises.

Henry Rosemont, Jr.

Rights-Bearing Individuals and Role-Bearing Persons*

I. Introduction

Throughout a productive and inspiring career, Herbert Fingarette has challenged received opinion on topics as diverse as alcoholism and the law, and on thinkers as diverse as Sigmund Freud and Confucius.[1] In doing so, he has combined logical rigor with sensitivity and insight into the human condition, enhancing measurably our understanding of ourselves and of the contemporary world in which we endeavor to lead meaningful lives.

His work is altogether original, and I would hypothesize that a measure of that originality can be traced to Fingarette's familiarity with, and respect for, non-Western philosophy, especially that of the early Chinese. He studied the classical language in order to read the texts on his own, and he has acknowledged a great philosophical debt to Confucius.[2] Also, some evidence for this hypothesis can be found in the fact that although he has had many important things to say about such matters as the law, treatment of disease, insanity, and criminal responsibility, Fingarette almost never employs the concept of rights – human, legal, or

---

* Portions of the present essay were taken from my "Why Take Rights Seriously? A Confucian Critique" in *Human Rights and the World's Religions*, ed. L. Rouner (Notre Dame, IN: University of Notre Dame Press, 1988).

1 See his *The Self in Transformation* (New York: Basic Books, 1963); *On Responsibility* (New York: Basic Books, 1067); *The Meaning of Criminal Insanity* (Berkeley: University of California Press, 1972); *Confucius – The Secular as Sacred* (New York: Harper and Row, 1972); *Heavy, Drinking* (Berkeley: University of California Press, 1989).

2 See my review of his *Confucius – The Secular as Sacred* in *Philosophy East and West* 26, no. 4 (October, 1976), his Response and my Reply in *Philosophy East and West* 28, no. 4 (October, 1978). He doses his response with the words, "I hoped Confucius might show others the vision, as he did me." I, too, have seen this vision, owing in significant measure to Fingarette's writings, and to several pleasurable conversations with him, all of which I am grateful for, and happy to acknowledge herein. "I have been encouraged where he agrees, and I have profited from exploring our differences" – as he was gracious enough to say about my work in his Response.

civil – in his analyses and evaluations; and the modern concept of rights is altogether absent in ancient Chinese thought.

In what follows, I would like to further test this hypothesis by making explicit what I thus take to be implicit but important in Fingarette's writings: a critique of the modern Western concept of rights, coupled with a sketch of an alternative view of what it is to be a person that is fundamentally Confucian. This "test," of course, is actually an extended invitation for him to respond to these fundamental issues as they bear on his philosophical views.

II. Rights-Bearing Individuals

It is a fairly bedrock presupposition of our moral, social, and political thinking – national and international – that human beings have rights. Both as scholars and as citizens of the Western capitalistic democracies we are strongly inclined to say that certain basic rights obtain independently of sex, color, age, ethnicity, abilities, time, or place; we have certain rights solely in virtue of being human. Which rights are basic, how conflicting rights-claims are to be adjudicated, the extent to which legal and political rights originating in a specific nation-state are to be differentiated from more universal moral rights, whether rights should be the foundation of moral and/or political theory are, among others, issues in dispute. But with a very few notable exceptions, the concept of individual human beings as rights-bearers is not itself in serious question in contemporary Western moral, social, and political thinking.

Nothing is more plain, however, than the facts that everyone of us does have a definite sex, a color, an age, an ethnic background, certain abilities; that we all live in a specific time, and a specific place. We are all born and reared in a specific cultural community, each with its language, values, religious orientation, customs, traditions, and concomitant ideas of what it is to be a human being. There are not, in short, any culturally independent human beings. Each of us has specific hopes, fears, joys, sorrows, values, and views which are inextricably linked to our definitions of who and what we are, and these definitions have been overwhelmingly influenced by the cultural community of which we are a part. F. H. Bradley has made this point – in another context – well:[3]

> Let us take a man, an Englishman as he is now, and try to point out that apart from what he has in common with others, apart from his sameness with others, he is not an Englishman – not a man at all; that if you take him as something by himself; he is not what he is ... he is what he is because he is a born and educated social being, and a

3 F. H. Bradley, *Ethical* 2nd ed. (New York: Oxford University Press, 1962), p. 166. I am indebted to David Wong for calling this passage to my attention.

> member of an individual social organism; ... if you make abstraction of all this, which is the same in him and in others, what you have left is not an Englishman, nor a man, but some I know not what residuum, which never has existed by itself, and does not so exist.

These considerations suggest a disturbing question: if, as is the case, a majority of the world's peoples live in cultures which do not have a concept of rights, or have concepts incompatible with that concept, then how could, or should, the members of those cultures imagine what it would be like to have rights, or that it would be right and good and proper for them to so imagine?[4] It should be clear that our own concept of human rights is closely related to our own views of human beings as freely-choosing autonomous individuals, views which are at least as old as the epistemological reflections of Descartes, and which found moral and political expression in such writings as those of John Locke, the Virginia Declaration of Rights, the Declaration of Independence, and the French Declaration of the Rights of Man. To be sure, this concept of human beings is embodied in the 1948 U.N. Declaration of Human Rights, and it might therefore be seen now as a more or less universal and not culture-bound concept. But let me quote the Preamble therefrom:[5]

> Now therefore the General Assembly proclaims this Universal Declaration of Human Rights as a common standard of achievement for all peoples and all nations to the end that every individual and every organ of society keeping this declaration constantly in mind, shall strive by teaching and education to secure respect for these rights and freedoms, and by progressive measures national and international, to secure their effective recognition and observance. ...

Note the key expressions here: "standard of achievement;" "shall strive by teaching and education;" "by progressive measures national and international" Clearly the framers of this Declaration, overwhelmingly drawn from the culture of the Western industrial democracies, were concerned to propose a particular moral and political perspective, an ideal not yet extant, as the standard toward which all nations, and all peoples, should strive.

But now, as we approach the celebration of the forty-third anniversary of the U.N. Declaration, it remains true that upwards of 70 % of the world's peoples have no intimate acquaintance with the culture of the Western industrial democracies. They never have lived, do not now live, and, because of economic,

4 Although he endeavors to rebut it in the course of his book, this argument has been well stated by A. J. M. Milne in his *Human Rights and Human Diversity* (Albany, NY: SUNY Press, 1985), pp. 3–6. Milne wishes to ground the concept of rights in the larger concept of a community, and thus a person's "rights (what he is entitled to as a member) consist of all that is due to him;" (p. 115).

5 As cited in ibid., p. 2.

environmental, and cultural circumstances, will not so live for a very long time, if ever.

Conjoining these two considerations, we seem to be forced to embrace what is highly fashionable philosophically these days, a form of relativism,[6] toward which two extreme responses have been given. On the one hand, we might wish to simply accept the "diff'rnt strokes for diff'rnt folks" idea, and cease believing that our philosophical efforts can find a purchase beyond our Western cultural heritage; at this extreme, it cannot ultimately make any sense to argue that a particular view of human beings is any better, or any worse, than any other, because there could be no culturally independent grounds for settling the argument. On the other hand, we can simply dig in our heels, and insist that all human beings *do* have rights even if they are not recognized in other cultures, that if other cultures don't have our concept of rights, they *should* have it, and will all of them be the worse morally and politically if they do not.

Now the first extreme has a commendable aura of tolerance about it, but has as well the untoward consequence of leaving us nothing significant to say ethically about the activities of such people as the Marquis de Sade, Aztec ritual cannibals, slave societies, or The Waffen S.S. Pessimism, cynicism, nihilism, are all predictable, if not logically necessary outgrowths of this position, evidenced, I believe, both in much of contemporary Western society, and in much contemporary Western philosophy.

The other extreme has the virtue of arguing for a moral ground from which culturally and historically independent judgments might be rendered, but has had the untoward consequence, for which there is a sorry superfluity of historical documentation, of grounding the morality in the culture of the Western industrial democracies, with the attendant chauvinism, imperialism, and, increasingly now, irrelevance for the more than three billion people who do not share that culture.

Strong words here, but I do not believe I have exaggerated, and have stated these positions in this way in order to throw into sharp relief an alternative I wish to pose for consideration: that there is a conceptual framework – what I will call a "concept-cluster" – within which both ethical statements and an ethical theory can be articulated which can be applicable to, understood and appreciated by, all of the world's peoples, but that before such a concept-cluster can be worked out by philosophers, *the* Western philosophical tradition will have to incorporate in the future more of the views of non-Western philosophies than it has in the past. If our own modern ethical, social, and political philosophies, in which the con-

6 "Relativism" is of course a loaded philosophical term today. For fuller discussion, see my "Against Relativism," in *Interpreting Across Boundaries:* ed. Gerald Larson and Eliot Deutsch (Princeton, NJ: Princeton University Press, 1988).

cept of rights is central, are outgrowths of a culture encompassing no more than 25 % of the human race, and if there are other rational ethical and political philosophies which more or less reflect the presuppositions and assumptions of the other 75 %, then those assumptions and presuppositions should be incorporated, if at all humanly possible, into any ethical and/or political philosophy which claimed to be universal. All the more so is this necessary if it is now the case that our own concept-cluster surrounding rights not only separates us from our fellows in other cultures, it is increasingly separating us from each other within our own culture, a point to which I will return toward the end.

If my alternative is to be made at all attractive, I shall have to talk more about rights and associated ethical concepts within the context of our culture, and then must endeavor to partially de-contextualize – not deconstruct – those concepts by considering some issues that are usually referred to vaguely as falling under comparative studies, and simultaneously to endeavor to bracket our Western ethical concept-cluster by contrasting it with another, in this case, the concept-cluster of the early Confucian philosophers.

On any given day, somewhere in the world a number of our fellows are being confined in highly inhospitable environments, are in fear for their lives, and are being subjected to a host of physical and psychological indignities. Some are incarcerated and being tortured basically because of their color, others because of their nationality, still others are imprisoned because of their political beliefs, and others yet are being persecuted in similar ways for their religious and attendant social convictions. And we also have many instances, either undertaken independently or in concert with one or more governments, of the taking of hostages, or random acts of terrorism and torture.

We are angry at these circumstances and events, indignant that they continue to take place, and probably feel frustrated that we are personally able to do so little to bring an end to such heinous practices.

Consider, now, the accounts we would typically give to describe and explain our feelings and beliefs about these practices. They are unjust, we say: no one should be imprisoned, tortured, or held hostage, simply due to their color, nationality, political or religious beliefs, because all human beings have basic rights, rights which are clearly being violated in these instances. When, having broken no reasonable law, individuals are denied their liberty, their livelihood, their property, and are in fear for their physical well being, they are being unjustly deprived of the opportunities to freely choose their actions, and therefore stand in loss of the self-governing autonomy which makes them uniquely human.

Such an account is sufficiently straightforward that virtually every reflective citizen of the English-speaking countries would accede to it, and consequently I do not wish to challenge it as an accurate reflection of our cultural perspective; it is the same perspective incorporated in the U.N. Declaration. Rather do I want to suggest that the complex philosophical notion of the individual, the self, which underlies this account may not be the most appropriate, or the most advanced, or the most humane way to characterize the members of our species. It is certainly not the account the vast majority of the human race would give.

Moreover, within the Western industrial democracies, especially in America, the concepts of rights and autonomous, freely choosing individuals is central not only to the problems of political prisoners, hostages, terrorist acts and torture in the international arena, but to virtually all of the pressing national ethical issues of our time as well. Speaking broadly, the abortion controversy is usually couched in terms of whether fetuses may be said to have rights, and if so, whether those rights take precedence over the rights of women to control their own bodies.[7]

Issues surrounding suicide and terminally ill patients are commonly analyzed by asking when, if ever, the rights of the individual to decide matters affecting his or her own life and death may be overridden by doctors or others on the basis either of sound medical practice or the premiss that where there's life, there's hope.[8]

Turning to environmental concerns, ecologists of varied persuasions commonly defend their positions by appealing to the rights of our descendants to inherit a maximally healthy and genetically diversified natural world,[9] and with respect to animals, a number of philosophers and others are asking whether or not animals may be seen to have rights solely in virtue of their being living things, rights which place sharp constraints on our right to manipulate them and/or the natural environments in which they live.[10]

And finally, I do not believe it is too grand a generalization to say that a number of domestic, ostensibly political issues – e.g., welfare, tax reform, capital

7 The discussions which have contributed to the second-order account of abortion touched on here and below are Judith Thomson, "A Defense of Abortion," in *Philosophy and Public Affairs* 1 (1972); Mary Anne Warren, "On the Moral and Legal Status of Abortion" in the *Monist* 57 (1973); L.W. Summer *Abortion and Moral Theory* (Princeton, NJ: Princeton University Press, 1981), and David B. Wong, *Moral Relativity* (Berkeley; University of California Press, 1984), with the possible exception of Wong, however, it is doubtful that any of the other authors cited here would concur with what has been said in the text on this divisive issue.

8 See, for example, James Rachels, "Active and Passive Euthanasia," in the *New England Journal of Medicine* 292, no. 2, (1975).

9 Beginning philosophically with John Passmore's *Man's Responsibility for Nature* (New York; Charles Scribner's, Sons, 1973); and now a major and diverse field of study.

10 A now somewhat dated, but still useful anthology is *Animal Rights and Human Obligations*, ed. Tom Regan and Peter Singer (Englewood Cliffs, NJ: Prentice-Hall, 1976); and there is much more recently written by both editors, and many others.

punishment, affirmative action – reduce to a more fundamental ethical tension between individual rights and social justice.[11]

If this all-too-hurried outline nevertheless seems roughly correct, we can appreciate that a great many of the major controversies of our time are described, analyzed, and evaluated within the conceptual framework of a rights-based morality. To be sure, once we move from the general public arena to the narrower domain of ethical philosophy there is much less uniformity. Here we might speak of goal-based, and duty-based moralities as well. Thinkers working in the Kantian tradition for example, accord rights a more basic place in their theories than do the adherents of any of the several forms of utilitarianism, and a few philosophers, such as MacIntyre, are turning away from contemporary moral theories altogether, forcefully arguing instead for the re-introduction of a virtue-based moral philosophy inspired by an updated Aristotle.[12]

But MacIntyre's work has not yet made significant inroads into discussions of rights, and however differently different Lockeans, Kantians, Benthamites, and others wish to ground our moral principles, the concept of rights is crucial to all of their views.

Most foundational is Robert Nozick, who states on the first line of the first page of his *Anarchy, State, and Utopia*[13] that

> Individuals have rights, and there are things no person or group may do to them (without violating their rights). (p. ix)

In his influential *A Theory of Justice*,[14] John Rawls formulates his First Principle as follows:

> Each person is to have an equal right to the most extensive total system of equal basic liberties compatible with a similar system of liberty for all. (p. 302)

And on behalf of the modern British tradition, the following passage from R. M. Hare's recent *Moral Thinking*[15] is fairly typical:

> It should be clear by now how lacking in substance is the common objection to utilitarianism which might be advanced against my own theory of moral reasoning too, that it can give no place to rights, and can ride rough-shod over them in the interests of utility ... If we take [rights] seriously enough to inquire what they are and what their

11 See A. MacIntyre, *After Virtue* (Notre Dame, IN; University of Notre Dame Press, 1981), esp. pp. 229–33.

12 The major thrust of *After Virtue*, op. cit. See also *Whose Justice? Which Rationality?* (Notre Dame, IN: University of Notre Dame Press, 1988). Although I am not convinced of the superiority of the Greek and Christian traditions over the Chinese, my debt to MacIntyre is great, evidenced herein and in other of my recent writings.

13 Robert Nozick, *Anarchy, State and Utopia* (New York: Basic Books, 1974).

14 John Rawls, *A Theory of Justice* (Cambridge, MA: Harvard University Press, 1971).

15 R. M. Hare, *Moral Thinking* (Oxford: Oxford University Press, 1981).

> status is, we shall discover that they are, indeed, an immensely important element in our moral thinking ..., but that this provides no argument at all against utilitarians. For utilitarianism is better able to secure this status than are institutionist theories. (pp. 154–55)

From these citations – chosen virtually at random – and our earlier considerations it should be clear that the concept of rights thoroughly permeates contemporary Western moral and political thinking, even for those philosophers who do not give it pride of place in their moral and political theories. And just because it permeates our thinking so pervasively, we should not be surprised that the term "rights" is seldom fully defined by those who employ the term most frequently.

The best example of this is the well-known, tightly argued work *Taking Rights Seriously*,[16] in which Ronald Dworkin reflects on this point, and deserves to be quoted at some length:

> Principles are propositions that describe rights; policies are propositions that describe goals. But what are rights and goals and what is the difference? It is hard to supply any definition that does not beg the question. It seems natural to say, for example, that freedom of speech is a right, not a goal, because citizens are entitled to that freedom as a matter of political morality, and that increased munitions manufacture is a goal, not a right, because it contributes to collective welfare, but no particular manufacturer is entitled to a government contract. This does not improve our understanding, however, because the concept of entitlement uses rather than explains the concept of a right. (p. 90)

In a not unrelated way, Patricia Werhane,[17] in attempting to ground her views on moral rights, begins with:

> I shall assume that all human beings, and in particular rational adults, have inherent value. Because human beings have inherent value they have certain rights. These rights are moral rights ... (p. 3)

Now Werhane's statement may appear unexceptionable to us, but it does exhibit the question-begging problem of defining rights mentioned by Dworkin, for one could certainly hold that human beings have inherent value without having the concept of rights at all. (The early Confucians are a cardinal example.)

If a definition of rights is not ready to hand, we may attempt to further elucidate the concept by examining how rights are distinguished, and by enu-

---

16 Ronald Dworkin, *Taking Rights Seriously* (Cambridge, MA: Harvard University Press, 1977). Because the concept of rights is intimately bound up with the legal systems of the English-speaking countries, and Dworkin is engaged significantly in the philosophy of law, he surely has a "right" to urge us to "take rights seriously."

17 Patricia Werhane, *Persons, Rights, and Corporations* (Englewood Cliffs, NJ: Prentice-Hall, 1985).

merating them. The right to life is taken to be a passive right – because it requires recognition by others – while the right of freedom is an active right because one must do something in order to exercise it. Rights are also distinguished as positive and negative, i. e., the right to security as opposed to the right not to be tortured. The most common division is between *prima facie* and absolute rights, or, as they are also described, defeasible and indefeasible rights. There is little agreement among philosophers about which rights are absolute, if indeed there are any, but the following have been defended as the most basic rights of all: H. L. A. Hart[18] and others have argued for the primacy of the right to freedom, Henry Shue[19] for the primacy of the right to security, and subsistence. Many philosophers consider the right to life as the most basic,[20] but Dworkin argues that the right to equal consideration (not equal treatment) underlies all of the others.[21]

We could go on further distinguishing the differing positions in contemporary Western moral philosophies, but need not for present purposes: what links them together, tautologically, is that they are all uniformly described as moral philosophies, and in this technical sense I should like to argue that early Confucianism should *not* be described as a moral philosophy. To show why this is so, and at the same time to allay any suspicion that despite my avowed intent, a radical moral relativism underlies my position, let us consider one of the sets of arguments commonly given on behalf of moral relativism based on examinations of other cultures, the arguments from anthropological evidence.[22]

We do not need to question, at least initially, the reliability of the wealth of ethnographic data which appear to demonstrate the regularity with which a particular human action has been loathed by one people, and at least tolerated, if not applauded, by another. But this evidence, by itself, will not do what a moral relativist might think it does; there is a logical point involved.

18 H. L. A. Han, "Are There Any Natural Rights?" *Philosophical Review* 64 (1955).

19 Henry Shue, *Basic Rights* (Princeton, NJ: Princeton University Press, 1980).

20 See Milne, op. cit., p. 139.

21 Dworkin, op. cit., pp. 180–83.

22 These arguments begin with Westermarck, and later Herskovits, in Europe, and with Boas and his students – especially Kroebler and Benedict – in the U.S. For summary, see G. Stocking, Jr., *Race, Culture, and Evolution: Essays in the History Of Anthropology,* (New York: Free Press, 1968), and E. Hatch, *Culture and Morality* (New York: Columbia University Press, 1983). For both anthropologists and philosophers, a number of articles discussing moral relativism are contained in *Rationality,* ed. Bryan Wilson (Worcester, MA: Basil Blackwell, 1970); *Rationality and Relativism,* ed. M. Hollis and S. Lukes (Cambridge, MA: MIT Press, 1982); *Relativism: Cognitive and Moral,* ed. M. Krausz and J. Meiland (Notre Dame, IN: University of Notre Dame Press, 1982). A recent anthropological statement is Clifford Gcertz's "Anti Anti-Relativism," in *The American Anthropologist* 86, no. 2 (1984). For a recent philosophical statement, see Wong, op. cit.

The farther we get from modern English and related Western languages, the farther do we get from lexical items which correspond closely to the term "moral." *All* languages of course have terms for the approval and disapproval of human conduct, and also have terms for concepts employed in the evaluation of that conduct; but a great many of the world's languages have no words which connote and denote uniquely a set of actions ostensibly circumscribed by the pair "moral-immoral" as against the nonmoral. In this light, we should not be surprised that morals, like rights, is a sufficiently foundational concept in Western philosophical thinking that it is almost never given a clear definition.

The simplicity of this linguistic fact should not obscure its philosophical significance: speakers (writers) of languages having no term corresponding to "moral" cannot logically have any *moral* principles (or moral theories), from which it follows that they cannot have any moral principles incompatible with other moral principles, our own or anyone else's.

Imagine attempting to describe uniquely the set of human actions which should be evaluated as moral or immoral, distinguishing them from those actions for which the evaluations would be inappropriate – to someone not raised in any of the modern Western cultures. What would be central, and possessed by all members of the set? But this question cannot be answered unless we assume the correctness of some particular philosopher's views: motives more or less for Kantians (i. e., based on the use of the categorical imperative), consequences for utilitarians, intrinsic worth, perhaps, or piety, for many Christians. The most that we could say was that under particular circumstances virtually any human action *could* have moral consequences. This is probably true, but notice that it is not particularly helpful to someone from another culture who did not already have our modern concept of morals in advance. (What might be said of the Confucians slightly misleadingly is that every human action *does* have what we – not the Confucians – would call moral consequences.)

Put another way, *we* might disapprove of an action which members of another culture approve. But if our disapproval rests on criteria essentially involving the concept-cluster of contemporary rights-based morality, a concept-cluster absent their culture (language), and if their approval rests on criteria involving a concept-cluster absent our culture (language), then it is simply a question-begging, logical mistake to say that the members of the two cultures are in basic *moral* disagreement; the term is ours, culturally defined, it is not theirs. The ethnographic argument for moral relativism gains force only if it can be shown that two different people(s) evaluated human conduct in the same way invoking similar criteria grounded and exhibited in the same or very similar concept-cluster – and that one approved the action, and the other disapproved.

It may seem that a big fuss is being made over a little word: why not simply find the closest approximation to the English "moral" in the language (culture) under investigation, and proceed with the analysis from there? This is exactly what most anthropologists, and not a few philosophers and linguists, have done. But now consider specifically the classical Chinese language in which the early Confucians wrote their philosophical views. Not merely does that language contain no lexical item for "moral," it also does not have terms, for example, corresponding to "freedom," "liberty," "autonomy," "individual," "utility," "principles," "rationality," "rational agent," "action," "objective," "subjective," "choice," "dilemma," "duty," "rights," and probably most eerie of all for a moralist, classical Chinese has no lexical item corresponding to "ought" – prudential or obligatory. (And we might suspect that the vast majority of other human languages which do not have a lexical equivalent for "moral" will not have equivalents for most of these other modern English terms either; which could hardly be coincidental.)[23]

No, it is not only a term corresponding to "moral" that must be sought in other languages if we are to speak cross-culturally about morals, for the sphere of contemporary Western moral philosophy is designated only roughly by the single term itself; a clear delimitation requires the full concept-cluster of terms just adumbrated, plus a few others. Now if contemporary Western moral philosophers can't (don't) talk about moral issues without using these terms, and if none of the terms occurs in classical Chinese, it follows that the early Confucians couldn't be moral philosophers in our modern sense, and we will consequently be guaranteed to miss what they might have to tell us about human conduct, and what it is to be a human being, if we insist upon imposing on their writings the conceptual framework constitutive of our modern moral discourse. (And the same may be said, *mutatis mutandis,* of members of other cultures who spoke or wrote about basic human conduct descriptively and evaluatively.)[24]

For this reason, and for others I have argued elsewhere,[25] I should like to distinguish "morals" from "ethics;" if the full and rich history of Western ethical thought and its variants in other cultures is to be fully intelligible to us, the subject must be defined so as to be inclusive of the ancient Greeks, their Christian successors, modern Western moral theorists, the early Confucians, and the relevant concept-clusters of many other non-Western cultures as well.

---

23 The notion of "concept-cluster" is important for translation matters here, because arguments endeavoring to show that *dao,* or *li,* or *yi,* or some other single Chinese graph, might appropriately be translated as "morals," cannot succeed unless one is also willing to offer Chinese lexical candidates for "subjective," "rights," "choice," and so forth – an altogether question-begging philological effort. See note 33 for further discussion.

24 For further discussion of the relations between concepts and terms, see my "Against Relativism," op. cit., esp. fn. 11.

25 Ibid.

ethics = df. (1) The systematic study of the basic terms (concepts) employed in the description, analysis, and evaluation of human conduct. (2) The employment of these basic terms (concepts) in the evaluation of human conduct.

It might be objected that this definition is too broad. Under it, one might decide to study, for example, the descriptions, analyses, and evaluations of such human activities as slurping soup, wearing inappropriate dress, the improper performance of rituals or making crude sexual advances; and surely we must distinguish rudeness from immoral conduct? Of course we must, if we are committed in advance to contemporary rights-based moralities as the be-all and end-all of *ethical* thinking. Unfortunately, such commitment, common though it may be, begs a large cultural question, for without the vocabulary of the concept-cluster of contemporary Western moral philosophy, it is fairly difficult to state clearly the purported distinction between "boorishness" and "immorality," as everyone who has contemplated the meaning and significance of *li* (ritual) knows full well. The above definition allows greater room for comparative studies than contemporary Western philosophical usage would encourage. It also, not irrelevantly, approximates fairly closely the more ordinary usages of "ethics" as found in standard dictionaries of English and simultaneously reflects the linguistic fact that whereas even philosophers speak of "social ethics," "medical ethics," "professional ethics," and so forth, they do not – nor does anyone else – speak of "social morals," or "professional morals."[26]

If the concept-cluster dominating contemporary Western moral philosophies is correctly seen, its variations notwithstanding, as only one among many possible ethical orientations, we must reflect on a number of consequences which follow from making this distinction. Returning now to the issue of moral relativism, the distinction between morals and ethics of course does not completely vitiate arguments given on behalf of ethical (or cultural) relativism, but it does call into question a number of their premisses; clearly the "moral" counter-arguments here are not confined to the ancient Chinese language, as already noted. Retranslations and reinterpretations must be carefully made before the extant ethnographic data can be called forth again in support of relativistic theses. Ethical relativism may be true, but it is not entailed by (rights-based) moral relativism.

Second, making this distinction shows that non-Western materials, despite the ever-increasing sophistication of comparative scholarship, continue to be approached from a strongly Western perspective. To be sure, no comparative scholar can come to another culture as a *tabula rasa*. One need not be committed

26 This is undoubtedly so because the basic vocabulary of the concept-cluster of contemporary Western moral philosophy is not sufficient for describing and analyzing issues that fall within these areas, and in some cases – e.g., religious ethics – it isn't necessary either.

to relativistic theses to admit that pure (culture-free) objectivity is a myth: again, physicists and physicians, scholars and scolds, plain men and philosopher queens are one and all ineradicably influenced by their cultural and historical circumstances. But it must equally be admitted that there are degrees of culture-boundedness, degrees which are in principle capable of being measured by all. Anthropologists of the late nineteenth century, for instance, made intelligence the determining characteristic of culture, and it was certainly a step toward reducing the Victorian English chauvinism underlying that concept when the focus shifted to learning as the determining characteristic.[27]

This approach, while cheerily optimistic, may yet appear to rest on a conceptual confusion. The vocabulary of contemporary Western moral philosophy is deeply embedded in the language we all speak both as scholars and as citizens, and it would therefore seem that Confucian ethics can't be all that different from contemporary Western moral philosophy, or else we couldn't understand accounts of it in English as ethical thinking. That is to say, in order to make a case for the Confucian persuasion, isn't it necessary to employ some at least of the English-language concept-cluster comprising contemporary Western moral philosophies? And if so, then isn't Confucian ethics after all not so very different therefrom?[28]

I maintain that the concept-cluster of early Confucian ethics is very different indeed from the philosophical concept-cluster I have been discussing. The vocabulary of English for making normative judgments and discussing ethics,

27 For the history of this development in anthropology, see Stocking, op. cit., and Hatch, op. cit.

28 This argument can also be put as a paradox of exposition and/or advocacy for claims of incommensurable belief systems. In the present case of ethics, it can be stated thus: if two ethical conceptual frameworks (concept-clusters) are taken to be total, and as sufficiently dissimilar as to be irreconcilable, then we could only make a case for the superiority of one framework over the other by assuming or presupposing the correctness of some at least of the ethical concepts embedded in the framework claimed to be superior. But on the first horn, if these assumptions or presuppositions are accepted by one's audience, it would seem that arguments wouldn't be needed to command conviction. On the other horn, if the relevant assumptions or presuppositions are not accepted by one's audience, it would seem that no arguments could command conviction. Either the assumptions or presuppositions will be accepted by one's audience, or they won't; in either case, it would seem that arguments are not simply irrelevant, but altogether worthless for commanding conviction. It is something akin to those considerations that led Davidson ("On the Very Idea of a Conceptual Scheme") to say "Most of our beliefs must be true." And if what is meant by "alternative conceptual frameworks" are totally and incompatibly different, then the claim is correct, and does imply the conclusion of the paradox. However, Davidson's use of "our" is ambiguous. If it simply refers to mature, English (and related modern Western language) speakers, it is unexceptionable. But if "our" refers to contemporary Western moral philosophers, his claim is suspect; and it is only the latter, and not the former that the Confucians challenge, dissolving the seeming paradox, as the text goes on to maintain. *(Proceedings and Addresses of the American Philosophical Association,* no. 47, 1974.)

however, is far richer than is found in contemporary rights-based moral philosophy. If I may put the matter bluntly, the most fundamental challenge raised by early Confucian ethics is that contemporary Western moral philosophy has become increasingly irrelevant to day in, day out, concrete ethical concerns; utilizing an impoverished – and largely bureaucratic[29] – technical vocabulary emphasizing law, abstract logic, the formation of policy statements, and employing altogether implausible hypothetical examples, contemporary rights-based moral philosophy, the Confucian texts suggest, is no longer grounded in the real hopes, fears, joys, sorrows, ideas, and attitudes of flesh and blood human beings. Since the time of Descartes, Western philosophy – not alone moral philosophy – has increasingly abstracted a purely cognizing activity away from concrete persons and determined that this use of logical reasoning in a disembodied "mind" is the choosing, autonomous essence of individuals, which is philosophically more foundational than are actual persons; the latter being only contingently who they are, and therefore of no great philosophical significance.

What the early Confucian writings reflect, however, is that there are no disembodied minds, nor autonomous individuals; to paraphrase Fingarette, unless there are at least two human beings, there can be no human beings.[30] By their lights, the writings of virtually every Western philosopher from Descartes to the present can only be seen as incantations for exorcising the human ghost from the calculating machine, to the current extreme that we cannot any longer even be certain that we aren't brains in vats. But to advance this challenge on behalf of the early Confucians is not to decry the Western cultural tradition, nor to applaud raw feeling, nor to claim that irrationality is somehow more human than rationality – all of which would involve a misreading of the Confucian texts, and would be fairly difficult claims to establish on the basis of rational argumentation given in a language central to the Western rational tradition. Rather is it to suggest that the contemporary philosophical stereotype of a disembodied, purely logical and calculating autonomous individual is simply too far removed from what we feel and think human beings to be, it has raised problems that seem incapable of solution, and it is therefore becoming increasingly difficult for moral, social, or political philosophies embodying this stereotype to have much purchase even on ourselves, not to mention the peoples who do not live as inheritors of the Western philosophical tradition.

We must pursue this issue in greater depth, because this stereotype does not fail descriptively merely for contingent reasons, it must fail necessarily. It is

29 The expression "bureaucratic rationality" is from Williams, *Ethics and the Limits of Philosophy* (Cambridge, MA: Harvard University Press, 1985), p. 206.

30 "Thc Music of Humanity in the Conversations of Confucius," in the *Journal of Chinese Philosophy* 10 (1983).

admitted on all sides that human beings are not simply self-conscious and capable of reason, they are agents, which means they can act purposefully, and will act in different ways depending on what purposes they have. Purposes are ends, and there is a great multiplicity of possible ends one might strive to achieve. The problem arises when we ask how we can decide which ends we ought to strive to achieve, because of the persuasiveness of Hume's argument that no imperative statement (encompassing values) is logically derivable from any set of declarative statements (encompassing facts). It has long remained unquestioned, that to decide how to act it is not enough to be aware of things as they objectively are. Something more is needed to get to values, but what? And from whence can it come? Hume's position (in the *Treatise* and the *Enquiry,* at any rate) entails that answers to these questions must be "nothing", and therefore "nowhere"; our values are ultimately ungrounded.

The spell of this problem of the gulf between facts and values was indeed first cast by Hume, but its enchanting powers derive from Descartes' view of what it is to be a human being, Hume's anti-Cartesianism notwithstanding. The plausibility of this form of skepticism about values requires that we see human beings as having bodies, each with a specific shape, weight, color, and spatial and temporal location, bodies which generate a mixed set of impulses, emotions, passions, attitudes, and so forth. Hovering over and above each of these lumps of matter and messy assemblages of psychological states is a pure (because disembodied) mind, supremely competent to ascertain how things are (the objective word of fact/science), and how things must be (the necessary world of logic/mathematics), but – Hume's contribution – altogether worthless for determining how things ought be (the world of ends/values). The break between mind and body is total. Moreover, the bodies we have are obviously contingent upon the way the world happens to be, and are subject to all of the causal laws which govern this contingent world; and how could such contingently existing, causally determined lumps of matter have value, be the source of value?

In one sense, it is philosophically irrelevant whether we accept this general picture of human beings as literally true, or simply as a Western conceit useful for theorizing about issues, akin in large measure to Hobbesian capitalists in a state of nature, or Rawlsian statesmen behind a veil of ignorance, or Quinean linguists who can never be certain of the meaning of 'gavagai'. Whether seen as fact or fiction, the picture is one of a sense-absorbent and logically calculating mind altogether discontinuous with an emotively evaluating (but probably valueless) body, with no moral, aesthetic, or spiritual equivalent of the pineal gland to bring them, or facts and values, together.

This Cartesian picture of what it is to be a human being has dominated Western moral, aesthetic, and religious thinking for almost three hundred years. Kant accepted much of the picture, but recoiled from a major inference Hume drew from it, namely, that reason had to be the slave of the passions. Instead, *he* endeavored to ground ends (and values) on purely rational grounds, insisting that reason be the master of the passions.

But Kant's reason can no more generate, or create values, than Hume's. Being purely formal, both the categorical imperative and the kingdom of ends principle do not, strictly speaking, embody values, and Kant's arguments for them do not rest on any basic values, but on the fear of logical self-contradiction which would follow from rejecting them. Reason, in short, is necessary instrumentally – to help us achieve goals – and it can be of assistance in ordering or re-ordering our values; but create values it cannot, and hence if we believe that human beings are, or can be, purposeful agents, we cannot simultaneously believe that they are altogether autonomous, disembodied, individual rational minds.[31]

To this critique any rights theorist would probably reply that of course the Enlightenment model of the rational, autonomous individual isn't to be seen as descriptive of human beings, but rather prescriptive. Obviously, people have values and just as obviously different cultures embody different values, which is what makes moral relativism the acute problem that it is today. By focusing on rationality, this reply might continue, and by showing the rationality of the concept of rights, we can hope to overcome what separates us (cultural differences) on the basis of what unites us (the capacity to reason); and we can hope thereby to overcome most, if not all of the problems of moral relativism by establishing the reasonableness of the view of human beings as rational, autonomous individuals, and as rights-bearers, no matter what their cultural background. The view is not descriptive, but normative: we *ought* to accept it.

The force of this imperative, however, weakens as soon as we look carefully for the moral relativism it is designed to overcome. Earlier I argued, on logical grounds, that true instances of moral relativism can arise only when two peoples employed the same or very similar evaluative concepts and criteria, and that one people approved a particular human and the other disapproved.

How much such examples of true moral relativism there may be between different peoples around the world I don't know, but suspect the number has been greatly exaggerated. Unfortunately we do not have to trek to exotic lands to find examples, however, for they are everywhere in contemporary American society. As hinted at the outset, abortion is a prime example. Within the conceptual framework of rights-based moralities, with its concomitant concepts of duty, rationality, autonomy, choice, self, and freedom, it may be impossible to resolve the issue of abortion. One might want to argue that abortion is funda-

31 For fuller discussion of these points, see Angus C. Graham. *Reason and Spontaneity* (London: Curzon, 1985), and my critique of the book, "Who Chooses?", in *Chinese Texts and Contexts*, ed. Henry Rosemont, Jr. (La Salle, IL: Open Court, 1991).

mentally a legal and not a moral issue, but for good or ill the vocabulary utilized in discussing the issue stems from the same conceptual framework. The matter could not be otherwise, for when both sides claim that basic human rights are at stake, then we cannot but have a paradigmatic moral issue. Nor can it be objected that abortion is an instance of moral conflict, not moral relativism, for this objection misses the logical point: an abortion is a human action tolerated by a fairly large number of people, and loathed by another group; precisely the same situation described in all purported instances of moral relativism based on anthropological evidence.

The examples can be multiplied, again, as hinted at the outset; animal rights, euthanasia, the rights of the not yet born to a healthy and genetically diversified natural environment; all of these and other issues are sharply dividing the American peoples, and our inability to effect reconciliation may well be due to the conceptual framework within which the dialogues and diatribes occur. More generally, where the moral and the political realms intersect – justice and fairness – there is even more *prima facie* evidence for irreconcilable differences, leading to the conclusion not that those who disagree with us are stupid, selfish, or evil, but rather to the conclusion that individual rights and social justice are very likely incompatible concepts when their implications are drawn out.

Other arguments can be advanced against the rational, autonomous, rights-bearing individual as a model of human beings, taken either descriptively or prescriptively. One of these is well known from work in Prisoner's Dilemma games, and from rational choice theory more generally.[32] If we add to the Enlightenment model of human beings – which virtually all thinkers since Hobbes have done – the additional quality of being self-interested, then, for a wide range of nonexcludable collective (or public) goods (or benefits), everyone behaving rationally guarantees that the collective good will never be obtained, and everyone will be worse off. To illustrate, let us consider the streets of our major cities. They are filthy, drug-filled, and dangerous. It would be a great collective or public good for the people, say, of New York, to clean up and reclaim their streets. But given that no one can be excluded from the streets, no rational self-interested individual will elect to contribute to the reclamation project. The streets will either be cleaned up, or they will not. If they are, the self-interested individual will enjoy the collective good without having to pay the costs of contributing. If the streets remain as they are, the individual has saved the costs of contributing. Each rational, self-interested individual must therefore decide not to contribute. And

32 Beginning in its present form with Mancur Olson's *The Logic of Collective Action* (Cambridge, MA: Harvard University Press, 1965). A good statement of the problem(s) is in *The Politics of Private Desires*, by Michael Laver (New York: Penguin, 1981), which contains a bibliography.

the streets of New York will remain as they are, and every individual will be worse off.

A great many attempts to escape from this and other "free rider" or collective action paradoxes have been made, all of them unsuccessful, suggesting that the streets of New York will only continue to deteriorate unless and until some new (or very old) ways of thinking about ethical and political issues gain currency.

An enormous body of literature has been produced assuming, elaborating, and defending the view that human beings are autonomous, rational, rights-bearing, and self-seeking individuals. Clearly I have not even begun to respond to the whole of that literature in this very brief and general critique. But because so much of that literature presupposes the model of human beings as purely rational, self-seeking, autonomous individuals, the many arguments in that literature cannot have any more plausibility than the basic presuppositions on which they rest. To be sure, that model – especially as it has been taken to imply human rights – has advanced significantly the cause of human dignity, especially in the Western democracies, but it also has a strong self-fulfilling prophetic nature, which is strengthened further by the demands of capitalist economies; and I believe that model is now much more of a conceptual liability than an asset as we approach the twenty-first century, continuing our search for how to live, and how best to live together on this increasingly fragile planet.

III. Role-Bearing Persons

The critique of rights can be broadened and deepened considerably, but I should like to shift the focus now to an alternative view, that of the early Confucians. Describing the early Confucian lexicon[33] – their concept-cluster – is beyond the

33 Some comments on the early Confucian lexicon: Categories of persons – i. e., the *shi* 士, *junzi* 君子, and *shengren* 聖人, especially as they are distinguished from *xiaoren* 小人, I have endeavored to describe briefly, along with the *shanren* 善人, and *chengren* 成人, in "Kierkegaard and Confucius: On Following the Way," in *Philosophy East and West* 36, no. 3 (1986). *Dao* 道, I think is translated well by "Way," so long as it is understood to also mean "to speak," and consequently "doctrines," as it must be rendered, for example, in *Lun Yu* 14:30 and 16:5. For *de* 德, I reject, as does Munro, "manna," Waley's "power," and everyone else's "virtue." *De* approximates "dharma" in denoting what we can do and be if we realize (i. e., make real), the full potential of our concrete physical, psychological, and cognitive endowments. This being a rather lengthy gloss for *de*, I would not translate, but transliterate the term.
Similarly for *li* 禮, for which "customs," "mores," "propriety," "etiquette," "rites," "rituals," "rules of proper behavior," and "worship" have been offered as semantic substitutes. If we can agree that appropriately contextualized each of these English terms can translate *li* on occasion, we should conclude that the Chinese graph must have all of these meanings on every occasion of its use, and that selecting only one of them can only lead to the result, to cite the shibbaleth, that "something is lost in translation." *Li* can only be *li*.

scope of the present paper, but this much should be said: the Chinese philosophical terms focus attention on qualities of human beings, as a natural species, and on the kinds of persons who exemplify (or do not exemplify) these qualities

---

Ren 仁 is commonly translated as "benevolence," occasionally as "humanheartedness," and less occasionally by the clumsy and sexist "manhood-at-its-best." I would render the term in English, as "human kindness," which I believe captures the spirit of the Chinese original even if less lofty than "benevolence," and it moreover greater play to the richness of English by simultaneously making reference to *Homo sapiens* – humankind – and to a characteristic of that species, human kindness.

Zhi 知, with or without the sun radical beneath it, is usually translated as "knowledge" or "wisdom." Donald Munro comes closer, I believe, by rendering it "moral knowledge," but this would return us to our own concept-cluster. Consonant with the arguments of Roger Ames I would render *zhi* as "realize." "Realize" has the same strong epistemic connotations as "know" or "knowledge." Just as a person cannot know that today is Thursday if it is indeed Friday, so a person cannot realize that today is Thursday if it is not. Furthermore, by translating *zhi* as "realize," a link forged between the Confucians and their post-Tang successors with respect to the doctrine described as the "unity of knowledge and action." If to personalize is to make personal, and to finalize is to make final, then "realize" must mean "to make real," again, an expression which exploits the richness of English without recourse to the vocabulary of rights-based moral theories. *Xin* 信 has been described by Ezra Pound, following his teacher Ernest Fenollosa, as a picture of a person standing by his word. No small number of people have excoriated Pound for his philological Chinese flights of fancy, but every sinologist must analyze this particular graph in the same way: the character for "man," or "person" 人 stands to the left of the character for "speech," or "words" 言. When it is now appreciated that the written language in which the early Confucians wrote had a very high percentage of terms which were pictographic or ideographic in nature, we might be willing to allow Pound and Fenollosa their translation of *xin* as "trustworthy," "sincere," or "reliable."Next is *yi* 義, the graph D. C. Lau will render – counter-intuitively – as "right" here, "duty" there, and as "moral" or "morality" more generally. Now if one is committed to following Lau in his description of the early Confucians as moral philosophers, then *yi* is admittedly the best candidate for a Chinese lexical equivalent of "morals" or "morality." However, several variants of the original Shang for *yi* suggest other interpretations. *Yi* is commonly described as an adumbrated picture of a sheep 羊 over a graph referring to the speaker, i. e., a first-person singular pronoun 我, the origins of which are unknown. But this pronoun *wo* is itself, in many of its representations, a picture of a human hand 扌 holding a dagger-axe 戈. If it is now remembered that sheep were offered (cf. *Lun Yu* 3:17) as sacrifices at large communal gatherings, we might wish to gloss *yi* as the attitude one has, the stance one takes, when literally preparing the lamb for the ritual slaughter. This attitude, this stance, must be one of attempted purification, to make oneself sacred, thereby purifying and making sacred the sacrificial victim. If this be so, then clearly *yi* should not be translated as "moral" or "morality;" "reverence" is the closest English analogue, even though it is regularly used to translate *jing* 敬. But the latter connotes fear – *pace* the club-wielding hand of the right side of the graph 攴 – in a way absent in the usage of *yi*, and therefore I would translate *yi* – most frequently found in a noun-form – as "reverence," and *jing* – most frequently encountered verbally – as "to fearfully respect."

Xiao 孝 is straightforwardly "filial piety," and the dual strands of Confucius's "One thread" – *zhong* 忠 and *shu* 恕- are, I think, just as straightforwardly to be rendered as "loyalty" and "reciprocity" respectively. *Zhi* 志 I would translate as "will," or "resolve," and as a modifier, "resolute," instead of the more common "upright," or "uprightness."

to a high degree. Where we would speak of choice, they speak of will, resolve; where we invoke abstract principles, they invoke concrete human relations, and attitudes towards those relations. Moreover, if the early Confucian writings are to be interpreted consistently, they must be read as insisting on the *altogether* social nature of human life, for the qualities of persons, the kinds of person they are, and the knowledge and attitudes they have are not exhibited in actions, but only in *interactions,* human interactions. While reflection and solitude are necessary ingredients of our human lives, we are never alone. And our cognitive and affective qualities can never be wholly divorced.

Against this background, let me attempt to sketch briefly the early Confucian view of what it is to be a human being. If I could ask the shade of Confucius "who am I?" his reply, I believe, would run roughly as follows: given that you are Henry Rosemont, Jr., you are obviously the son of Henry, Sr. and Sally Rosemont. You are thus first, foremost, and most basically a *son;* you stand in a relationship to your parents that began at birth, has had a profound influence on your later development, has had a profound effect on their later lives as well, and it is a relationship that is diminished only in part at their death.

Of course, now I am many other things besides a son. I am husband to my wife, father of our children, grandfather to their children; I am a brother, my friend's friend, my neighbor's neighbor; I am teacher of my students, student of my teachers, and colleague of my colleagues.

Now all of this is obvious, but note how different it is from focusing on me as an autonomous, freely choosing individual self, which for many people is the *raison d' être* of contemporary philosophy, especially rights-based moral philosophy. But for the early Confucians there can be no me in isolation, to be considered abstractly: I am the totality of roles I live in relation to specific others. By using the term "roles" here I do not wish to imply that the early Confucians were the forerunners of the discipline of sociology. They emphasize the interrelatedness of what I am calling "roles", that is to say, they are cognizant of the fact that the relations in which I stand to some people affect directly the relations in which I stand with others, to the extent that it would be misleading to say that I

There are, of course, other lexical items in the early Confucian concept-cluster, but I only wish to consider one more at this time, the graph *xin* 心. Even though the early forms are clearly pictures of the human heart, the term has often been translated as "mind." There is much justification for this, because a number of passages in the texts can only be rendered intelligible on the basis of the *xin* thinking. Nevertheless I believe it is closer to the mark to render *xin* by the more awkward "heart/mind." With this translation it will seem somewhat less perverse to claim that the concept of choice is absent in the early Confucian texts.

There are other lexical items – *xue, wen, su,* etc. – included in the early Confucian concept-cluster, but the above are at least a beginning. For fuller discussion, and citations of philological sources, see my *Classical Confucianism and Contemporary Ethics,* forthcoming from Open Court, 1992.

"play" or "perform" these roles; on the contrary, for Confucius I *am* my roles. Taken collectively, they weave, for each of us, a unique pattern of personal identity, such that if some of my roles change, others will of necessity change also, literally making me a different person.

My role as father, for example, is not merely one-to-one with my daughters. In the first place, it has a significant bearing on my role as husband, just as the role of mother bears significantly on my wife's role as wife. Second, I am "Samantha's father" not only to Samantha, but to her friends, her teachers, someday her husband, and her husband's parents as well. And Samantha's role as sister is determined in part by my role as father.

Going beyond the family, if I should become a widower, both my male and my female friends would see me, respond to me, interact with me, somewhat differently than they do now. A bachelor friend of mine, for instance, might invite me as a widower to accompany him on a three-month summer cruise, but would not so invite me so long as I was a husband.

It is in this epistemologically and ethically extended meaning of the term "roles" that the early Confucians would insist that I do not play or perform, but am and become the roles I live in consonance with others, so that when all the roles have been specified, and their interconnections made manifest, then I have been specified fully as a unique person, with few discernible loose threads with which to piece together a free, autonomous, choosing self.

Moreover, seen in this socially contextualized way, it should become clearer that in an important sense I do not achieve *my* own identity, am not solely responsible for becoming who I am. Of course, a great deal of personal effort is required to become a good person. But nevertheless, much of who and what I am is determined by the others with whom I interact, just as my efforts determine in part who and what they are at the same time. Personhood, identity, in this sense, is basically conferred on us, just as we basically contribute to conferring it on others. Again, the point is obvious, but the Confucian perspective requires us to state it in another tone of voice: my life as a teacher can only be made significant by my students, my life as a husband by my wife, my life as a scholar only by other scholars.

All of the specific human relations of which we are a part, interacting with the dead as well as the living, will be mediated by the rituals of *li,* i.e., the courtesy, customs, and traditions we come to share as our inextricably linked histories unfold, and by fulfilling the obligations defined by these relationships we are, for the early Confucians, following the human Way. It is a comprehensive "Way." Quickly sketched, by the manner in which we interact with others our lives will clearly have an ethical dimension infusing *all,* not just some, of our conduct. By the ways in which this ethical interpersonal conduct is effected, with reciprocity, and governed by civility, respect, affection, custom, ritual, and tradition, our lives will also have an aesthetic dimension for ourselves and for others. And by specifically meeting our defining traditional obligations to our elders and ancestors on the one hand, and to our contemporaries and descendants on the other, the early Confucians offer an uncommon, but nevertheless spiritually authentic form of transcendence, a human capacity to go beyond the specific spatio-temporal circumstances in which we exist, giving our personhood the sense of humanity shared in common, and thereby a sense of strong continuity with what has gone before and what will come later. There being no question for the early Confucians of the meaning *of* life, we may nevertheless see that their view of what it is to be a human being provided for everyone to find meaning *in* life, and to have the possibility of becoming, to quote Fingarette on Confucius, "a holy vessel."[34]

This is a woefully brief account of one basic element of early Confucianism.[35] But if it at all accurately captures the thrust of the classical texts, I would suggest that those texts reflect a view of what it is to be a person – Chinese or American, young or old, male or female, capitalist or socialist, past or present – that is more

34 *Confucius – The Secular as Sacred,* op. cit.

35 A fuller account will be forthcoming in *Classical Confucianism and Contemporary Ethics,* op. cit. Classical Chinese society was certainly patriarchal, and thus to a significant extent misogynous. Arguably, patriarchal privilege extended far beyond what Confucius and his followers would have condoned, but it cannot be denied that the classical texts see women in basically subordinate roles. It is thus all the more paradoxical that what I am attempting to describe as the Confucian interdependent person very nearly approximates what some contemporary researchers describe as a *female* concept of persons.
For example, Carol Gilligan has said:

> Consequently, relationships, and particularly issues of dependency, are experienced differently by women and men. For boys and men, separation and individuation are critically tied to gender identity since separation from the mother is essential for the development of masculinity. For girls and women, issues of femininity or feminine identity do not depend on the achievement of separation from the mother or on the progress of individuation. Since masculinity is defined through separation while femininity is defined through attachment, male gender identity is threatened by intimacy while female gender identity is threatened by separation. The males tend to have difficulty with relationships, while females tend to have problems with individuation. *(In a Different Voice* [Cambridge, MA: Harvard University Press, 1982], p. 8)

Relatedly, in "Feminism and Epistemology: Recent Work on the Connection Between Gender and Knowledge," Virginia Held writes:

> ... [N]on-Western [epistemological] approaches have often been based far more than the Anglo-American views with which we are most familiar on a relational and more holistic view of reality. Such continental and non-Western views have usually been more misogynous than have Anglo-American views, yet they seem epistemologically closer to what is now being suggested as a more characteristically feminine approach. *(Philosophy and Public Affairs* 14, no. 3 [1985], p. 300)

If these feminist arguments can be sustained, the case for a Confucian-like concept-cluster of ethics and the *li*-governed person is even stronger than is suggested in this text.

realistic and humane than the view of us as purely rational, autonomous, rights-bearing individuals. (As noted above, such individuals will not be able to reclaim the streets of New York. But families, friends, and neighbors might.)

I do not wish to imply that the early Confucian writings are the be-all and end-all for finding answers to the multiplicity of questions I have posed. I do want to suggest that they are a highly salutary beginning, for just as no Ptolemaic astronomer could consider seriously that there were fundamental problems with his view of the heavens until the Copernican view had been articulated, just so we cannot seriously question our concepts of rights, and of what it is to be a human being, until there are alternatives to contemplate. Is it possible to have an ethical and/or political theory that did not employ the concepts of autonomous individuals, or choice, or freedom, or rights, and did not invoke abstract principles? Could there be such a theory, grounded in a view of human nature as *essentially* involving interpersonal relations, a theory that accorded both with our own moral sentiments, and those three billion plus human beings who do not live in the Western capitalist countries? If there were such a theory, could it conceivably be conflict-free?

I do not know the answers to these questions, but do know that if the early Confucian ethical alternative can genuinely alter our perspectives, it will not only have made a contribution to ethics, it will have made an important contribution toward reconstituting the entire discipline of philosophy.

If one is still inclined to think that the Master and his followers are simply too remote from us in time, space, and culture to teach us anything of basic import, a few historical facets of Confucianism should be borne in mind. First, simply in terms of its longevity, and the sheer numbers of people directly influenced by it-who lived and died in accordance with its vision Confucianism is arguably the most important philosophy ever put forward; it should not be too quickly dismissed merely on the grounds of its antiquity.

Further, it must be remembered that Confucianism was attacked at its inception by Daoists, Moists, Legalists, and proponents of others of the "Hundred Schools" of classical Chinese thought. Later on it was almost totally eclipsed by Buddhism for several centuries. Later again it was challenged by Christianity, first by the Jesuits and Franciscans of the late sixteenth and seventeenth centuries, and afterward by both Protestant and Catholic missionaries of the nineteenth and twentieth, these latter being buttressed by the gunboat diplomacy attendant on the imperialistic "coming of the West" to China. And of course Western democratic/capitalist, and Marxist thought too, have contributed much to onslaughts on the Confucian philosophical tradition. From all of these past and present challenges Confucianism has recovered (and it is recovering once again in the land of its birth); it has been strengthened, it has endured.

Moreover, in responding to these challenges Confucianism has never had recourse to supernatural support. It is entirely a secular philosophy, grounded in this life, making no appeal to divinity or divinities; one need not surrender contemporary common sense nor need to be skeptical of the physical description of the world put forward by natural scientists in order to understand and appreciate Confucian thought. Yet this secularism notwithstanding, Confucianism addresses simultaneously issues taken in the West to be religious, and it offers in its secularity a means whereby what may correctly be called the "sacred" can be approached, as Herbert Fingarette has so persuasively argued in his *Confucius – The Secular as Sacred.*

And finally, Confucian ethical and social thought can be relevant today because it directly addresses the issue of how a society best distributes the basic necessities of life when these are in short supply, and how human lives can be dignified, and significant, in such circumstances. Western philosophers from the time of Plato have simply presupposed at least a minimal amount of overall affluence when constructing their ideal societies, from the *Republic* to the present. The great majority of the world's peoples, however, do not live in affluent societies, and consequently Confucianism may have more to say to them than do most Western moral and social theories.[36]

For all these reasons, we should not think that the Confucian tradition must be irrelevant to contemporary issues of ethical concern, nor that it has been, or ought to be put to rest. Rather should we consider seriously the possibility that there be much in that tradition which speaks not only to East Asians, but perhaps to everyone; not only in the past, but perhaps for all time.

While I do believe there is a concept-cluster within which similar ethical judgments might be made inter- and intraculturally, I do not believe that concept-cluster is now ready to hand in precisely the language I am now using. Some Western philosophical concepts will, and should, remain with us; some others will have to be stretched, bent and/or extended significantly in order to represent more accurately non-Western concepts and concept-clusters; and still other Western philosophical concepts may have to be abandoned altogether in favor of others not yet extant, but which will issue from future research as new (and old) concept-clusters are advanced and examined. If we are reluctant to participate in the requiem mass currently being offered for philosophy, if we wish instead to seek new perspectives that might enable the discipline to become as truly all-encompassing in the future as it has mistakenly been assumed to have been in the past, we must begin to develop a more international philosophical language which incorporates the insights of all of the world-wide historical tradition of

36 I have argued for the importance of these economic constraints in "State and Society in the *Hsün Tzu,*" in *Monumenta Serica,* vol. XXIX, 1970–71.

thinkers who addressed the questions of who and what we are, and why and how we should lead our all-too-human lives; a tradition enriched considerably by the work of Herbert Fingarette.

Henry Rosemont, Jr. / Roger T. Ames

Family Reverence (*xiao*) as the Source of Consummatory Conduct (*ren*)

Does "family reverence" (*xiao* 孝) – the ground of the Confucian vision of a moral life – lead inevitably from nepotism to cronyism and then in turn to political corruption? Or is *xiao* a necessary condition for the cultivation of consummatory conduct (*ren* 仁)? We have read with interest and have gained insight from many of the recent articles proffered in response to this timely issue.[1] Indeed, as the Leviathan China continues to struggle on a long march to democracy, it is perhaps endemic corruption that is its greatest challenge.

Professor Liu Qingping and his supporters have mounted a well-reasoned attack on a position Confucius and Mencius endorse that would seem to protect law-breaking family members from state retribution. Such obstruction of justice would, on anyone's definition of the term, seem to be a rather egregious form of "corruption." To oversimplify somewhat, according to the Liu position, the culprit that ultimately produces corruption is *xiao*, conventionally rendered "filial piety" in English (but which we render as "family reverence," or "family feeling" to avoid the close Christian associations with the word "piety" today).[2] That is, *xiao* as the privileging of intimate relations is the source of immoral conduct.

Ably defending the Confucian tradition, on the other hand, is Professor Guo Qiyong and others who claim that the priority given to family feeling does not necessarily lead to any untoward favoritism, and hence should not be seen as leading inevitably to corruption.

1 Articles by Liu Qingping and Guo Qiyong are included in a special issue of *Contemporary Chinese Thought* (2007) 6 on "Filial Piety: The Root of Morality or the Source of Corruption?" with an introduction by guest editor Yong Huang. Guo Qiyong published a summary collection of articles in 儒家倫理爭鳴集：以親親互隱為中心 *Debates on Confucian Ethics: The Mutual Concealment among Family Members* (Wuhan: Wuhan Education Press, 2004). There is a relatively complete collection of the articles in this debate at www.confucius2000.com.

2 For details of our semantic and philosophical analysis of this term, see our "Introduction" to *The Chinese Classic of Family Reverence: A Philosophical Translation of the* Xiaojing 孝經 (Honolulu: University of Hawai'i Press, 2009).

In the end we will offer a defense of the Confucian position. But we will do so by approaching the debate at least initially from a meta-ethical position. That is to say, we will argue that to the extent that the classical Confucian texts – the *Lun Yu* and *Mengzi* – are being interpreted in this debate against the background of modern Western moral theory, they can provide neither an adequate account of the passages under scrutiny nor the vision needed for a way forward in moral thinking that they might otherwise yield. Indeed, we will attempt to show ways in which these ancient texts, taken on their own terms, offer a perspective on key ethical (and political) issues that are at least as worthy of our attention as any of the competing Western views.[3]

Let us take the first of the three passages referenced in this debate – (*Lun Yu* 13.18 and *Mengzi* 5 A3 and 7 A35) – as a representative example that we can draw upon in our discussion:

> The Governor of She in conversation with Confucius said, "In our village there is someone called 'True Person.' When his father took a sheep on the sly,[4] he reported him to the authorities."
>
> Confucius replied, "Those who are 'true' in my village conduct themselves differently. A father covers for his son, and a son covers for his father. And being true lies in doing so."[5]

In the first instance we must be clear about what is at stake in the dispute as we see it. Within a (roughly) Confucian framework, the contributors to the debate so far seem to have structured the discussion around the question of whether it is "family reverence" (*xiao*) or "consummatory conduct" (*ren*) that should be taken as most fundamental for the Master and his illustrious successor. Liu and the critics claim that this emphasis on family is at the expense of *ren:* after all,

3 We are acutely aware that many, perhaps most, of our Chinese colleagues *on both sides of this debate* may disagree with much of our stern critique of modern Western moral and political philosophy. Having enjoyed the moral and political fruits of these theories in a democratic society throughout our own lives, we can feel comfortable in criticizing these views in ways that perhaps our fellow philosophers in other countries who have yet to enjoy such fruits would not want to do.

4 This passage goes to the centrality of both family reverence and moral imagination in Confucian role ethics. On Zhu Xi's reading, the father is in dire straits – *rang* 攘 means "to steal when in difficult straits" – and thus steals out of abject need. But on such a reading, the putative "crime" of the father evaporates, and the son is just rotten. Perhaps Confucius has a more serious situation in mind: indeed, a hard case.

5 See interesting and amusing developments of this anecdote in *Hanfeizi* 韓非子 49.9.2 (*Hanfeizi suoyin* 韓非子索引 Beijing: Zhonghua shuju, 1982) , *Lüshichunqiu* 呂氏春秋 (Xu Weiyu 許維遹, Beijing: Wenxue guji kanxingshe, 1955):449, and *Huainanzi* 淮南子 13/125/14 (*Huainanzi zhuzisuoyin* 淮南子逐字索引 (Hong Kong: Commercial Press, 1992). Here and throughout this essay all translations from the *Lun Yu* are from our *The Analects of Confucius: A Philosophical Translation* (Random House/Ballantine Books, 1998).

consummatory human conduct can hardly be made to square with tolerating or indeed abetting illegal and immoral activity (and hence corruption). Upholders of the canon like Guo, on the other hand, claim there is no inconsistency between the way *xiao* and *ren* are employed in the texts. The priority of *xiao* is necessary for the achievement and maintenance of *ren*, that is, family feeling is a prior and necessary condition for later extending and developing fellow feeling for all others.

But concern about the respective priority of *xiao* and *ren* does not address the fundamental problem. In all three cases referenced and analyzed in the debate, it is clear that *xiao* is central – that is, protect family members at any cost, even when they are wrongdoers. We believe that although Guo Qiyong and the defenders of the canon are taking the argument in the right direction, there is a missing subtext to this debate on which the matter turns.

This subtext is discernible by noting that in all three textual examples familial loyalty trumps loyalty not to humanity writ large – as focusing on *ren* would require – but rather, family reverence takes priority over loyalty to the state, (those who govern, and the regulations they enforce). This is a crucial distinction. The charge of nepotism qua corruption carries little opprobrium if it is merely the favoritism I show my cousin in hiring her as the bookkeeper for my store. It only becomes an issue if my cousin is the less competent candidate for keeping the books in the district for whose financial concerns I am the responsible political person, appointed by the government.[6]

More directly to the textual examples from the *Mencius*, few would question the morality of our decision to carry our father or brother off to some remote place if they were abusing our mother or sister-in-law, but in the three examples given in the classical Confucian texts, it is not familial but legal wrongdoing that is

6 It might be argued that Liu Qingping and his pro-*ren* colleagues would claim that the alternative to the family is the community (other persons) rather than the state. The two – the community and the state – may indeed be distinguished (as we have done in our example below). But the moral issue in the passages under discussion remains one between the family and the government representing the community rather than the community of persons itself, whether that community be local, state, or national. Liu Qingping himself clearly sees the opposing sides just as we do when he argues that "it is wrong to obstruct the legal punishment of a relative's criminal act," and further, that protecting wrongdoing relatives "is an abuse of the law." Again, Shun's concern for his father "protected [the father] from just legal punishment and deprived his victim of his right to justice." (Liu, p. 6). What else is the state besides the impersonal enforcer of community norms? What else could it be? But there is another issue here. "Remonstrance (*jian* 諫)" – that is, the obligation that a child has to protest the conduct of an erring parent – has a prominent role in the Confucian literature on *xiao* 孝. That being the case, we would have to assume that in each of these cases (indeed, this is made clear in the case of the banishment of Shun's brother), an effort would be made by the concerned son to set the ledger right with members of the community who had suffered any loss on account of the conduct of the members of his family.

under consideration: robbery, manslaughter (if not murder), and attempted fratricide. To be sure, spousal abuse is and ought to be a crime, and it might well be that in the extreme case we would be obliged to call in the police to halt the violence. However, as far as our family is concerned, and very probably our neighbors and friends as well, there are priorities in our response to situations. Calling in the police is not what we would do first, but only as a last resort; initially at least we would almost surely try other means to remedy the problem.

This question of one's ultimate loyalties is a very old one in Western philosophy, beginning at least with the *Euthyphro.*[7] Socrates seems to be only mildly interested in the criminal charge of murder that Euthyphro is bringing to the court until he discovers that Euthyphro is prosecuting his own father, and that he has justified this indictment as an act of piety demanded by the gods. Only then does Socrates speak of how uncommonly advanced in spiritual wisdom the young man must be to know that his religious duty requires him to accuse his own father of murder in a court of law. The elderly stonemason is clearly incredulous that Euthyphro would do such a thing. But by the end of the dialogue, only at the meta-ethical level is it illuminating for us (although illuminating it surely is). On the practical level, we gain no insight from the *Euthyphro* as to whether our highest loyalty should be to the family or to the state; all we learn is that Euthyphro cannot give good reasons for doing so.

It is perhaps a distinguishing characteristic of the history of Western philosophy that Plato is not alone in this regard: No later thinker has answered the question of divided loyalties between family and state at all satisfactorily, and indeed, for most of the past two and a half centuries, none of our philosophers have even asked it.[8] The reasons for this neglect are, we believe, instructive for everyone participating in the debate on the relationship between *xiao*, corruption, and *ren.*

Throughout the Western philosophical narrative evolving with the discovery of the soul by the classical Greeks, the dominant view of human beings has tended to be that of abstract, individuated selves: autonomous, rational, free, and (usually) self-interested. This view of what it is to be human has been pretty much un-

7 *The Collected Dialogues of Plato,* edited by Edith Hamilton and Huntington Cairns (Princeton: Princeton University Press, 1961). The section from the *Euthyphro* we discuss here is 4a–b.

8 The history of moral ideas pertaining to family has been studied at length by Jeffrey Blustein, who noted: "After Hegel, philosophers did not stop talking about the normative aspects of parent-child relations altogether. What happened was that they no longer attempted to systematically apply their most dearly held moral and social values to the study of parenthood. The resolution of problems relating to the upbringing of children and to our expectations of them became a sideline, and the most profound issues of the lives of human beings in society were seen to lie elsewhere." *Parents and Children: The Ethics of the Family* (Oxford: Oxford University Press, 1982), p. 95. Blustein does not, however, attempt to account for the philosophical neglect of such a basic pattern of human interaction.

questioned from the time of Locke, and has become thoroughly entrenched as an unannounced presupposition by the time of Hume and Kant.[9] Indeed, a foundational individualism is the Enlightenment model of humanity, and has been a key motivating factor in those populist revolutions instigated to curb the excesses of authoritarian governments. At the same time, appeal to the institution of family as a source and model of moral order has been markedly absent from the Western philosophical tradition.

If we understand what it means to be human in this individualistic manner, it would seem to follow that in thinking about how we ought to deal morally with our fellows, we should seek as abstract and general a viewpoint as possible. If the dignity of everyone is derived from the (highly valued) qualities associated with this individualism – autonomy, equality, rationality, freedom – then it is just these qualities we must respect at all times, and hence gender, age, ethnic background, religion, skin color, and so on, should play no significant role in our decisions about how to interact with others.

On this orientation it is thus incumbent upon us to seek universal principles and values applicable to all peoples at all times. Otherwise the hope of a world at peace, devoid of group conflicts, racism, sexism, homophobia, and ethnocentrism will never be realized. Moreover, the best way to arrive at these universal principles is to transcend our own spatio-temporal location and cultural tradition – to overcome, that is, our personal prejudices, hopes, fears, likes and dislikes – and on the basis of impersonal reason alone ascertain beliefs and principles that should be compelling to all other rational persons equally committed to transcending their specific locations, backgrounds and biases. Our

9 This concept of the abstract and universal individual has become a commonplace, and as such, is often insinuated into interpretations of classical Confucianism. For example, in this present collection of essays, Yong Huang in his "Introduction" rehearses an argument by Liu Qingping that Mencius is inconsistent because he allows for the possibility of love itself not being based on family love. That is, on Liu's interpretation, Mencius's notion of *renxing* 人性 articulated by appeal to the "four beginnings (*siduan* 四端)" defines a universal conception of human individuality that is more fundamental than family relations. Although Huang disputes this particular example of a Mencian inconsistency, he provides his own in citing the "child in the well" passage as a more compelling case for a love for others that is not derived from family love. For us, the problem here lies in ascribing a conception of discrete individuality to a classical Confucian tradition that understands person as irreducibly relational. The "four beginnings," for example, describe the initial conditions of a person as lived within a family context. For the debate on Mencius and the ongoing arguments against essentializing Mencius's notion person and of *renxing*, see 孟子心性之學 *Studies on the Mencian Notions of Heart-and-Mind and "Human Tendencies"* edited by James Behuniak, Jr. 江文思 and Roger T. Ames 安樂哲 (Beijing: Shehuikexue wenxian chubanshe, 2005). For an argument against this individualistic reading of person in classical Confucianism, see also Roger T. Ames, "What Ever Happened to Wisdom? A Confucian Philosophy and 'Human Becomings'" Special *Festschrift* issue of *Asian Major* in honor of Nathan Sivin. Edited by Michael Nylan, Henry Rosemont, Jr. and Li Waiyee, 2008.

differing heritages, personalities, sexual orientations, religious beliefs and much more that divide us, are all sources of possible conflict. But normal human beings have the capacity to reason that thus unites us all, and consequently offers a greater hope for a less violent human future than has been the case in the past, and at present.

This emphasis on reason, on objectivity, impartiality, and abstraction has provided a strong impetus for seeking universalism in ethics. Many people, and most Western philosophers, have been influenced by this perspective, and not unreasonably so; it is complete with a vision of peace, freedom, and equality. From this position, the rare challenges to it heard within the corridors of the Western academy seem either hopelessly relativistic, authoritarian, or both.

The two dominant universalistic ethical theories, grounded in the concept of the individual we have just outlined, reflect this orientation: deontological ethics, emphasizing our moral duties, and utilitarianism, which focuses on attending to the consequences of what we do in the moral sphere. While the participants in the current *xiao* debate are no doubt familiar with these theories, we want to rehearse them briefly in order to make clear how we contextualize them in the tradition of moral philosophy.

The deontological theory is associated with Immanuel Kant, whose fundamental moral principle, the Categorical Imperative, is roughly "Always act on a maxim you could will to become a universal law." Kant sought to establish a certain, universally valid basis for human moral behavior that could withstand relativistic and skeptical challenges: that is, he believed he had structured the logic of moral arguments such that they would reveal our unconditional moral obligations without reference to historical experience, inclination, or personal values. The substance of our autonomy, for Kant, is thus an inner rational faculty uncorrupted by external circumstances, enabling us to develop and then comply with moral imperatives; an autonomy, that is, devoid of our particularities as unique individuals living in a specific time, place, and culture, grounded only in the principle of non-contradiction.[10]

Utilitarianism was developed by Jeremy Bentham and John Stuart Mill three-quarters of a century after Kant, and its most fundamental principle is to act so as to maximize the utility or happiness of the greatest number of people (with the minimal disutility and unhappiness for the rest). For Kant, logic reigns, the primary focus being on compliance and consistency more than on consequences; for Bentham and Mill the situation is more nearly – but not quite – reversed, since inductive probabilities instead of deductive certainties must weigh heavily in a moral agent's calculations about the consequences of his or her actions in ac-

10 The *locus classicus* for Kant's views here are *The Critiques of Practical Reason,* various editions.

cordance with the Principle of Utility. For Bentham and Mill, calculating benefits or happiness is the proper employment of reason as applied in our moral deliberations. Like Kant's Categorical Imperative, however, the Principle of Utility is universal, is based on reason alone, and is applicable to any and all moral situations, in which each individual counts for one, and no one counts for more than one. It is only by ignoring individual particularities – again, time, place and culture – that Utilitarians believe true justice and equality can be achieved.[11]

Both of these universalistic ethical theories have had, and continue to have numerous champions in philosophy, theology, and political theory, and they have had, and continue to have, a great deal of influence in other circles as well. In general, the influence of Kant can be seen fairly clearly in the courts of the United States, where consistency and precedent are prized, even if at times the consequences of the decision are untoward (witness famous cases such as Dred Scott, or Miranda). Legislators, on the other hand, typically look to consequences when enacting laws, and find no problem in repealing a law when the consequences of the law appear to become adverse (repeal of prohibition, the draft, and so on).

If our analyses of these positions and issues have merit, we can begin to see not only why questions of family versus state loyalties cannot be answered by these Western moral theories: they cannot even be asked. Indeed, no moral questions concerning the family can even be framed for examination because, by definition, family members are not abstract, autonomous individuals, parts of the public, but are flesh and blood, highly specific young and old, male and female fellow human beings related to ourselves in highly intimate ways.[12] Thus all moral questions pertaining to family matters have been swept under the conceptual rug of a "private" realm that involves personal matters of taste and religious belief – a realm wherein moral and political philosophy do not enter.

Only by divesting persons of any uniquely individuating characteristics can we begin to think of developing a theory of moral principles that will hold in all instances. With respect to family, this is precisely what we cannot do if we are even to attempt to formulate the relevant moral questions about loyalties and obligations coherently, for as soon as we use the expression "my mother" in a moral question, we are not dealing with an abstract, autonomous individual, but

11 The *locus classicus* is Mill's *Utilitarianism,* various editions.

12 An excellent, although surely unintentional example of this conceptual difficulty was the comment by feminist philosophers Martha Minow and Mary Lyndon Shanley in a special issue of *Hypatia* on the family, when they note "a paradoxical characteristic of family life," namely, that "the individual must be seen simultaneously as a distinct individual and as a person fundamentally involved in relationships of dependence, care, and responsibility." (vol. 11, no. 1, Winter, 1996), p. 22. Unfortunately, it is no more possible to "see" others simultaneously in this way than to see the Wittgensteinian image as both duck and rabbit at the same time.

one who carried us, brought us into this world, nurtured and comforted us, giving of herself extraordinarily for our benefit.

Thus to search for a universalistic principle of some sort in the Confucian writings is to try to square the circle, for Confucianism is paradigmatically particularistic – resolutely particularistic – just as Kant, Bentham, and Mill endeavor to be universalistic. To seek a principled ground for moral judgments in the classical Chinese texts is, to our minds, like expecting a Kantian to take specific cultural differences into account as conditions that qualify his Categorical Imperative, when in fact the Categorical Imperative is the very test for principle as unconditional universal law. Stated succinctly, we cannot appeal to Western moral theory to adjudicate the decidedly Confucian problem of family loyalty versus loyalty to the state.[13]

Against this meta-ethical background, we should like now to advance some arguments that suggest that the *Lun Yu* and the *Mengzi* offer insights into our manifold moral and political predicaments that Kant, Bentham and Mill (and John Rawls, for that matter) cannot provide, and taking this a step further, that these dominant Western views are in significant measure responsible for much of our contemporary moral and political malaise. If this be true, then a sensitivity to the Confucian persuasion is not only important for the Chinese world today, but to everyone.

In order to make these arguments, we will have to understand the several passages from the Confucian classics that focus this debate from within their own interpretive context. We will argue that, taken on their own terms, these classical Confucian texts appeal to a relatively straightforward account of our actual life experience rather than abstract principle, and in so doing, provide a justification for reinstating the intimacy of family feeling as the concrete ground of an always emergent moral order. We will argue further that there is a difference between Western ethical theories that are directed at best at enabling people to think and to talk about ethics more coherently, and a Confucian vision of a moral life that

13 As we will note below, it is of course possible to derive generalizations from the Confucian canon, but these are a long way from claims about universal "principles," because the latter can be refuted by a single counter-example. Generalizations, however, are defeated not by a counterexample – or even several of them – but rather by a better generalization; we should not be thinking of English "all" so much as "many," or "most." Some might wish to claim that the "negative golden rule" found in *Analects* 5.12, 12.2 and 15.24 is paradigmatically a universal principle. We believe it is more correctly and incisively seen as a rough generalization about an attitude one should have for determining what is most appropriate in one's relations with others that does not presume to know from the beginning what is right for everyone. We cultivate a sense of deference (*shu* 恕) initially in our family relations, and then extend this sensibility with imagination to those who are much different from us as our lives unfold. Indeed, far from being an argument *for* universalism in ethics, it is an argument *against* it. But then this is the topic of another paper.

seeks to inspire people to be better persons. We will refer to this Confucian vision as a Role Ethics, although we do not intend to advance it as an alternative moral theory so much as a vision of human flourishing, one that integrates the social, political, economic, aesthetic, moral and the religious dimensions of our lives.[14] In this view, we are not individuals in the discrete sense, but rather are interrelated persons living – not "playing" – a multiplicity of roles that constitute who we are, and allow us to pursue a unique distinctiveness and virtuosity in our conduct. We are, in other words, the sum of the roles we live in consonance with our fellows.

Let's begin then with a reconstruction of the Confucian project as it is enunciated in the seminal texts of classical Confucian, the *Four Books.* The central message of these canonical documents is that while familial, social, political, aesthetic and cosmic (religious) cultivation is ultimately coterminous and mutually entailing, still it must always begin from the Confucian project of personal cultivation. We become moral not by divesting ourselves of our particular roles and relationships in order to apprehend those universal principles that provide moral justification, but on the contrary, we become worthy by cultivating these same roles and relations that constitute us as the ultimate source of moral meaning. Each person is a unique window on their own family, community, polity, and so on, and through a process of personal cultivation and growth, they are able to bring the resolution of their relationships into clearer and more meaningful focus. That is, the production of meaning is both radial – beginning from one's own roles and relations – and collateral, because it is resolutely contextual. Cultivating one's own person grows and adds meaning to the cosmos, and in turn, this meaningful cosmos provides a fertile context for the project of one's personal cultivation.

Another way of putting this point is to say that personal cultivation is what we should see as the basic spiritual discipline in Confucianism, coming to a deepening and broadening sense of belonging, a strong feeling of being a part of something larger and more enduring than ourselves, a feeling that begins in and with the family (*xiao*), and with increasing effort, can culminate in a feeling of close affinity with all fellow human beings dead and alive, and with the cosmos (*ren*). But the family must clearly be the basis of this discipline.[15]

---

14 Many if not most contemporary comparative philosophers, especially in the English-speaking world, are now portraying Confucianism as a "virtue ethics," more or less on the model of Aristotle and his contemporary champions. Our own view is that Confucianism no more fits a Western "virtue" model of ethics than a deontological or consequentialist one, and indeed, that it is not a "moral theory" in the Western sense. For discussion of this point, and for an extended argument on how Confucian role ethics differs from a classical Aristotlelian model of virtue ethics, see our translation and commentary on the *Xiaojing* cited in fn. 2 above.

15 Whether speaking cosmologically (the cosmos), or religiously (a sense of belonging), we wish

Such personal cultivation is prerequisite not only for one's own personal life and family, however, but also for the development of a better world. This is the fundamental message of the *Great Learning*. This shortest of texts asserts unambiguously that it is only by committing oneself to a regimen of personal cultivation that one can achieve the quality of intellectual understanding that can change the world, and ourselves, for the better. In this singularly important respect, we must get our priorities right. And the priority is that the cultivated person as constituted by intimate family relations, far from being in competition with the state, is the root of effective governance, and as such, must be properly tended in order to sustain a healthy political canopy. This continuity between family and state is clear in the concluding paragraph of this text:

> From the emperor down to the common folk, everything is rooted in personal cultivation. There can be no healthy branches when the root is rotten, and it would never do for priorities to be reversed between what should be invested with importance and what should be treated more lightly. This is called both the root and the height of wisdom.

In the same way, in *Analects* 14.35, Confucius insists that moral order starts here and goes there: "I study what is near at hand and aspire to what is lofty," and again in 12.1 he is adamant that becoming consummate as a person must be self-originating. It is this local nature of the source of consummate conduct that makes any moral guidelines not principles, but generalizations from particular situations. In the *Analects* 1.2, Youzi claims that becoming *ren* begins at home. That is, the ground of our consummate humanity is family feeling:

> Exemplary persons (*junzi* 君子) concentrate their efforts on the root, for the root having taken hold, the way will grow therefrom. As for family reverence (*xiao*) and fraternal responsibility (*ti* 弟), it is, I suspect, the root of becoming consummate in one's conduct (*ren*).

Since family feeling is the ground of Confucian role ethics, and since polity in this tradition is a direct extension of the family – literally "country-family" (*guojia* 國家) – Confucius can further claim that being a responsible and productive member of one's family is tantamount to governing the country:

> Someone asked Confucius, "Why are you not employed in governing?"
> The Master replied, "The *Book of Documents* says: 'It is all in family reverence! Just being reverent to your parents and a friend to your brothers is carrying out the work of

to make clear that we are speaking of *this* world, the world in which our family ties are bound, the only world of classical Confucianism. There is no transcendental realm, in the Judaic-Christian sense of something on which our world is utterly and wholly dependent, but which is in no way dependent on us or our world. For the cosmological side, see David L. Hall and Roger T. Ames, *Thinking Through Confucius* (Albany: State University of New York Press, 1987), and for the religious, Henry Rosemont, Jr., *Rationality & Religious Experience* (La Salle, IL: Open Court Publishing Co., 2001).

> government.' In doing this I am employed in governing. Why must I be 'employed in governing?'"

This passage can be easily misunderstood as minimalist – each one of us in our families makes our own small contribution to the greater political order. Confucius's point, however, is quite the opposite. Most of our political lives are lived out close to home. If we ask after the relative importance of the state and the family in effecting cosmic harmony, we must allow that family is the ultimate ground of political order, and without it, political order is a sham. It is for this reason that any formal pretence to democracy independent of the flourishing community is hollow, what Whitehead would call "misplaced concreteness." And taken one step further, any discussion of a flourishing community without reference to a robust family life is again an empty abstraction.

This "idea" that personal cultivation pursued within the context of the inherited world is the ultimate source of cosmic meaning, is reiterated in *Focusing the Familiar* (*Zhongyong*), providing us with a moral vocabulary:

> This notion of equilibrium and focus (*zhong* 中) is the great root of the world; harmony (*he* 和) then is the advancing of the proper way in the world. When equilibrium and focus are sustained and harmony is fully realized, the heavens and the earth maintain their proper places and all things flourish in the world. Citation information

To repeat what we have said earlier, Confucian role ethics is not an abstract theory that provides principled moral judgments for those particular problematic situations we might encounter along the way, nor does it suggest developing a deliberate rational means to some moral end. Rather the Confucian project is a vision for developing the moral life as a whole in which one acts morally in order to be moral (and aesthetic, religious, and so on). It is a way of trying to live consummately through relational virtuosity (*ren* 仁). It is the ongoing cultivation of an aesthetic, moral and religious imagination that will enable one to achieve optimal appropriateness and significance in what one does (*yi* 義). It is an attempt to use personal artistry in one's roles and relations to live life most significantly.

This being the case, the Confucian issue in these several passages is not a legal one about an individual's conduct. To take the example above, the Confucian question is not "Is it just for a son to cover for a father who has committed a crime?" It is rather a matter of priorities: what the *Great Learning* describes metaphorically as setting the roots as a precondition for a luxurious canopy. Indeed, the focus is not upon the father as a discrete, autonomous individual perpetrating a crime against the state, but rather on how the mutually constitutive father-son relation can continue to be "true" when strained by circumstances. How should one behave to best sustain the quantum of harmony within the existing configuration of roles and relations that constitute this family and this community, and by extension, this state?[16] The assumption here would be that endorsing a litigious course of action on the part of a son as the appropriate way to act in such cases would not only be anathema to the ultimate interests of familial and communal harmony, but ultimately it would be detrimental to the prospects of a prosperous state.

We might take a case perhaps more familiar in our modern world. If a person discovers that his or her child has been shoplifting, what is the most efficacious response? Should one dial 911 and the city desk to allow the authorities and the public to resolve the situation by trying the criminal in the courts and in the press, thereby bringing the criminal quickly to justice? Surely there are laws against stealing.

A more imaginative approach to the situation might be to accompany a good child who has done a bad thing back to the scene of the crime, and allow the child to negotiate the situation with the shopkeeper whose property has been taken. The outcome presumably would be to remedy the situation for the short term by restoring the property to its rightful owner, and for the long term by not only educating the child, but also by reinforcing the communal solidarity of all concerned. It is in everyone's interest – the parent's, the child's, the shopkeeper's, and the state's – that this case be resolved in an imaginative manner that makes the best of a bad situation. And it is in no one's interest, because of a lack of imagination, to abandon a child to a path that might well lead ultimately to a career of crime.

Perhaps an immediate objection to this position would be the putative differential in moral competence between the child and the adult father who stole the sheep. The rejoinder would be: Where did the adult come from? The Confucian tradition is preemptive in trying to establish a social fabric that would reduce the possibility of crime, rather than adjudicating hard cases after the fact. We might be better off creating a community that does not give rise to spousal abuse rather than struggling to find a fail-safe procedure for retribution after the victim has been injured or worse – all the more so as the preponderance of the evidence shows that the threat of retribution is not really a deterrent against criminal activity.

In *Analects* 1.13 we read: "Making good on one's word (*xin* 信) gets one close to being optimally appropriate (*yi* 義) because then what one says will bear repeating." When we ask after the source of moral meaning, the answer might lie

16 It is important to frame the question in this way, for it might be tempting to ask instead, based on a Western orientation, "What should we do when the other person is not keeping his or her side of the role bargain?" But this, of course, is to beg the question against the Confucians by demanding a principle, and if we are correct, such cannot be found in the early canon. Even those who would appeal to principle have the idea of extenuating circumstances, or excuse conditions. Fn 4 suggests one possible case, and the fact that Shun's father is blind might suggest another; but we can only speculate here.

in exhorting the community to embrace honesty as a way of life rather than in a post hoc auditing procedure for weeding out corruption. In the Confucian tradition, it is the fabric woven of strong family bonds rather than inviolate laws that enables the community to thrive. In fact, appeal to law is perceived broadly as a dehumanizing (although sometimes necessary) last resort. In this world, invoking the law is a clear admission of communal failure

In setting priorities, then, the initial response in Confucian role ethics is to appeal to the moral resources within our family and community to reestablish a communal harmony that has been diminished by sometimes thoughtless conduct. The challenge is how to draw upon these resources most imaginatively to make the best of the situation. Family reverence (*xiao*), far from being the source of corruption, is our best hope in avoiding it by serving as the ground for consummate human conduct, and is the best hope for a social and political order much more humane than those in which we currently live.

Of course there are tradeoffs in surrendering the individual autonomy that undergirds much of Western ethical and religious thinking. This way of thinking about the human experience brings with it much that we hold in high regard: A quality of individual freedom and independence, equality, privacy, rights and entitlements, personal integrity, and indeed the sacredness of human life, are for most of us, good things. But it must be seen that when we give these qualities pride of place in prioritizing our values, we do so at an important cost. Individualism can bring with it a diminished sense of shame and responsibility, and a reduced appreciation of our interdependence. Each of us has a moral obligation to respect the civil and political rights of all others. Governments have often been remiss, and worse, in granting such respect, but for persons, it is very easy, for we can fully respect those rights simply by ignoring the others: You surely have the right to speak, for example, but not to have us listen. Indeed, individualism in its extremes can precipitate feelings of alienation, depression, and selfishness, and a continuing tendency to "blame the victim" when confronted with gross social injustice, despite the absurdity of the denial of community responsibility. Too much freedom becomes license, too much independence becomes loneliness, too much autonomy becomes moral autism, and too much sacralizing of the human being comes at the cost of massive species extinction.

Our overall argument here is simple. A careful consideration of Confucian role ethics prompts us to ask after the benefits that come with an increased awareness of the centrality of family feeling. What do we get in exchange – ethically, socially, politically, and religiously – for what we have to give up when we surrender in degree our emotive attachment to personal autonomy and all that it entails? And is the tradeoff worth it? This then is the question that we have raised and reflected upon in these pages, and is the question that we would leave with our readers for their own consideration.

Roger T. Ames / Henry Rosemont, Jr.

Family Reverence (*xiao* 孝) in the *Analects:* Confucian Role Ethics and the Dynamics of Intergenerational Transmission

Abstract

We begin this chapter on family reverence (*xiao* 孝) from the assumption that within the interpretive framework of the *Analects*, associated, interpersonal living is taken to be an uncontested, empirical fact. Every person lives and every event takes place within a vital natural, social, and cultural context. Association being a fact, our different roles lived within family and society are nothing more than the stipulation of specific modes of associated living: mothers and grandsons, teachers and neighbors. While we must take associated living as a simple fact, however, the consummate conduct that comes to inspire and to produce virtuosity in the roles lived in family, community, and the cultural narrative broadly – what we have called Confucian role ethics – is an achievement; it is what we are able with imagination to make of the fact of association.

Confucian role ethics are perpetuated through family lineages that have complex political, economic, and religious functions. One way of understanding the dynamics of "family reverence" (*xiao*) as intergenerational transmission is to appeal to two cognate characters that are integral to the continuities of the family lineage: *ti* 體 ("body," "embodying," "forming and shaping," "category, class") and *li* 禮 ("ritual," "achieving propriety in one's roles and relations"). The living body and our embodied living is the narrative site of a conveyance of the cultural corpus of knowledge – linguistic proficiency, religious rituals, the aesthetics of cooking, song, and dance, the modeling of mores and values, and so on – through which a living civilization is perpetuated.

"Family Reverence" (孝 *xiao*) and the Primacy of Relationality

A quick survey of the chapter titles in the Table of Contents of *Dao Companion to the Analects* should persuade the reader of the centrality of lived roles and relations in defining the philosophical narrative as it is recounted in the pages of the *Analects*. Beginning from the enormous value Confucius invested in the term (*ren* 仁) – which we translate as "consummate conduct" – it is the relationality of persons rather than their individuality that is primary in describing, analyzing, and evaluating their quality as people and the efficacy of the social institutions of family and of community in which they live their lives.[1] Several other essays in this anthology take up the matter of moral philosophy, but we must note quickly here that by focusing on the dependent relationality of persons rather than their independent individuality, Confucius is not a moral philosopher in the same way, if at all, that Aristotle, Immanuel Kant or John Stuart Mill are moral philosophers, or almost every other Western moral philosopher for that matter. Indeed, we would go so far as to say that the Master has no moral theory as such; the *Analects* instead provides us with a *vision* of the moral life, a narrative vision of interrelational and embodied, consummate conduct (*ren*).

An important *dramatis persona* in the *Analects* who in his own conduct underscores this primacy of relationality is Confucius' protégée, Master Zeng 曾子, who throughout the classical corpus is the paradigmatic figure most closely associated with the fullest expression of "family reverence" (*xiao* 孝):[2]

> Master Zeng was gravely ill, and when Meng Jingzi questioned him, Master Zeng said to him, "Baleful is the cry of a dying bird; felicitous are the words of a dying person. There are three habits that exemplary persons consider of utmost importance in their vision of the moral life: By maintaining a dignified demeanor, they keep violent and rancorous conduct at a distance; by maintaining a proper countenance, they keep trust

1 Earlier we have translated *ren* as "authoritative conduct," and others have rendered it "benevolence," "humaneness," "human-heartedness," and the clumsy and sexist "manhood-at-its-best." It would probably be best to provide a competent gloss for the term, and thereafter simply transliterate it; but herein "consummate conduct" captures fairly well what we are saying about *xiao* 孝, and about the roles in which people endeavor to live *xiao* throughout their lives.

2 Here and throughout, all quotations from the text are based on our translation, *The Analects of Confucius: A Philosophical Translation* (Ames, Rosemont 1998). Master Zeng is best remembered as a proponent of *xiao* – the devotion and service that the younger generation directs to their elders and ancestors, and the pleasure that they derive from doing so. A natural extension of this affection for one's family is friendship, and Master Zeng is portrayed in the *Analects* as being able to distinguish between the sincerity of his fellow student, Yan Hui, and the rashness of another student, Zizhang. In exploring the meaning and function of *xiao* in the *Analects* by recourse to those seminal passages that shed light on this untranslatable term, we will also be able to appeal to the references to Master Zeng himself where he appears as the personal embodiment of *xiao*. *Xiao* 孝 has conventionally been rendered "filial piety" in English but we translate it as "family reverence." What recommends "family reverence" as a translation is that it in degree disassociates *xiao* from the duty to God implied by "piety" and from the top-down obedience that is assumed in *paterfamilias*. "Family reverence" also retains the sacred connotations that are certainly at play in the ritualized culture of ancestral sacrifices. For details of our semantic and philosophical analysis of this term, see Rosemont, Ames 2009: "Introduction."

> and confidence near at hand; by taking care in their choice of language and their mode of expression, they keep vulgarity and impropriety at a distance. As for the details in the arrangement of ritual vessels, there are minor functionaries to take care of such things."[3]

In this passage, Master Zeng, clearly aware of his own impending demise, begins by exhorting the listener to pay serious attention to what he is saying, for he believes that his last words as he utters them on his deathbed are of real consequence.

Master Zeng's message then is that all three of the habits of deportment considered by exemplary persons to be vital to the moral life – that is, a dignified demeanor, a proper countenance, and a commitment to effective communication – are essential to the productive growth of interpersonal relations. And it is this growth in relations that is the substance of Confucian ethics. On the other hand, the failure to cultivate such dispositions precipitates vulgarity, impropriety, and violent and rancorous actions – behavior that as an immediate source of diminution and disintegration in relations is for the Confucian the substance of immoral conduct. In contrast with this vital concern about the quality of relations, the material aspect of a refined life – the arrangement of ritual vessels, for example – is perceived to be of marginal significance.

Associated Living, Virtuosity, and Confucian Role Ethics

Heeding Master Zeng's dying words, we will begin this chapter on family reverence (*xiao* 孝) from the assumption that within the interpretive framework of the *Analects*, associated, interpersonal living is taken to be an uncontested, empirical fact.[4] Every person lives and every event takes place within a vital

3 *Analects* 8.4: 曾子有疾，孟敬子問之。曾子言曰：「鳥之將死，其鳴也哀；人之將死，其言也善。君子所貴乎道者三：動容貌，斯遠暴慢矣；正顏色，斯近信矣；出辭氣，斯遠鄙倍矣。籩豆之事，則有司存。」

4 And a negative implication of this claim would be that the notion of the autonomous individual is a modern fiction that has little relevance for this classical Confucian text. The concept of the autonomous individual that underlies modern moral and political philosophy has at least two malevolent effects. First, it enables libertarians, growing in their numbers in the U.S., Europe, and Asia, to claim moral purchase in justifying an unfettered human freedom as the basis of political justice, and then to reject any conception of social justice that retards such freedom as fundamentally immoral. The notion of the autonomous individual thus continues to provide a moral basis for a more or less *laissez-faire* free market capitalist global economy that is exponentially compounding gross inequalities of human well-being within and between nation states. The second reason the concept of the autonomous individual is pernicious is its pervasiveness in the consciousness of Western intellectuals, entrenched at a depth that makes it almost impossible for them to see any alternative to an individualism so defined except a more or less faceless collectivism. Indeed, we would claim the assumption that the essential cha-

natural, social, and cultural context. Association being a fact, our different roles lived within family and society are nothing more than the stipulation of specific modes of associated living: mothers and grandsons, teachers and neighbors. While we must take associated living as a simple fact, however, the consummate conduct that comes to inspire and to produce virtuosity in the roles lived in family, community, and the cultural narrative broadly, is an achievement; it is what we are able with imagination to make of the fact of association.

The means and the goal of healthy living is an achieved equilibrium in which we are able to make the most of the transactional human experience by achieving proper measure in our social and natural activities, and in so doing, to avoid both excess and insufficiency in giving and getting, in doing and undergoing. As explained by anthropologist ZHANG Yanhua:

> Harmony defined here is related to the Chinese sense of *du* 度 (degree, extent, position) … In other words, in a dynamic interactive environment, harmony is brought about when each particular unfolds itself in its unique way and to an appropriate *du* such that "each shines more brilliantly in the other's company" (*xiangde-yizhang* 相得益彰). (Zhang 2007: 51)

Parents, for example, may dote on their children but shouldn't fawn over them; young children must learn to be obedient without being servile; siblings should assist each other without demanding payback, criticize each other without mean-spiritedness. Love, sadness, affection, and joy may be expressed in many ways, and every youngster learns the social conventions of interacting with strangers from learning and participating in the homely little rituals of family life from greetings to leave-takings to the sharing of food together.

It is thus that the familial and social roles themselves come to have normative force, serving as guidelines for how we ought to proceed and what we should do next. Indeed, it is this continuing process of elevating and refining our lived roles and relations to make the most of associated living that prompts us to describe Confucian morality as an ethics of roles, and to claim that Confucian role ethics is, in our view, a *sui generis* orientation with no proximate moral counterpart in Western philosophy.

In this ongoing collateral and radial process of associated living, cultivation of one's unique person within one's specific and often changing relations is the root from which a canopy of interdependent personal bonds grows to define the various social spheres of family, lineage, neighborhood, community, and village, each of which makes its own contribution to the prevailing social ethic. As the *Great Learning* (大學 *Daxue*) enjoins us, in the singularly important project of

racteristics and actions of human beings are best evaluated by treating them as fundamentally free, autonomous, and rational individuals has itself become an unquestioned ideology.

becoming consummate persons, personal cultivation is fundamental, and we must give it our highest priority:

> From the emperor down to the common folk, everything is rooted in personal cultivation. There can be no healthy canopy when the roots are not properly set, and it would never do for priorities to be reversed between what should be invested with importance and what should be treated more lightly.[5]

In Confucian role ethics, social and political order emerges from and is dependent upon personal cultivation within the institution of the family. The renowned sociologist FEI Xiaotong reflects upon the contemporary configuration of the Chinese kinship-based sociopolitical model of governance that can be attested to as early as the canons and the bronze inscriptions of the early Zhou dynasty.[6] He contrasts those rule-governed social organizations that function with clearly defined boundaries and that are constituted by groups of discrete individuals – what he calls "the organizational mode of association" (*tuantigeju* 團體格局) – with the Chinese kinship model that he likens to "the concentric circles formed when a stone is thrown into a lake" (Fei 1992: 63). We might note that Fei's analogy is reinforced by the fact that the character for "ripples" (*lun* 淪) is cognate and homophonous with the graph for "relational order" (*lun* 倫), where the assumption is that a life well-lived is the rippling process of extending (*tui* 推) oneself outwards in increasingly capacious social circles to participate fully in defining the order of the cosmos itself.[7]

Fei provides us with a terminology that is useful in clarifying the implications of a tradition in which primacy has been given to kinship and relationality. He notes that the term "relational order" (*lun* 倫) denotes not only specific family and social relations themselves (husbands and wives, rulers and subjects), but also the meaning that it is possible to achieve in these same relations (nobility or baseness, intimacy or remoteness). That is, *lun* refers to both the specific roles themselves and the process of growth and refinement within the roles that we are

5 *Daxue* 1969: 2b: 自天子以至於庶人，壹是皆以修身為本。其本亂而末治者否矣，其所厚者薄，而其所薄者厚，未之有也！

6 Yiqun Zhou argues, "The home, where one engaged in daily practices of kinship-centered moral precepts and religious ceremonies, was the site for the most fundamental education in Zhou society (Zhou 2010: 147)."

7 This process of cosmic co-creativity is the defining theme of the *Zhongyong* 中庸 – a text that we have translated as *Focusing the Familiar* to underscore family and community relations as the ultimate source of cosmic growth. Zhu Xi 朱熹 (1130–1200), the Southern Song philosopher who compiled the *Four Books*, takes the *Zhongyong* as the fourth and highest expression of the Confucian project. The cosmic proportions of a sage such as Confucius is pervasive in the literature. For example *Analects* 19.24: 他人之賢者，丘陵也，猶可踰也；仲尼，日月也，無得而踰焉。"The superior character of other people is like a mound or a hill that can still be scaled, but Confucius is the sun and the moon that no one can climb beyond." See also *Zhongyong* 30.

describing as Confucian role ethics.[8] We might note that the considered translation of the English word "ethics" in the modern Chinese and Japanese languages as it is derived from early Han dynasty sources is *lunlixue* 倫理學 (Jp. *rinrigaku*) – that is, "the study of the meaningful coherence achieved in human relations." This being the case, we would have to allow that the expression "*lunli*" itself means "role ethics," and that to say "Confucian ethics" is in fact to say "Confucian *role* ethics."[9]

Further, Fei Xiaotong would claim that the predominant pattern of kinship relations in hierarchically defined roles and relations – what he calls "the differential mode of association" (*chaxugeju* 差序格局) – that "is composed of webs woven out of countless personal relationships" produces its own distinctive kind of morality (Fei 1992: 78).[10] Fei insists that "Confucian ethics cannot be divorced from the idea of discrete centers fanning out into a weblike network" (Fei 1992: 68). This being the case, simply put, for Fei "no ethical concepts … transcend

8 That *lun* 倫 means "class," "category," and "order" as well as "relations" might seem somewhat odd at first blush, but it suggests that classification is dependent upon analogy and association rather than on some essential feature or characteristic. The later Wittgenstein is making a similar point when he insists that words are not defined by core meanings present in all uses of that word. Rather, we should approach words historically and contextually, mapping them through "a complicated network of similarities, overlapping and criss-crossing" (Wittgenstein 1953: Sec. 66). Wittgenstein surrenders his earlier concern for certainty and exactness and fixed boundaries when he introduces the expressions "family resemblances" and "language games" – that is, when he appeals to similarities and associations rather than strict identity and formal definitions.

9 That is, to say "Confucian role ethics" more explicitly in Chinese as *ruxue juese lunlixue* 儒學角色倫理學 would in fact make "role" redundant. See Liu 1995: 316 for the Han dynasty sources of this term *lunli.*

10 In their comparison of Greek and Chinese philosophy and science, Geoffrey Lloyd and Nathan Sivin add their authority to an analogous contrast in modes of inquiry that has long been argued for: that is, a proclivity of the early Greeks for an exclusive dialectic in pursuit of apodictic truth and a classical Chinese search for a relationally constituted, inclusive harmony and consensus:

> The dominant, but not the only, Greek way was through the search for foundations, the demand for demonstration, for incontrovertibility. Its great strengths lay in the ideals of clarity and deductive rigor. Its corresponding weaknesses were a zest for disagreement that inhibited even the beginnings of a consensus, and a habit of casting doubt on every preconception. The principal (though not the sole) Chinese approach was to find and explore correspondences, resonances, interconnections. Such an approach favored the formation of syntheses unifying widely divergent fields of inquiry. Conversely, it inspired a reluctance to confront established positions with radical alternatives (Lloyd and Sivin 2002: 250).

Lloyd and Sivin underscore the primacy and dominance of relationality and synthetic growth in this classical Chinese worldview as producing the predominance of a distinctive mode of inquiry. Such a claim reinforces Fei Xiaotong's argument that an emphasis on hierarchical kinship relations also produces a distinctive kind of morality, a family-centered relational conception of moral competence we have termed Confucian role ethics.

specific types of human relationships" (Fei 1992: 74). That is, kinship as the root of human relations is defined by the values of "family reverence" (*xiao* 孝) and "fraternal deference" (*ti* 悌). And friendship as the way of extending this pattern of kinship relations to include non-relatives is pursued through an ethic of "doing one's utmost" (*zhong* 忠) and "making good on one's word" (*xin* 信).[11] All of these ethical values are achieved within the specific personal relationships of family and community.

This ethics of roles also has important political implications for Confucius. A well-known passage in the text has him using the specific roles themselves as guidelines, claiming that the proper use of these names is as necessary for effective governance as it is for achieving a flourishing family. When he is asked about effective governing by Duke Jing of Qi, he quite simply replies: "The ruler must rule, the minister minister; the father father, and the son son."[12] The Duke is delighted, exclaiming that if we do not live our roles effectively, social and political order is lost utterly.

There are solid warrants for interpreting this passage as more concerned with the roles and the ideals expressed though them than with their names merely as linguistic units, while not neglecting the latter. Throughout classical Confucianism, the contention is that the proper and effective use of language (*zhengming* 正名) is the substance of relationships, and is basic to the flourishing community in all of its overlapping dimensions. Using language properly is how we achieve what is most *appropriate* in our associations, and hence what is most *meaningful*. Indeed, both of these qualities of conduct – appropriateness and meaningfulness – are captured in the Confucian term *yi* 義, a central vocabulary in this tradition's vision of the moral life. This power of language as the primary source for effecting social order is not lost on Confucius:

> "Were the Lord of Wey to turn the administration of his state over to you, what would be your first priority?" asked Zilu.
> "Without question it would be to insure that names are used properly (*zhengming*)." replied the Master.
> "Would you be as impractical as that?" responded Zilu. "What is it for names to be used properly anyway?"

11 See for example *Analects* 1.4 and 1.8. There is an ambiguity in the expression "associates and friends" (*pengyou* 朋友) as it is used in the documents of the Western Zhou and Spring and Autumn period where these texts do not distinguish between non-related friends and agnatic male relatives – that is, paternal relatives such as brothers, uncles, nephews, cousins, and so on. Some have argued that *pengyou* becomes a term commonly used to denote non-kin friends specifically only in the Warring States period. See Zhou 2010: 110–111 and 137–139.

12 *Analects* 12.11: 齊景公問政於孔子。孔子對曰：「君君，臣臣，父父，子子。」公曰：「善哉！信如君不君，臣不臣，父不父，子不子，雖有粟，吾得而食諸？」For an explanation of why our rendering of this passage concludes ungrammatically, see the Introduction to our translation of the text, Ames, Rosemont 1998: 28–44.

> "How can you be so dense!" replied Confucius. "Exemplary persons defer on matters they do not understand. When names are not used properly, language will not be used effectively; when language is not used effectively, matters will not be taken care of; when matters are not taken care of, the achievement of a ritual propriety in roles and relations and the playing of music will not flourish; when the achievement of ritual propriety and the playing of music do not flourish, the application of laws and punishments will not be on the mark; when the application of laws and punishments is not on the mark, the people will not know what to do with themselves. Thus, when exemplary persons put a name to something, it can certainly be spoken, and when spoken it can certainly be acted upon. There is nothing careless in the attitude of exemplary persons toward what is said."[13]

In these two passages, the Master focuses on how the proper use of names conduces to achieving meaning in those relations that constitute a thriving family, community, and polity. He does not appeal to value terms, he offers no abstract principles, he does not warn us of using euphemisms. That is, he does not urge us to refrain from describing mediocre things as " good", he does not exhort us to be honest and temperate, he does not recommend that we avoid using "collateral damage" to describe the killing of civilians. Rather, he observes that our roles and relations require that we relate to each other effectively. It is not, however, just by means of our verbal conduct that we relate to each other, important though that clearly is, but also through non-verbal consummate conduct exemplified in the performance of the other dimensions of our roles. Thus,we should also understand Confucius as exhorting us in these passages, especially in 12.11, "See here, you know what it is to be a good father (minister, ruler, son); now be one!"

In understanding more deeply how deference in social and political relationships functions without degenerating into servility or even an untoward humility we might want to reflect on the nature of hierarchy that holds between "those above" (*shang* 上) and "those below" (*xia* 下). Even though the graphs certainly carry these meanings, readers can appreciate the text more if they see Confucius describing interpersonal conduct not between individuals, equal or otherwise, but largely between *benefactors* and *beneficiaries*. And when we keep in mind that we are all of us benefactors and beneficiaries much of our daily lives, the negativity usually associated with the hierarchical nature of the early Confucian family system can perhaps be replaced by a more appreciative attitude, for the hierarchy – if that is even the proper term for the relationship – is not at all

13 *Analects* 13.3: 子路曰："衛君待子而為政，子將奚先？"子曰： "必也正名乎！"子路曰："有是哉，子之迂也！奚其正？"子曰："野哉由也！君子於其所不知，蓋闕如也。名 不正，則言不順；言不順，則事不成；事不成，則禮樂不興；禮樂不興，則刑罰不中；刑罰不中，則民無所措手足。故君子名之必可言也，言之必可行也。君子於其言，無所苟而已矣。"

elitist or exclusive. And we do not simply have the roles of benefactor and beneficiary with different people, but not infrequently with the same persons: we are the beneficiary of our parents when young, move to being their benefactor when they become infirm; we are beneficiary of our friend when we need her help, benefactor when she needs ours. These, too, are empirical facts about our lives as we live them.

Family Lineages as the Mode of Cultural Conveyance

It is because the entry point for developing moral competence in the Confucian vision of the moral life is family relations that *xiao* 孝 as "family reverence" has a singularly important place in the *Analects.* But before we turn to *xiao* itself, we first must clarify the nature and significance of the institution of family within this Confucian context. Again, Fei Xiaotong, draws a contrast between the nuclear "family" that for anthropologists takes its major significance from being the site of reproduction, and the dominant historical pattern of premodern Chinese families as lineages of persons with the same surname (*shizu* 氏族), and by extension, as clans (*jiazu* 家族) made up of several lineages who share the same surname. While lineages also have the function of reproduction, Fei insists that within the Chinese experience they serve as "a medium through which all activities are organized" (Fei 1992: 84). That is, in addition to the perpetuation of the family, lineages have complex political, economic, and religious functions that are expressed along the vertical and hierarchical axes of the father-son and mother-daughter-in-law relationships. Lineage relations are again reinforced socially and religiously through the institutions of ancestor reverence, a continuing practice that archaeology tells us dates back at least to the Neolithic Age (Keightley 1998).[14]

14 In the early Shang, the ancestors – at least those of the king and the noble families – were believed to be directly and significantly responsible for the good or ill fortune in the lives of their descendants, necessitating a propitiating of them through sacrifice. This belief died out only slowly, which helps to explain *Analects* 2.24: The Master said, "Sacrificing to ancestral spirits other than one's own is being unctuous." A part of the genius of Confucius was to see and appreciate that these ritual sacrifices could provide a good deal of meaning to human lives, and serve as a binding force in society overall – even when the supernatural *raison d' etre* for their performance was no longer credited, at least among the intelligentsia. A not dissimilar sentiment was expressed by the American philosopher George Santayana: "I reject altogether the dogma of the Roman Church; but rejoice in the splendor and the beauty of the Mass." Yiqun Zhou in her analysis of the dominance of kinship and the inalienable bond between ancestors and their progeny in early Zhou society points out that "Nearly one-sixth of the *Odes* pertain to ancestral sacrifices, including the ceremony proper and the subsequent feast. These pieces demonstrate the central importance of the ancestral banquet for our understanding of the Zhou discourse of sociability (Zhou 2010: 104)." And further, that

Of course, given the fact that the structure of Chinese family lineages have changed dramatically over time, such generalizations must be qualified by time and place – by regional and temporal variations. Having said this, Yiqun Zhou marshals scholarly consensus behind her claim that premodern Chinese society was "for several thousand years largely a polity organized by kinship principles" (Zhou 2010: 19). In weighing the extent to which social order was derived from and dependent upon family relations, Zhou insists that in contrast with the Greeks, "the Chinese state was never conceived as a political community that equaled the sum of its citizens," and that "the relationship between the rulers and the ruled was considered analogous to the relationship between parents and children" (Zhou 2010: 17–18n51). She cites the late Qing scholar YAN Fu who claims that imperial China from its beginnings was "seventy percent a lineage organization and thirty percent an empire" (Zhou 2010: 19n55). It is this persistent family-based sociopolitical organization of Chinese society that has within this antique culture, late and soon, elevated the specific family values and obligations circumscribed by the term *xiao* to serve as the governing moral imperative.

"Family Reverence" (*xiao*) as the Governing Moral Imperative

With the primacy of kinship relations in family lineages in mind, what then does *xiao* denote? The character translated "familial reverence" (*xiao* 孝) is constituted by the combination of the graph for "elders" (*lao* 老) and that for "son, daughter, child" (*zi* 子), encouraging an existential rather than a formularaic understanding of what this particular combination of images would convey. Like *ren* 仁 that requires us to access and to build upon our own existential sense of what it would mean to become consummate as a "person" in our relations with specific others, *xiao* too has immediate reference to our lived experience in a narrative of succeeding generations as we remember our own parents and grandparents, and attend to our own children and grandchildren. In fact, if we examine the earliest form of the character "elders" (*lao* 老) found on the oracle bones, it depicts a old person with long hair leaning on a walking stick  that later in the Small Seal script becomes stylized closer to its present form of 老 as . In comparing this character for "elders" with the earliest form of the character for "family reverence" (*xiao*) found on the oracle bones , the image of a youth has

"ancestor worship entails not only memorial rituals that are regular, systematic, and continuous, but also, more important, incorporation of the dead into a descent group as permanent members endowed with an essential role in forging group solidarity (Zhou 2010: 112)."

taken the place of the walking stick as a source of support on which the elders can lean. *Xiao* is certainly the support that succeeding older generations enjoy from the progeny that follows, but it is also the vital process whereby the younger generation is transformed into and becomes a novel yet persistent variant of those to whom they have deferred. The older generation literally lives on in the bodies and in the lived experience of the generations that follow.

The centrality of *xiao* to the Confucian project of becoming consummate in one's conduct (*ren* 仁) becomes immediately apparent on examining one familiar passage from the *Analects:*

> Exemplary persons (*junzi* 君子) concentrate their efforts on the root, for the root having set, one's proper path in life (*dao* 道) will emerge therefrom. As for family reverence (*xiao* 孝) and fraternal deference (*ti* 弟), these are, I suspect, the root of becoming consummate in one's conduct (*ren* 仁).[15]

What does it mean to take the practical activities of revering family members (*xiao* 孝) and of deferring appropriately to elders (*ti* 弟) as the *root* (*ben* 本) of becoming consummate in one's conduct as a person (*ren* 仁)? In the first instance we must remind the reader that when Confucius insists again and again on the importance of obedience when young or when in an official capacity, and on the weight of deferential conduct throughout one's life, he is not teaching manners, or worse, servility, to children. His listeners are all *adults*. And while he is surely claiming that these patterns of interpersonal behavior are necessary for family flourishing and societal harmony, he is equally guiding his protégées toward a path of spiritual self-cultivation in which appropriate conduct expressed through a reverential attitude to family elders is a mark of refinement:

> Those today who are filial are considered so because they are able to provide for their parents. But even dogs and horses are given that much care. If you do not respect your parents, what is the difference?[16]

But such reverence and deference only begins with family; it must become a pattern of conduct that, with unrelenting attention, is extended to all members of the community:

> Zhonggong inquired about consummate conduct. The Master replied, "In your public life, behave as though you are receiving honored guests; employ the common people as though you are overseeing a great sacrifice. . . ."[17]

Treaders of the way must, in other words, attend carefully at all times to the appropriateness of their conduct with others, *and* cultivate the proper attitude

15 *Analects* 1.2: 君子務本，本立而道生。孝弟也者，其為仁之本與.
16 *Analects* 2.7: 子曰：「今之孝者，是謂能養。至於犬馬，皆能有養；不敬，何以別乎？」
17 *Analects* 12.2: 仲弓問仁。子曰：「出門如見大賓，使民如承大祭。。。。」

toward that conduct, and those others, at the same time.[18] Confucius elaborates upon this point further:

> Deference unmediated by ritual propriety is lethargy; caution unmediated by observing ritual propriety is timidity; boldness unmediated by ritual propriety is rowdiness; candor unmediated by ritual propriety is rudeness.[19]

On our reading, such *xiao* and *ti* activities as a practical expression of *ren* are not descriptive of a human nature *ab initio*. If we take "human nature" as the product rather than the ultimate source of human conduct, are we not putting the cart before the horse?[20]

To us, these passages make the point that human nature and the cultivation of ourselves as persons are inseparable from the context of the roles we live within family and community, and that they are constantly undergoing change and development. Relationally constituted persons are born into their family and community relations – they do not exist exclusive of them, nor can they grow without them. By locating the notion of human nature within the relational cosmology that serves as interpretive context for the *Analects*, we can argue that terms such as "root," "potential," "cause," and "source" that are sometimes taken to be unilateral and exclusive terms generally associated with a given human nature have to be reconceived as referencing a collateral, reciprocal and reflexive

18 In earlier work (Rosemont 2001) we have argued that despite great theological and metaphysical differences the world's religions have a number of interesting parallels, one among them being the provision of a variety of instructions very similar across the traditions for how to practice approaching the sacred from our decidedly profane daily lives – *spiritual disciplines*, as we believe they are – in their sacred writings that adherents may follow in order to live with dignity, learn to maximally appreciate the pleasures of this earth that come to them, and learn as well to deal with the sorrows that must also attend every human life. Above all they proffer paths for developing a sense of *belonging*, an attunement with something larger than oneself, the experience of which may legitimately be described as religious experience, in our opinion. Because the texts of classical Confucianism also contain such instructions, we take it to be a religion on all fours with the others, despite the absence of any theology, or much metaphysics. There are, moreover, no churches, monasteries, nunneries, ashrams, synagogues, or mosques in early Confucianism, but as our quotes from the *Analects* throughout this essay demonstrate, the basics of the spiritual discipline are centered in another edifice – that is, the family home – thus making "family reverence" all the more felicitous as a translation for *xiao* than "filial piety." Cf. fn.1.

19 *Analects* 8.2: 子曰：「恭而無禮則勞，慎而無禮則葸，勇而無禮則亂，直而無禮則絞。君子篤於親，則民興於仁；故舊不遺，則民不偷。」

20 Much commentarial ink has been spilled on trying to argue against the claim of this passage that *xiao* as the root produces *ren*. ZHU Xi in his commentary on the *Analects* worries over this problem, and cites the interpretation of his philosophical predecessors, the Cheng brothers 二程, that disputes this claim. The Cheng brothers argue for a distinction between "becoming *ren*" (*weiren* 為仁) and "practicing *ren*" (*xingren* 行仁), insisting that *ren* as integral to human nature must be prior to *xiao*, and that *xiao* only enables us to "practice" *ren* rather than to "become" *ren*. See Ames 2011: 88–90.

process. That is, taking "root" as our example, the tree and its roots are an interactive and organic whole, and they grow together or not at all. While the root may be thought to grow the tree, the tree also in turn grows its roots. The *Record of Rites* (*Liji* 禮記) version of the *Great Learning* that we cited above as setting the Confucian project of personal cultivation concludes this seminal text by declaring that giving priority to achieving personal excellence is wisdom at its best. In the words of the text itself:

> This commitment to personal cultivation is called both the root and the height of wisdom.[21]

Here again, personal cultivation as the "root" and its product, "wisdom," are to be perceived as an organic whole that in growing together are two ways of viewing the same phenomenon. Said another way, just as individual persons are abstractions from the concrete reality of their continuing friendship, root and wisdom are abstractions from the concrete process of becoming consummately human within the relations of family and community. *Ren* has no meaning or possibility independent of our family and community relations.[22] In sum, in addition to thinking of *xiao* in terms of root and source it will perhaps will be best understood fundamentally as a *resource* – a resource for consummate conduct at the aesthetic, ethical, social, and spiritual levels.[23]

21 Lau and Chen 1992: 43.1/164/30: 此謂知本，此謂知之至也。

22 The graph *zhi* 知, uniformly translated as "to know," "knowledge," or "wisdom," is less abstract than these English terms, as each of us has argued in the past (Hall and Ames 1987), (Rosemont, unpublished manuscript). In our *Analects* translation we used "to realize," and "realization" for *zhi* whenever possible in an attempt to convey the performative as well as the cognitive dimension of knowing – that is, the importance of the activity and experience of knowing. If "to finalize" is to make final, then "to realize" can be taken as "to make real."

23 The contrast with Kierkegaard on these planes of living could not be more stark. Without denigrating the work of the great Dane in any way, it is clear that his planes are exclusive: once you leave the aesthetic life for the ethical, you do not – cannot – return; and to leave the ethical plane for the religious requires "a leap to faith" of great proportions. The Confucian planes on the other hand are always subject to change, are intertwined, mutually dependent and interdependent, and they must be integrated throughout our lives. See Kierkegaard 1985, especially "The Preamble of the Heart." The reader might also want to contrast our treatment of *xiao* with that of P.J. Ivanhoe, who takes it to be a virtue in the philosophical (Aristotelian) sense of the term. See Ivanhoe 2004.

"Family Reverence" (*xiao*) as the Inheritance and Conveyance of Meaning

This understanding of the root and the tree as a symbiotic process stands in contrast to thinking of the root as an independent, single source, and reflects the holistic cosmological assumptions that require a situated answer to one of our most fundamental and perennial philosophical questions: "Where does meaning come from and how is it conveyed?" In the Abrahamic traditions, the answer is simple: Meaning comes from a Divine source beyond and independent of the individual: Yahweh, or God, or Allah provides us with a continuing vision of life's purpose, and we must return to this source when we lose our way. For the Confucian project, on the other hand, without appeal to some independent, external principle, meaning arises *pari passu* from a vital network of meaningful relationships. A personal commitment to achieving relational virtuosity within one's own family relationships is both the starting point and the ultimate source of personal, social, and indeed, cosmic meaning. That is, in cultivating our own persons through achieving and extending robust relations in our families and beyond, we enlarge the cosmos by adding meaning to it, and in turn, this increasingly meaningful cosmos provides a fertile context for the project of our own personal cultivation.

We must bear this alternative meaning of "root" and "source" in mind when we reflect upon a passage in which Confucius in the *Analects* describes himself in the following terms:

> The Master said: "Following the proper way, I do not forge new paths; with confidence I cherish the ancients – in these respects I am comparable to our venerable Old Peng."[24]

Many commentators across the centuries have read this passage as a portrait of Confucius as a cultural conservative. As early as the *Mozi*, for example, Confucius is taken at his word as being wholly a transmitter, and is criticized roundly for offering the world a lifeless conservatism:

> Again the Confucians say: "Exemplary persons follow and do not innovate." But we would respond by saying: "In ancient times, Yi introduced the bow, Yu introduced armor, Xizhong introduced the carriage, and the tradesman Qiu introduced the boat. Such being the case, are today's tanners, smiths, carriage-makers, and carpenters all exemplary persons, and are Yi, Yu, Xizhong, and the tradesman Qiu simply petty persons? Further, since whatever it is the Confucians are following had to be introduced by someone, doesn't this mean that what they are in fact following are the ways of petty persons?"[25]

---

24 *Analects* 7.1: 子曰："述而不作，信而好古，竊比於我老彭。"
25 *Mozi* 63/39/19: 又曰：「君子循而不作。」應之曰：「古者羿作弓，杼作甲，奚仲作車，

This Mohist criticism of Confucianism is alive and well in the commentarial tradition that extends down to the present day. The contemporary political philosopher, HSIAO Kung-chuan [XIAO Gongquan], describes this ostensive Confucian conservatism at length as "emulating the past" (*fagu* 法古) (Hsiao 1979: 79–142). More recently, Edward Slingerland, in interpreting this same passage from the *Analects*, aligns himself with a retrospective understanding of a Confucianism that harkens back to the Golden Age of the Zhou dynasty. He observes:

> It is more likely that transmission is all that Confucius countenanced for people in his age, since the sagely Zhou kings established the ideal set of institutions that perfectly accord with human needs (Slingerland 2003: 64).

Contra this conservative reading of Confucius – a position that we disagree with fundamentally – we want to suggest that this passage speaks rather to Confucius' understanding of the nature and the dynamics of intergenerational transmission. And in this process of transmission, the patterns of deference captured in the notion of "family reverence" (*xiao*) serves as a key factor.[26] Borrowing the language of the *Yijing*, we would argue that Confucius as he is remembered historically is in fact a particularly good example of the cosmological assumptions that grounds this canonical text. He, like the *Yijing*, assumes that the unfolding of the natural and cultural narratives can best be expressed in the language of "persistence and change" (*biantong* 變通) and of "ceaseless procreation" (*shengsheng buyi* 生生不已). That is not to deny that with Confucius' reliance upon the core canons of the tradition, he is an effective transmitter of the persistent and abiding "common sense." At the same time, however, with his own contribution to the development of a specific philosophical vocabulary, he is also a source of novel insight. Indeed, appreciating his modesty in demurring at the suggestion that he has been an innovator, we still have substantial evidence to comfortably assert that Confucius was both a transmitter and someone who sought to break new ground.

In broad strokes, Confucius does self-consciously continue a tradition that reaches back into the second millennia BCE:

巧垂作舟，然則今之鮑函車匠皆君子也，而羿、杼、奚仲、巧垂皆小人邪？且其所循人必或作之，然則其所循皆小人道也？」 See also 81/46/50.

26 Translating *shu* 述 as "to follow the proper way" enables us to maintain the "path" (*dao* 道) metaphor that it suggests and that is a key to a coherent reading of the text. Throughout the early corpus, the term meaning "to initiate" (*zuo* 作) – translated here as to "forge new paths" – is frequently associated with the term "sageliness" (*sheng* 聖). Hence Confucius' description of himself might be read as an expression of modesty. "Old Peng" is Peng Zu 彭祖, a minister to the court during the Shang dynasty whom legend has it lived to be some 800 years old. With the name "Peng Zu" – literally "Peng the Ancestor" – and with his remarkable longevity, Old Peng is certainly emblematic of historical continuity.

> The Master said: "The Zhou dynasty looked back to the Xia and Shang dynasties. Such a wealth of culture! I follow the Zhou."[27]

But at the same time, Confucius has also been responsible for introducing, re-defining, and reinvesting in such key notions as *ren* 仁 (consummate conduct), *junzi* 君子 (exemplary person), *yi* 義 (optimizing appropriateness), and *li* 禮 (achieving propriety in one's roles and relations) as an authorized philosophical terminology. Again, it is Confucius who promotes personal cultivation as defining of the Confucian project and who grounds Confucian role ethics and the vision of the consummate life in "family reverence" (*xiao* 孝).[28]

To ground a vision of the consummate human life in "family reverence" is to assert that each succeeding generation is the teacher of the generation that is to follow. It is important to keep this idea of generational continuities and changes *via* lineages in mind when reading the *Analects*, for (at least) two reasons. First, while Confucius regularly cites the *Odes* (*Shijing* 詩經) and the *Book of History* (*Shujing* 書經), and urges his disciples to read and re-read them, he lived when oral instruction was still the norm in education. As Michael Nylan has argued, China did not become a true "manuscript culture" until the Han (202 BCE-22CE) – several centuries after the death of Confucius – with the appearance of libraries, archives, book shops, and other signs of such a culture (Nylan 2011). Thus, just as with other schools of thought in early China, early Confucianism as a "school" is probably best understood in terms of lineages transmitted orally – personally and interrelatedly – beginning with the Master himself and his own disciples, some of whom later took on disciples themselves, and continuing, with the dominant pattern of education not being book learning, but formal and informal discussion among and between a group of learners centering around a talented teacher. Today's reader would be well advised to attempt to recapture this sense of

27 *Analects* 3.14: "'周監於二代，郁郁乎文哉！吾從周。'" See also *Analects* 8.20: "舜有臣五人而天下治。武王曰：'予有亂臣十人。' 孔子曰：'才難，不其然乎？唐虞之際，於斯為盛。有婦人焉，九人而已。三分天下有其二，以服事殷。周之德，其可謂至德也已矣。'" Shun had only five ministers and the world was properly governed. King Wu also said, "I have ten ministers who bring proper order to the world." Confucius said, "As the saying has it: 'Human talent is hard to come by.' Isn't it indeed the case. And it was at the transition from Yao dynasty to Shun that talented ministers were in greatest abundance. In King Wu's case with a woman, perhaps his wife, among them, there were really only nine ministers. The Zhou, with two thirds of the world in its possession, continued to submit to and serve the House of Yin. The excellence of Zhou can be said to be the highest excellence of all."

28 This being the case, it is not surprising that Zhu Xi 朱熹 canonizes the *Analects* as the second of the *Four Books* for the explicit reason that it not only provides the fundamental vocabulary of the tradition, but it also provides a narrative example of personal cultivation that is at the heart of the Confucian project described in the first of his *Four Books*, the *Great Learning* (*Daxue* 大學).

learning through direct conversation that is reflected throughout and definitive of the *Analects;* the task is not easy, but surely worth a try.

A second reason for attending carefully to the idea of lineages (and roles) for teachers and students no less than for family and clan members is that at least six of the disciples who appear in the received *Analects* went on to establish their own lineage, and thus "school," which they saw as originating with the Master. Consequently there can be no "orthodox" interpretation of classical Confucianism in general nor of the *Analects* in particular. The text, although uniformly read and revered, did not itself achieve full canonical status until well over a millenium after achieving its present form when the interpretation of the text by the great neo-Confucian scholar ZHU Xi, became "orthodox," and a basis of the imperial civil service examinations for over seven hundred years.[29]

The Master himself may be an exception to the rule of school lineages and oral transmission of their *dao* (道); we do not know who his teachers were, or indeed, even if he had any. When asked who was the teacher of Confucius, his student Zigong replies:

> The way of Kings Wen and Wu has not collapsed utterly – it lives in the people. Those of superior character have grasped the greater part, while those of lesser parts have grasped a bit of it. Everyone has something of Wen and Wu's way in them. Who then does the Master not learn from? Again, how could there be a single constant teacher for him?[30]

The source of Confucius' education, then, has been the aggregated culture of the generations that have preceded him as it lived on in the people of his own day. As he says when confronted by a perilous situation in Kuang:

> With King Wen long dead, does not our cultural heritage reside here in us? If *tian* were going to destroy this legacy, we latecomers would not have had access to it. If *tian* is not going to destroy this culture, what can the people of Kuang do to us![31]

29 Indeed, before ZHU Xi's time it is not even accurate to refer to "Confucianism" at all – there is no graph for it in classical Chinese – because it was basically the learning of the literati or "gentlefolk" (*ruxue* 儒學). And thus it bears repeating, we think, that the classical texts that have been classified as "Confucian" should be read on their own, and not as collectively cohering as to have a "correct" interpretation that it is ours to find; there are far too many inconsistencies among and between them, the *Mencius* and the *Xunzi* being among the more notorious examples. At the same time, if its use be clear, "Confucianism," especially in its classical forms, may be conceived as an extension of the *xiao* dynamic, where each generation inherits the cultural tradition, uses it to address the pressing issues of the age, and thus reauthorizing it, passes it along to the next generation with the recommendation that they do the same.

30 *Analects* 19.22: 子貢曰：「文武之道，未墜於地，在人。賢者識其大者，不賢者識其小者，莫不有文武之道焉。夫子焉不學？而亦何常師之有？」

31 *Analects* 9.5: 文王既沒，文不在茲乎？天之將喪斯文也，後死者不得與於斯文也；天之未喪斯文也，匡人其如予何？According to the biography of Confucius in Sima Qian 1959: 1919, Confucius had left Wey and was on route to Chen when he passed through Kuang. The

"Family Reverence" (*xiao*) and the Embodying (*ti* 體) of Propriety (*li* 禮)

One way of understanding the dynamics of "family reverence" (*xiao*) as intergenerational transmission is to appeal to two cognate characters that are integral to the continuities of the family lineage: *ti* 體 ("body," "embodying," "forming and shaping," "category, class") and *li* 禮 ("ritual," "achieving propriety in one's roles and relations").

In the pre-Qin documents, the graph for "body" (*ti* 體) appears with three alternative semantic classifiers – "bones" (*gu* 骨), "lived, vital body" (*shen* 身), and "flesh" (*rou* 肉). We can appeal to these different ways of writing the graph as a heuristic for attempting to give full value to the notion of one generation "embodying" the one that comes before.[32] We must allow that *ti* with the "bones" classifier (*gu* 骨) references the "discursive body" as a process of "structuring," "configuring," "embodying," and thus "knowing" the world not only cognitively and affectively, but also viscerally. Each of us inherits a worldview and a cultural common sense, and collaborates with the world to discriminate, conceptualize, and theorize the human experience, embodying and giving form to our culture, our language, our habitat.

Ti with the "lived body" classifier (*shen* 身) highlights another dimension of embodying experience by referencing the vital, existentially aware, lived-body in its dynamic social relations with others. Experience always has a subjective dimension, an inside as well as an outside, and we come to understand and express what it means to become fully human intuitively as well as objectively through the actual process of becoming human.

And *ti* with the "flesh" classifier (*rou* 肉) references the carnal body – the body as flesh and bone. The modalities of our experience are rooted in and are always mediated through a unique localizing physicality, and are temporally and spatially constrained by this fact.[33] And all of our thoughts and feelings are grounded in a complex physical sensorium that makes specific demands on our conduct, and that registers our pleasures and pain.

At the most primordial level, the body via these three mutually entailing modalities – the discursive, vital, and carnal bodies – serves as the bond that correlates our subjectivity with our environments and that mediates the proces-

people of Kuang had recently been ravaged by Yang Huo, also from the state of Lu, and mistook Confucius for him. See also 11.23.

32 For a fuller discussion of this sense of embodiment, see Ames 2011: 102–113. For more on the *ti* body, see Sommer 2008.

33 A popular written form of the character for "body" (*ti* 體) that has become the standard script in Japanese and the simplified Chinese form is (*ti* 体) that combines the character "person" (*ren* 人) and the graph for "root" (*ben* 本).

ses of thinking and feeling with our emerging patterns of conduct. Human procreativity is the birthing of distinctive and unique persons from those who are genealogically prior. At the same time, within the ongoing, ceaseless process of embodiment, the many prior progenitors persist and live on in this continuing process of transforming into someone else. That is, while persons emerge to become specifically who they are as unique individuals, the parents and grandparents of such individuals continue to live on in them, just as they too will live on in their descendents. The focus-field language that we have proposed as a way of thinking about the relationship between particulars and the totality seems immediately relevant to this kind of holography in which the entire field of the physical and cultural experience is implicated in the narrative of each person.

This "living on" is not meant merely rhetorically. A very large number of people, we suspect, look very much like one of their great-grandparents, which, thanks to photography, can be seen directly in several ways. Change the hairstyle, the dress, and then squint a bit, and today's Susan looks very much like her Great-grandmother. Susan will also bear the surname of one of those great-grandparents, and perhaps her ancestral look-alike was also named Susan, the source of her given name. And if Susan keeps alive any memories she may have of her great-grandmother, then here, too, the earlier Susan may be said to be "living on." But even more obvious and significant than this physical transmission are the continuities of the cultural tradition itself – its language, institutions, and values.[34]

In the Confucian tradition, the body is understood as an inheritance we receive from our families, and as a current in a genealogical stream that reaches back to our most remote ancestors. It brings with it a sense of continuity, contribution, and belonging, and the religious significance that feelings of felt worth inspire. To show respect for our own bodies – both the physical body and its function as the residence of the cultural corpus that they bequeath to us – is to show reverence for our ancestors and the relationship we have with them, while disregard for our bodies is to bring shame upon our family lineages. What is significant in this reflection on our embodied persons is that physically, socially, and religiously, our bodies are a specific matrix of nested relations and functions that are invariably a collaboration between our persons and our many social, cultural, and natural environments. "Nobody" and no "body" – not the discursive, vital, or the carnal body – does anything by itself.

In this Confucian tradition, we can correlate "body" (*ti* 體) and its cognate character "achieved propriety in one's roles and relations" (*li* 禮) by arguing that

34 The sense of immortality implied by the expression "living on" is difficult to see if the body is taken as "belonging" only to an individual. The *Xiaojing* makes clear that for Confucius, it does not, as evidenced in the several quotes below in fns. 38–40. See also Rosemont 2007.

they express two ways of looking at the same phenomenon: That is, these two characters reference "a living body" and "embodied living" respectively. The notion of *li* 禮 denotes a continuing, complex, and always novel pattern of invested institutions and significant behaviors that is embodied, authored, and reauthorized by succeeding generations as the persistent cultural authority that serves to unify the family lineages (*shizu* 氏族) and clans (*jiazu* 家族) as a specific lineage of people (*minzu* 民族). For this holisitic Confucian philosophy, our unique persons in their physical and narrative entirety penetrate so deeply into human experience that it would be a nonsense to try to separate out some reality that stands independent of them. Said another way, reality is our lived, embodied experience and nothing else.

"Family Reverence" (*xiao*) and Transmitting the Cultural Body Intact

It should be clear that what we are referencing here is not simply the transmission of a physical lineage. But it is that, too. The living body and our embodied living is the narrative site of a conveyance of the cultural corpus of knowledge – linguistic facility and proficiency, religious rituals and mythologies, the aesthetics of cooking, song, and dance, the modeling of mores and values, instruction and apprenticeship in cognitive technologies, and so on – through which a living civilization itself is perpetuated. Our bodies are certainly our physicality, but they are so much more. They are also the conduits through which the entire body of culture is inherited, interpreted, elaborated upon, and reauthorized across the ages.

There is an important passage in the *Analects* in which Master Zeng on his deathbed surrounded by his students expresses a deep sense of relief in having preserved his body intact:

> Master Zeng was ill, and summoned his students to him, saying, "Look at my feet! Look at my hands!
> The *Book of Songs* says:
> Fearful! Trembling!
> As if peering over a deep abyss,
> As if walking across thin ice.[35]
> It is only from this moment hence that I can at last know relief, my young friends."[36]

It is clear that Master Zeng is rejoicing in the fact that he has reached the end of his life without having desecrated his physical form, and that he is able to return

35 *Book of Songs* 195.

36 *Analects* 8.3: 曾子有疾，召門弟子曰：「啟予足！啟予手！《詩》云『戰戰兢兢，如臨深淵，如履薄冰。』而今而後，吾知免夫！小子！」

this carnal body to the ancestors without issue. But the first chapter of the *Classic of Family Reverence* (*xiaojing* 孝經) in providing us important commentary on understanding this exchange between the dying Master Zeng and his students suggests that we might want to read "body" in a broader cultural sense:

> Confucius was at leisure in his home, and Master Zeng was attending him. … "It is family reverence," said the Master, "that is the root of personal excellence, and whence education itself is born. Sit down again and I will explain it to you.
> Your physical person with its hair and skin are received from your parents. Vigilance in not allowing anything to do injury to your person is where family reverence begins;[37] distinguishing yourself and walking the proper way in the world; raising your name high for posterity and thereby bringing esteem to your father and mother – it is in these things that family reverence finds its consummation. This family reverence then begins in service to your parents, continues in service to your lord, and culminates in distinguishing yourself in the world.[38]

We would argue that Confucius in elaborating upon the importance of *xiao* here is not simply referencing respect for the body in its physical sense, but is also alluding to its function as the site of intergenerational cultural transmission. He reinforces the claim in the *Analects* that *xiao* is indeed the "root" of human excellence, and perhaps playing with the cognate relationship between the character *xiao* 孝 and "education" (*jiao* 教), defines the substance of Confucian education as the serious responsibility of each generation to transmit the culture that they have inherited in its fullness and without diminution to the generation that follows.

Thus, keeping the "body" intact is the inclusive process of embodying the tradition, drawing upon it creatively as a resource for distinguishing oneself in the world, and contributing to its cultural resources by establishing a name for oneself and one's family that will be remembered by posterity. The body of the cultural tradition is embodied in each generation as it is perpetuated for those that follow.

37 In the *Record of Rites*, the *Liji* 25.36/128/6 it says: The Master said: "Among those things born of the heavens and nurtured by the earth, nothing is grander than the human being. For the parents to give birth to your whole person, and for one to return oneself to them whole is what can be called family reverence. To avoid desecrating your body or bringing disgrace to your person is what can be called keeping your person whole."

38 仲尼居，曾子侍。。。。 子曰：「夫孝、德之本也，教之所由生也。復坐，吾語汝。身體髮膚，受之父母，不敢毀傷，孝之始也。立身行道，揚名於後世，以顯父母，孝之終也。夫孝始於事親，中於事君，終於立身。。。」

Conclusion

We opened this chapter with the claim that in the interpretive context of the *Analects*, mutually beneficial associated living is an uncontested empirical fact. We now want to close it by enumerating several corollary entailments that can be drawn from the primacy of lived relations as the ground of Confucian role ethics, corollaries readily illustrated by passages from the *Analects*. There is a fundamental uniqueness of persons as they are defined by their specific patterns of relations,[39] an interdependence among persons as they live these relations,[40] a correlative, engaging and reflexive nature to all personal activity,[41] and an underlying processive, provisional, and emergent conception of both the natural and the social order.[42] And as we have seen, there are also mutually entailing historical and cosmological implications that follow from this primacy of relations. For example, there is the holistic, unbounded, and nested nature of relationships, a holographic conception of person as defined in focus-field rather than part-whole terms, and Confucianism as a philosophical aestheticism that registers all relationships as being relevant in degree to the totality of the effect.

Because many of the relationships are among and between family members, much of the totality of the effect will be seen therein. But the relationships must also extend outward from family (and clan) to the larger social order. The relationships will be intergenerational, as we have noted earlier, and understood in terms of roles between benefactors and beneficiaries. And these totalities in turn will go beyond social to authentically religious effects. The *Analects* consistently seems to be saying that a full and flourishing human life requires that some of our

---

39 *Analects* 15.36: 子曰：「當仁不讓於師。」 The Master said, "In striving to be consummate in your person, do not yield even to your teacher."

40 *Analects* 6.30: 夫仁者，己欲立而立人，己欲達而達人。能近取譬，可謂仁之方也已。」 "As for consummate persons, they establish others in seeking to establish themselves; they promote others in seeking to get there themselves. Correlating one's conduct in those near at hand can be said to be the method of becoming consummate in one's conduct."

41 *Analects* 7.8: 子曰：「不憤不啟，不悱不發，舉一隅不以三隅反，則不復也。」 The Master said, "I do not open the way for students who are not driven with eagerness; I do not supply a vocabulary for students who are not trying desperately to find the language for their ideas. If on showing students one corner they do not come back to me with the other three, I will not repeat myself." And 7.22: 子曰：「三人行，必有我師焉。擇其善者而從之，其不善者而改之。」 The Master said, "In strolling in the company of just two other persons, I am bound to find a teacher in them. Identifying their strengths, I follow them, and identifying their weaknesses, I reform myself accordingly."

42 *Analects* 9.17: 子在川上，曰：「逝者如斯夫！不舍晝夜。」 The Master was standing on the riverbank, and observed, "Isn't life's passing just like this, never ceasing day or night!" ; 2.11: 子曰：「溫故而知新，可以為師矣。」 The Master said: "Reviewing the old as a means of realizing the new – such a person can be considered a teacher." and 15.29: 子曰：「人能弘道，非道弘人。」 The Master said: "It is the person who is able to broaden the way, not the way that broadens the person."

relations be with those younger than ourselves, others with our peers, and still other relations with the generations that have preceded us. And it is in this religious sense that we interpret the Master's autobiographical response when asked by his disciple Zilu what he would most like to do:

> I would like to bring peace and contentment to the aged, share relationships of trust and confidence with friends, and to love and protect the young.[43]

Bibliography of Works Cited

Ames, Roger T. 2011. *Confucian Role Ethics: A Vocabulary.* Hong Kong and Honolulu: Chinese University Press and University of Hawai'i Press joint publication.

Ames, Roger T. and Henry Rosemont, Jr., trans. 1998. *The Analects of Confucius: A Philosophical Translation.* New York: Ballantine.

Chan, Alan K.L and Sor-hoon Tan. 2004. *Filial Piety in Chinese Thought and History.* London: Routledge Curzon

Daxue 大學 (*Great Learning*). 1969. Zhu Xi 朱熹. *Sishu jizhu* 四書集註 (Collected Commentaries on the Four Books). Taibei: Yiwen yinshuguan.

Fei, Xiaotong. 1992. *From the Soil: The Foundations of Chinese Society.* A translation of *Xiangtu Zhongguo* 鄉土中國 by Gary G. Hamilton and Wang Zheng. Berkeley: University of California Press.

Hall, David L. and Roger T. Ames. 1987. *Thinking Through Confucius.* Albany, NY: State University of New York Press.

Hsiao, Kung-chuan. 1979. *A History of Chinese Political Thought* Volume 1. Translated by F. W. Mote. Princeton: Princeton University Press.

Ivanhoe, Philip J. 2004. "Filial Piety as a Virtue." In Chan and Tan above.

Keightley, David N. 1998. "Shamanism, Death, and the Ancestors: Religious Mediation in Neolithic and Shang China, ca. 5000–1000 B.C." *Asiatische Studien* 52: 763–828.

Kierkegaard, Soren. 1985. *Fear and Trembling.* Hammondsworth: Penguin Books.

Liji 禮記 (*Record of Rites*) 1992. *A Concordance to the* Liji. Lau, D. C. and Chen Fong Ching. Hong Kong: Commercial Press.

Liu, Lydia H. 1995. *Translingual Practice: Literature, National Culture, and Translated Modernity – China, 1900–1937.* Stanford: Stanford University Press.

Lloyd, Geoffrey, and Nathan Sivin. 2002. *The Way and the Word: Science and Medicine in Early China and Greece.* New Haven: Yale University Press.

Nylan, Michael. 2011. *Yang Xiong and the Pleasures of Reading and Classical Learning in China.* New Haven: American Oriental Society.

—,Henry Rosemont, Jr. and Li Waiyee. 2008. *Star Gazing, Fire Phasing, and Healing in China: Essays in Honor of Nathan Sivin.* Special issue of *Asia Major,* 3rd Series, vol. XXI, Part I.

43 *Analects* 5.26: 子路曰：「願聞子之志。」子曰：「老者安之，朋友信之，少者懷之。」

Rosemont Jr., Henry 2001. *Rationality and Religious Experience.* Chicago & La Salle, IL: Open Court Publishing Company.

—,2007. "On the Non-finality of Physical Death in Classical Confucianism." *Acta Orientalia Vilnensia,* 8:2, pp. 13–31.

Rosemont Jr., Henry and Roger T. Ames, trans. 2009. *Xiaojing: The Chinese Classic of Family Reverence: A Philosophical Translation of the* Xiaojing 孝經 . Honolulu: University of Hawai'i Press.

Sima Qian 司馬遷. 1959. Shiji 史記 (*Records of the Historian*). Beijing: Zhonghua shuju.

Slingerland, Edward, trans. 2003. *Analects: With Selections from Traditional Commentaries.* Indianapolis: Hackett Publishing.

Sommer, Deborah. 2008. "Boundaries of the *Ti Body.*" In Nylan, Rosemont, and Li above.

Wittgenstein, Ludwig. 1953. *Philosophical Investigations (PI).* G.E.M. Anscombe and R. Rhees (eds.), G.E.M. Anscombe (trans.), Oxford: Blackwell.

Zhang Yanhua (2007). *Transforming Emotions with Chinese Medicine: An Ethnographic Account from Contemporary China.* Albany: State University of New York Press.

Zhongyong. 2001. *Focusing the Familiar: A Translation and Philosophical Interpretation of the* Zhongyong. Translated by Roger T. Ames and David L. Hall. Honolulu: University of Hawai'i Press.

Zhou, Yiqun. 2010. *Festival, Feasts, and Gender Relations in Ancient China and Greece.* New York: Cambridge University Press.

Henry Rosemont, Jr.

Travelling through Time with Family and Culture: Confucian Meditations

We shall not cease from exploration
And the end of all our exploring
Will be to return to where we started from
And know the place for the first time.

T. S. Eliot

Introduction

One might argue that 'travelling' – that is, 'making one's way' (*dao*) – is the governing metaphor of the *Analects* of Confucius specifically, and other Confucian writings more generally: 'It is the human being that extends the way …' (15.29).[1]

When we normally think of travelling, it is through space; we go from place to place as we work and play throughout our adult lives. Even though highway and airport gridlock have become an ever more frustrating series of obstacles to overcome, we still tend to think positively about travel overall: the underlying assumption behind the question 'Where are you going on vacation?' is that you *should* be going somewhere during that time in order to enrich your life.

One of the most important reasons for the approbation generally given to travel, especially long-distance travel, is that it acquaints us with ways of living different from our own, presumably what the cliché 'Travel broadens one' is intended to convey. To be sure, climate and geography can and do contribute much to the excitement and wonder of travel, but it is how our fellow human beings live in differing environments that most captures and sustains our interest. And even more important than experiencing distinctive architecture, dress, cuisine and customs is attempting to understand the hopes, fears, dreams, beliefs and value-orderings of the peoples who embody those and related cultural determinants different from our own way of life.

Such experiences will almost certainly affect our own future lives, and consequently the metaphor of the 'way' of Confucius should be interpreted tem-

1 Here and throughout the parenthetical numbers refer to the *Lunyu*, specifically the translation by Ames and Rosemont, 1998.

porally no less than spatially, which means that the philosophical significance of travel for illuminating the human condition *tout court* must take both dimensions of the metaphor into account. And it is this temporal dimension of 'travel' that Roger Ames and I want to concentrate on herein as we attempt to elucidate certain features of our interpretations of classical Confucianism as an ethics of roles, especially those features linked to their conception of what it is to be a human being, and their consequent instructions on how we might best lead our altogether human lives meaningfully as we traverse the spatiotemporal distance from birth to death.

For my part, I will first take up briefly the concept of *individualism* – especially with respect to constancy, independence and freedom – which, although it is being questioned in some quarters, remains definitive of contemporary Western moral, political, economic and most religious thought, and I will contrast that view with the strong Confucian relational view of human beings that emphasizes change over time, interdependence and behavioural constraints. Imposing individualism on Confucian persons guarantees we will not understand who they are at any given moment, or desire to become in the future.

Thereafter I will take up some features of the most basic group to which we must all belong, namely the family, focusing on our temporal journeys as sons or daughters, parents and grandparents, aunts, uncles, nephews, nieces, cousins and in-laws, and I will do so in the context of the contemporary world, suggesting some lessons the ancient texts might have for us today. The key term here is *xiao*, translated commonly as 'filial piety', but which Roger and I translate as 'family reverence'.[2]

Along the way I will make an occasional reference to another group with which persons may identify, of signal importance to Confucius and his successors, namely, the scholar-literati, the *ru*, or our own choice, the 'classicists', i. e. those responsible for inheriting, maintaining and altering the cultural heritage of the society in which they live.

Roger will then in the last essay in this volume take up the *ru* in some depth, focusing on the dynamics of Chinese inter-generational cultural transmission of these processes of maintenance and transmission, and how the Confucian *ru* committed to them were formed, re-formed and transformed over time. He will also make additional remarks about *xiao* and the family, in order to more closely analyse and explore cultural transmission within living family lineages, and in this way deepen our understanding of the changing cultural landscape as it is conserved and reconfigured across the centuries in ways that are not uniquely Chinese.

2 See Ames and Rosemont, 2008.

Central for both of us is, first, a conception of *morality* that derives from a focus on families and family life, a conception significantly at odds with most contemporary thinking, especially those moralities associated with the deontological writings of Immanuel Kant, the Utilitarianism of Jeremy Bentham and John Stuart Mill, or the virtue morality found in Aristotle's *Nicomachean Ethics.* Equally central for us is the altogether non-supernatural conception of *religion* or *spirituality* that we believe emerges from Confucian familial and cultural orientations.[3]

On individualism

Ever since the time of Hegel – and usually before then as well – the family has not been much of a concern for philosophers, especially moral philosophers. One very important reason for this neglect is that the dominant Western moral theories on offer today – deontological, utilitarian and virtue-based – are all grounded in the idea of human beings as fundamentally *individuals*, individuals who are, or certainly ought to be, rational, free and autonomous (and usually self-interested). Whether this idea (presupposition, actually) is taken descriptively or prescriptively is not important here; the thrust of it is to see and treat all other human beings *as if* they are free, rational and autonomous individuals (and usually self-interested).

In addition to the ontological or normative individualism of philosophers, there is a *methodological* variant to the concept employed by psychologists and sociologists. The former assume, first, that psychological states can be individuated and studied independently of other psychological states, and second, that individual persons can exist and be studied independently of other persons. In sociology the claim of methodological individualism is that individual selves aggregated constitute the primary reality, with *society*, or the polity, being a second-order, abstract construct – a view common in the field since the days of Max Weber.[4]

A foundational individualism is also easily discernible in epistemology, as, for example, in the view that human beings can come to knowledge of the world as individuals independent of a cultural perspective, that they can 'see' the world as it 'really is'. Closely linked to the concept of objectivity at the empirical level, it is

3 For more detail on these two themes, see the introduction to Ames and Rosemont, 2008. David Hall and Roger Ames (1995, pp. 271–7) have argued for the family being the most foundational of all metaphors in Chinese thought; see also their references to the sociological work of Ambrose King.

4 For an overview of methodological individualism, see Udehn, 2004.

usually linked as well to subjectivity – more specifically, to the claim that the ontic individual self can *know* itself as an individual self.

A moment's reflection should make clear that none of these individualistic conceptions of being a human being will be of much use in accounting for the hopes, fears, dreams, deeds or the simple joys and profound sorrows of family life. We cannot explain the dynamics of family interactions, nor our feelings about those interactions, by seeing and treating our parents, grandparents and children (not to mention neighbours and friends) as *individuals.* Family relations, especially the most basic of them – namely, between parents and children (and grandparents) – cannot be described, analysed or evaluated on the basis of free and rational autonomous selves interacting with one another, for parents are implicated in the lives of their children, and children in the lives of their parents; a significant part of how both parents and children define who they are is in terms of the other, and hence cannot be autonomous in any important sense because their roles define them in terms of each other. (In a number of situations the most appropriate answer to a question asking me to identify myself might well be 'Connie Rosemont's father', or 'JoAnn Rosemont's husband', or 'Timmy Healy's grandfather' – or, in an extended sense of family, 'close friend of Roger Ames'.)

I have changed significantly in my travels through time, becoming a different person when I married, when my first child was born and then her sisters in turn. All of these and numerous similar events have contributed a great deal to the definition of who I have been and who I am now, just as I have contributed significantly to their definitions of and by themselves, and by others. Hence, when it is 'my daughter' that must be used in the description of a supposedly moral situation involving me, the possibility of formulating and acting upon some abstract principle vanishes; if I do not have the requisite resources within me to ascertain the most appropriate means of dealing with the situation, Kant can no more assist me than Bentham or Mill – or any other universalist moral philosopher, for that matter; I do not seek a rule that will apply to all abstract individuals all of the time, but what I should do *right now*, with *Connie*, my daughter. The obviousness of this point becomes apparent when we imagine that I might well address the immediate problem by asking her 'What would you like me to do?' – which is not what will be found in universalist moral theories, or pluralistic ones either.[5]

Despite the non-universalistic orientation of an ethics grounded in familial relations, the neglect of thinking seriously about the family and family life when dealing with morality must end, because families are going to continue their dominant role in the lives of the peoples of all cultures, and must therefore be

5 David Wong (2009) argues long and well for a plurality of acceptable moral codes, with constraints, as an alternative to universalism in moral philosophy.

taken into account when addressing the Herculean economic, social, political and environmental tasks the world faces today. While a great many families today can be characterized as sexist, oppressive, and/or just generally dysfunctional, many more of them the world over are not, and families are not going to disappear as an institution no matter what some people might wish. Moreover, admitting that 'family values' has regularly been employed conceptually – especially in the United States – in the service of arch-conservative social, political and/or religious organizations reinforcing patriarchy, sexism, homophobia and worse, nevertheless, family values do *not* have to be monopolized by extremists spiritual or secular; I want to suggest that family values can be modified along much more progressive social, political and economic lines when placed in an updated Confucian conceptual framework.

Roger will take up that framework more specifically in its early Confucian context; for the nonce, let me say only that within this framework each of us will be a unique person, but not an individual as delineated above; not isolatable, but interrelated; not autonomous, but interdependent; and not altogether free – even in principle – but encumbered by our responsibilities to those who define us, and whom we contribute to defining. Perhaps most important for the diverse societies of today, a family-oriented ethic can foster cultural pluralism even when not universalistic.

How, then, might family values be seen as progressive rather than reactionary (while allowing for differing orderings of them)?

A family travelling through time in today's world

We must, in the first instance, think about the *present* when attending to that dimension of our paternal role as caretakers – seeing, that is, to the needs of our children for food, shelter, clothing, books, and more basically, security and love. From birth on, however, the relationship is *reciprocal:* the children are an outlet for the love and care parents feel and express, and provide as well the means for taking pride and satisfaction in meeting parental responsibilities, a necessary condition for human dignity in virtually all societies. As they grow, children can express love and care for their parents more actively by being obedient.

Blind obedience, of course, is not to be encouraged, but it is a keen insight of Confucius that one significant way children show respect as well as love for their parents is by obeying them. (They know well, for example, that parents become increasingly distressed as the hour passes by which time the youngster was told to be home.) Thus family relations should be seen as reciprocal at all times (but of course not analysed as contractual).

In addition to the responsibility of *caring* for them, however – meeting their needs – we are also aware as parents of our responsibility for *raising* our children to become adults, which obliges us to think long and carefully about the *future* as well as the present. This is no more than to say that I must not only attend to my children as they are right now but also as I believe it would be best for them to become in the future. There are certain ways I should like my children to be when they grow up, and certain ways I do not want them to be, the details of which will be largely dependent on my children's mental, physical and psychological makeup, our socio-economic circumstances, and of course the cultural milieu in which we live. These details will also depend on my own (and my wife's) family history, our ethnicity, citizenship, and other social factors that have largely determined the hopes, fears, dreams and goals we have not only for ourselves, but altogether naturally have for our children as well – without which we would not be who we are, nor would we be a family in any meaningful sense of the word. As parents, in other words, we must emulate the *ru* at least in part, as we are obliged to carry on, and transmit the *culture* we have inherited, modifying dimensions of it that are no longer consonant with the times and/or our values, or conducive to the well-being of our children.

Anyone committed to an individualist morality in which autonomy and freedom are central may well take exception to this contemporary Confucian analysis thus far, because in raising children in this manner our concern is not solely, or perhaps even mainly, to seek to maximize the possibility of their later becoming fully autonomous and free *individuals*, as moralities grounded in individualism would insist.

Today's world is nowhere near as monocultural morally as was the China of Confucius, but his concerns are still important to consider in our contemporary and diversified societies. I attempt to live in accordance with an ordering of values that influences importantly who I am and what I do. I have that value ordering because I believe it is a very good one, and endeavour to exemplify it in my conduct with my offspring no less than with others. So, of course, does my wife, although she may have a slightly different ordering than my own. Needless to say, we will endeavour to instil our orderings in our children, for a major part of our parental responsibilities are to have them become value-oriented, and if we do not orient them toward our own value orderings, which others might we use? This is not at all to suggest that we should attempt to make our children copies of ourselves. We are different people, obviously, and we must take those differences into account at all times, especially in matters of taste and personal preferences. But matters of morals, or basic political or religious matters, are different from matters of aesthetics or personal inclination. In these latter areas I have accepted a worldview and attendant ordering of values because in the end I believe that ordering *better* than other possible orderings. Consequently, in today's increasingly pluralistic cultures we all have a fundamental responsibility to show our children that there are very decent and intelligent people who order their values somewhat differently than I do. But surely I am not in any way being derelict in my parental duties in endeavouring to orient my offspring toward what I believe is the best among the candidates? If not my own, then which?[6]

Consider a man whose chosen career has been that of a union organizer. He has enjoyed his work overall, and been extremely proud and happy when another work unit, through his efforts, voted in a union to represent their interests in negotiations with the corporate hierarchy. His career has not made him rich, but has provided the wherewithal to send his son to college, and to law school thereafter, a goal the boy has embraced since his sophomore year. Now, after passing the bar exam, the son announces that the best job offer he has had came from the largest union-busting firm in the state, and he has accepted it.

My personal intuition here is that any pride and joy the father might take at this turn of events – the son has a job, which he has clearly chosen on his own – would almost immediately leave him and be replaced by severe depression; not simply because of the choice the son has made, but because of the way the father now had to view his role as a father in a very different, much more negative manner, namely as a failure in several important ways. It is not merely that the father secretly might have wished for the son to choose to become a labour lawyer; had the son chosen real estate law, criminal law, become an assistant district attorney or public defender, the father might have been a bit disappointed, yet not more than that. But for the son to embark on a career that was the antithesis of the values of solidarity and social justice his father has lived for and attempted to embody was proof positive to him that his fathering had been radically deficient in crucial respects.

It might be tempting to think that the father is just being self-centred, either by wanting to live vicariously through his son's work, or by being a dogmatist, or pressing his own socio-political agenda, or simply not thinking of how the son might take pride in the knowledge of his independence and ability to make up his own mind. But now shift attention directly to the son himself as he begins a career

6 We emphasize the prioritization of values to make it clear that we do not believe it is possible to 'take on a new set of values' as most people would be inclined to say. One cannot logically take on a whole new set of values, but only re-order the values they (and everyone else except sociopaths) already have. How, for example, could one ever get you to change your mind about the worth of a particular value except by appealing to a more basic value you both share? Everyone values security, everyone values freedom; but different people order those values differently. And if members of one camp convince some members of another to change their minds, these latter have not 'taken on a whole new set of values', but have simply re-ordered the values they have long held, sometimes, but not always, permanently. In situation X, freedom trumps security, but in Y the opposite ordering might obtain.

devoted to undoing his father's life work and dreams: what would we think of him?

Notice that so long as we merely see him as *a free and autonomous individual* who has made a rational choice, we will probably just shrug our shoulders and say 'So what?', or 'It's a private matter, and his father's problem, not a moral issue'. My strong sense, however, is that if we focus on him as a *son* of *this* father we would not think much of him, and think of him as somehow a *moral* failure despite the private nature of the behaviour; we would see the son as fairly unfeeling, and certainly characterize him as *self-centred* for being so unmindful of the significance of his decision for his father, who, because of that decision, has now become a very different person, and not merely because of his sadness. The son has clearly been not simply ungrateful, but highly irreverent toward his family, with untoward consequences for the others with whom his life has been intertwined, and that is why we will hold him in low regard. And I suspect this would hold true even for people who hated unions. This, then, is role ethics in action, and how it differs from moralities built on the idea of individualism: if father and son are only autonomous (unencumbered) individuals, there is no moral issue here, only, at best, a personal one.

Every parent must, of course, balance their guiding conduct toward their children on the one hand with an appreciation of the uniqueness of each of them on the other; the desired goal would be to have them take on a value-ordering similar to the parents – not merely because it is theirs, but because they believe it is a *good* ordering, an ordering worth maintaining in the future, and committed themselves to it accordingly. And it seems to me that this goal can only be achieved on the basis of the *love* of the parents for their children, and exemplary conduct in raising them, with few if any abstract moral rules or principles playing a role. Returning to the union-organizing father, how could he possibly assign a higher place in his value-ordering to the categorical imperative or the utility principle than to the overall ordering which has given his life meaning, purpose and satisfaction? Moreover, the father's love of his work should have been exemplary for the son, too, and thus causes even more depression in the present case, for if the son hates his new job and is doing it only for the money, then the father's example of pride and satisfaction in his work was also for naught as a model – depressing to contemplate. But not as depressing as the other possibility: that the son really *likes* to break up unions. Note that whatever concerns about the young union-busting lawyer we may have, these are not generated by saying he has a 'poor character' or has no proper sense of 'morals'; he has failed significantly as a *son*, the most basic role he has lived – our opprobrium applies to role-bearing unique persons, not autonomous individuals.

(It might be objected here that all of this is well and good, but what do we do with fathers who don't love their children very much, and are rigid dogmatists to boot? A full response to this straightforward objection falls beyond the scope of this paper, but an adumbrated reply is given in the following endnote).[7]

The moral of the story thus far should be clear from a contemporary Confucian perspective: when dealing with relationships between parents and children we cannot see any of the participants as free, autonomous individuals, for they are too intimately bound up with one another not only in their interactions, but in their sense of who they are, have been and will become as well – in all cases, bonded by love, through time. What it means, in large part, to be a father or a mother is to be sensitive to the personalities, abilities and feelings of their children at all times, taking these into account both when caring for them *now*, and raising them with an eye to the *future*. And what it means to be a son or daughter is to be sensitive to the beliefs and feelings of one's parents before electing and following any significant goal in their lives, a sensitivity that must be maintained throughout their parents' lives as a matter of loyalty. This loyalty does not preclude remonstrating with them, of course (or others in authority), as all the texts of classical Confucianism make clear.[8]

There is yet a third time factor that parents must take into account in meeting their responsibilities both to care for and raise their children, and that is the *past*. Here, it seems to me, the Confucians have perhaps the most to say to everyone today, with their detailed concern for rituals, especially that involving ancestor veneration. It is in their emphasis on the importance of keeping yesterday before us in order to properly live today and plan for tomorrow that Confucian family

7 Usually couched as a conflict arising from the fact that good Confucians are supposed to serve in government when called upon, on the one hand, and the fact that the ruler you are now serving is a thoroughgoing rotter: what to do? What rule or principle will Confucius follow? If we are correct in our interpretation, however, there are no such rules or principles to be found in the early texts. But we may nevertheless resolve the conflict easily. Rather than searching for an abstract principle, we must ask, as one who is serving in government, whether *this* ruler, here now – is he re-formable? If the answer is affirmative, we must ask a second highly specific question: do we have the qualities and skills to reform him? If the answer to this question is also affirmative, King Wen becomes our model exemplar, and we continue to serve, remonstrating all the while. If the answer to the first question is 'yes', but is 'no' to the second, Confucius himself becomes our model, as we return to family and community, and 'serve government' from there, as *Lunyu* 2.21 makes clear, and 7.16 and 8.13 reinforce. And if we answer the first question 'no, we don't believe he is re-formable', then we must raise the flag of rebellion, with King Wu as our hero and precedent-setter. In sum, no conflicts; there is always a decision procedure. It is always highly particularistic – but none the worse for that, it would seem. The argument carries over, *mutatitis muntandis,* to fathers and other figures of authority.

8 Indeed, we want to claim that *all* interpersonal relations and interactions can be fruitfully described, analysed and evaluated on the model of parents and children, benefactor and beneficiary, as I have sketched here: the interrelations between friends, neighbours, colleagues and others. Nothing of ethical significance, we are arguing, will be lost, and much gained, by abandoning a foundational individualism altogether.

reverence can perhaps be seen most vividly in its religious no less than moral dimensions.

Much of who and what we are may be traced fairly directly to our ancestors, from our physical appearance to our native tongue, from our ethnicity to the specifics of the socialization processes we have undergone. Many of our tastes in food, music, dress, avocations and more can also often be traced directly to our parents and grandparents, and their grandparents in turn. (In a number of cases we can also trace our antipathy to certain of these tastes, or others, directly to them, too.) Like it or not, we belong to a family, and moreover, a family with a history – and in most cases, more than one. It follows from this that the more we know of our familial past, and the more we stay in touch with it, the better we can know who we are now, and envisage possibilities of who we might, or should, become, and define ourselves accordingly.

This point is obvious to the families of the rich and the powerful: every Rockefeller, Kennedy, Bush, Vanderbilt, and so on, has a strong sense of who they are, and a sense of belonging to a special group, with a special history; all of the adults in these families, I would guess, can name in full not only their four grandparents, but seven if not all eight of their great-grandparents as well. But the point is not to celebrate snobbery, for it applies to all families, even when misfortunes like being poor, a refugee or an immigrant have made it almost impossible to keep even a two-generation family genealogy intact, and remembered. Each of us almost surely has a hero or heroine or two in the family tree, and very probably an occasional villain as well. Each of us has eight great-grandparents, and it is obvious to me that all of us will have a better sense of who we are if we know who *they* were. Their fame or infamy may have been great or local, or they may have been simply 'ordinary' folk, but the histories of all families are special – extraordinary, if you will – to the members thereof. Yet in order to obtain that sense of *belonging* to a family with a history (which every family has), you must know about that history, especially the lives of the ancestors who have made that history. It behoves all of us, then, to learn of our family's history, to listen carefully to the stories told to us by our grandparents and their siblings, to look at old photographs, and/or do a bit of genealogical detective work. Knowing where we have come from provides major clues as to who we are, and might become, as we continue developing the history of our family – and contributing to it.

In my opinion there is no better way to obtain this sense of belonging, of feeling the continuity of a family line, than by a ritual honouring of the ancestors on occasion, especially for parents and grandparents. It should thus be a significant dimension of my role as parent to instil in my children this sense of coming from, and belonging to, a family with a history, that I have responsibilities to my own parents and their parents in turn, responsibilities that do not cease at their deaths; it is my responsibility to my forbears to see that their memory is not entirely erased by time. Hence, in order to be an appropriate model for my children I should periodically engage in a ritual which honours our ancestors, a ritual that might be widespread throughout my culture, or more locally; or it might be a ritual unique to our own family's heritage; it might even be a ritual my wife and I create for our descendants. I enrich the lives of my children by continuing to discharge my responsibilities toward my parents and grandparents after they have died by rituals of remembrance. I personally know of no culture that does not have such rituals.[9]

It may seem strange to think that we owe a debt to the dead, but it is not. Even atheists can understand the obligatory nature of keeping a deathbed promise. And doesn't every son and daughter raised in a loving home 'promise', even if only implicitly, not to forget them, nor to let our own children forget them? Rituals, especially family rituals, have tended to occupy the thoughts of most Western philosophers no more than the family has, but rituals can form a basic glue for families, and significantly affect the self-identification of its members, as well as their sense of worth. To see this point another way, consider the fact that a great many people invariably 'talk' to the tombstone when they visit a cemetery to pay respects to a deceased relative, teacher or friend. There is nothing surprising about this, it is altogether human; we *know* the deceased cannot hear us, but we speak anyway 'as if they were present' (3.12).

For this insight, if for no other, we owe a continuing debt to the early Confucians. In the past, these practices undoubtedly stemmed from the almost universal belief in ghosts and spirits, benign and malevolent, in keeping with the theologies of the world's religions. This occurred in China too, of course, and here is where the peculiar genius of the early Confucians is of such great relevance today, over and above the social, political and economic insights they can provide us as we undertake the task of seriously re-thinking the family: they also show us how rituals and customs of respect for our ancestors can be moving, satisfying and sustaining even for the increasing number of us the world over who give no credence to the idea of ghosts and spirits.[10]

9 For more on the temporal and non-physical sense of immortality attendant on the performance of mourning rituals, see Rosemont, 2012, especially Chapters XI and XII.

10 It might well be objected that the overall view of the family portrayed herein is so wildly idealistic as to not be worth taking seriously. Two quick replies: 1) The picture I have suggested might be more realistic than a number of accounts of the family – East and West – have been. Individualism is supposed to have been a characteristic only of the family in the West. Until the nineteenth century children were seen largely in economic terms. The nuclearization of the family in the West contributed greatly to the rise of capitalism, and many more stereotypes of the history of the family, whether compiled by sociologists (Western families), anthropologists (non-Western families), or by historians, comparative or otherwise, are deserving of careful scrutiny. 2) 'There is nothing wrong with building castles in the sky', said Thoreau; 'That is where they belong. Now put the foundations under them.'

But the satisfaction will come, I believe, only to those who can come to appreciate their interrelatedness and interdependence with others, and thus define themselves as role-living unique persons, not autonomous individuals, who may all too easily be seen as the nineteenth-century champion of women's rights Elizabeth Cady Stanton saw them: 'We come into the world alone [...] and we leave it alone. Each of us must make the voyage of life alone [...]' (Nussbaum, 2006, p. 29). Equally stark, Aldous Huxley noted a century later:

> We live together, we act on, and react to one another; but always and in all circumstances we are by ourselves. The martyrs go hand in hand into the arena; they are crucified alone. (Huxley, 1963, p. 12)

Against this brief background, Roger will continue our narrative of travel through time by moving from a family's specific ordering of values to the more general norms definitive of the larger Chinese culture in which families and their role-living member were embedded, and through which they also travelled.[11]

References

Ames, R. T. and Hall, D. (1995), *Anticipating China.* Albany: SUNY Press.

Ames, R. T. and Rosemont, H. Jr. (trans.) (1998), *The Analects of Confucius: A Philosophical Translation.* New York: Ballantine.

— (trans.) (2008), *Classic of Family Reverence: A Philosophical Translation of the Xiaojing.* Honolulu: University of Hawai'i Press.

Huxley, A. (1963), *The Doors of Perception: Heaven and Hell.* London: Penguin.

Nussbaum, M. (2006), 'In a lonely place'. *Nation*, 282, (8), 26–30.

Rosemont Jr., H. (2012), *A Reader's Companion to the Confucian Analects.* London: Palgrave Macmillan.

Udehn, L. (2004), *Methodological Individualism.* London: Routledge.

Wong, D. (2009), *Natural Moralities.* Oxford: Oxford University Press.

11 Parts of this paper were first read at a panel honouring the work of Joel Kupperman at the University of Hawai'i in the summer of 2010. I am grateful to the audience there and to my fellow participants at the conference of the Académie du Midi in Alet-les-Bains in spring, 2012 for their many useful comments and encouragement.

Roger T. Ames / Henry Rosemont, Jr.

Were the Early Confucians Virtuous?

We respond negatively to the question entitling our essay. While the vocabulary of virtue ethics for describing the early Confucian vision of the moral life (*dào* 道) is superior to those linked to Kantian or Utilitarian principle-based ethical theories, that vocabulary, too, forces the Master and his followers more into the mold of Western philosophical discourse than they ought to be placed, in our opinion, and hence make it difficult to see the Confucian vision as a genuine *alternative* to those with which we are most familiar.

Instead, we will claim: (1) That early (pre-Buddhist) Confucianism is best described as a *role ethics;* (2) This role ethics is *sui generis* in both philosophy and religion, East and West; (3) it embodies first, a specific vision of human beings as relational persons constituted by the roles they live, rather than as individual selves; and (4) embodies as well a specific vision of the moral life that takes family feeling as the entry point for developing a consummate moral competence *and* a religious sensibility grounded in *this* world.

Giving a detailed account of role ethics is beyond the scope of the present essay, except as part of our overall argument against efforts to link the early Confucians to Aristotle, or to Kant, Bentham and Mill – or their contemporary champions – by showing the far more central place of roles, especially family roles, in Confucianism, and simultaneously to argue *for* the importance of incorporating the concept of roles and family values into any view of morals or ethics that can claim the allegiance of reflective and sensitive citizens of the twenty-first century across ethnic, national, and religious boundaries.

Aristotle first. Many competent comparative philosophers have weighed in on the question of whether or not classical Confucianism is a form of virtue ethics, with a seeming preponderance of them affirming this claim. Some of them are not altogether Aristotlelian in their commitments to virtue ethics – Ivanhoe, Yearley, and others – but many others make the comparisons seriously; two recent studies (Sim 2007, Yu 2007), for example, are committed entirely to a comparison of Aristotle and the canonical Confucian texts on ethics, and to reinforcing the majority position. All of these philosophers and others have raised the bar considerably in our attempt to formulate a dissenting position.[1]

The philosophical reasons for our dissent will be proffered below. But we want first to note our unhappiness more generally with narrative and methodological approaches in these comparisons that are presumed to be philosophically neutral when in fact they are not. Consider, for example, another essay by Yu. With an admirable command of both the Aristotelian and early Chinese texts, Yu argues that Aristotle's *politick zoon* bears a close resemblance throughout to the relational self of Confucius and Mencius. But unfortunately, once the comparisons have been made, it turns out that something "... *is lacking* in Confucian ethics" (2005, 295); "what Aristotle regards as primary happiness *is missing* in Confucius" (296); "Confucius ... appears *to ignore* the theoretical ..." (297) (our italics). If Aristotle and Confucius are saying pretty much the same thing, but the former is saying it more adequately and thus better, then why bother reading the latter? We do not mean to be unfair to Yu. Similar statements abound in writings in comparative philosophy juxtaposing Confucius not just with Aristotle, but with most other Western philosophers as well. In virtually all these comparisons, something always seems to be missing in Confucianism. But we never seem to see converse statements such as "The concept of the sage *is lacking* in Aristotelian ethics," or "the centrality of ritual for human flourishing *is missing* in Aristotle," or "Kant, Mill and others ... appear *to ignore* the importance of the exemplary person (*jūnzǐ* 君子)," and so on. Why not?

We want to resist the unfortunate asymmetry that continues in the work of comparative philosophy, bolstering as it does the unannounced but persistent premise that Chinese philosophy's encounter with Western philosophy has been its defining moment, with such a definition being more flattering to the West than to the Middle Kingdom.[2] In this particular instance, we want to resist tailoring what we take to be a distinctively Confucian role ethics into a familiar category of Western ethical theory. We shall follow contemporary scholars of Chinese philosophy back to the classical Aristotelian model of virtue ethics and try to articulate the ways in which we believe the Confucian vision of human flourishing and the moral life are importantly different from Aristotle's *eudemonia.*

1 A few of our criticisms of Sim (2007) have been anticipated by Ni Peimin in his close and careful critique of her book, "How far is Confucius an Aristotelian?" *Dao: A Journal of Comparative Philosophy* 8 no 4 (2009). Supporting the claim that Confucianism is a virtue ethic are the papers in Ivanhoe and Walker (2006). See also Wilson (2002) and Yearley (2003), among others.

2 Shun (2008) underscores this persistent asymmetry. We are comfortable asking if Mòzǐ 墨子 is a utilitarian, but not whether or not Wittgenstein subscribes to a doctrine of "the proper use of language" (*zhèngmíng* 正名).

We shall argue for an alternative Confucian basis of normativity by establishing a contrast between an Aristotelian notion of "virtue (*arête*)" as acquired character traits and a much less abstract Confucian conception of family-based relational virtuosity. For Confucius, family feeling is clearly the entry point for developing moral competence,[3] and as such, we shall insist that Confucian normativity is defined in terms of living one's family roles to maximum effect. A person becomes good by living her life as a good daughter to her father and mother, and then by extending these developed moral sensibilities to the larger community. On our reading, lived family roles – mothering, brothering, granddaughtering – are themselves normative standards that, informed as they are by existential embodiment, are much clearer and more concrete than putative moral principles.

It is important to note that while the general terms denoting familial and other roles might be said to be abstract, they are just barely so, unlike the key terms in Western ethics, beginning with *individual* – the locus of moral analysis in Western ethical theorizing. What is known about a person when we are told she is an "individual," as contrasted with "mother?" There are levels of abstraction, seen clearly if we think of laws. There is the bare concept of *law*, below which we will find *criminal law*. And below that, laws *against stealing another's property;* lower down the abstraction scale we have *burglary*, *robbery*, and related laws, and down again we can find *pickpocketing*, *identity theft*, and so on.

Equally important, role terms are much less abstract than terms for the virtues on the basis of the differences in instantiation. If we see someone doing something seemingly risky, how will we tell without detailed examination whether that person is an exemplar of courage or foolhardiness, or was simply unthinking in his action? Or that we misperceived the situation? But our mother is a concrete and immediate instantiation of *mother* at all times (even when she is acting in a less than praiseworthy fashion), about which we cannot be in doubt, because who we are, in significant measure, is because of who she is. Similarly with our sister, our grandma, and our Aunt Jenny. It is through knowing these people as they define *our* lives and determine in large measure the course *our* lives will take, that we come to know and internalize the roles that model the activities of the peoples who live in our society, many of which we already occupy ourselves, or soon will.

3 We must remember, however, that "moral competence" is a Western term; as we shall argue below, there is no term for "morals" in classical Chinese. What *we* single out as distinctly moral and immoral behavior as opposed to legal, polite, religious, ceremonial, or other behaviors would not be parsed in anywhere near the same way within Confucian sensibilities, and it is this multiplicity of behaviors that give rise to what we are calling "family feelings," integrated feelings of responsibility, love, security, respect, loyalty, reverence, and more. On different categories of normative behavior, see Rosemont (1976). We follow standard usage in rendering *arete* as "virtue," but "excellence" captures the Aristotelian sense much better, we believe.

We thus begin with the very concrete, with the particular, that is to say, and then extrapolate to a more abstract level when we need to – but not to the highly abstract – the universal principle – unless we are philosophers besotted with pure rationality. Mothers may occasionally lay down the law, but to see the two as equally abstract is to misunderstand the nature of both mothers and laws.

Here, then, is another significant difference between Aristotle (and most other virtue ethicists) and the early Confucians: The virtues characteristic of the excellent individual inhere in him, and can be described, analyzed and evaluated without specifying any role or relationship to or with others, which Confucians would never do, and they can only be thought to do so by presupposing that they have more or less the same notion of human beings as individuals that Aristotle does.

Another difference we must call attention to is Aristotle's reliance upon reason in determining moral conduct as opposed to the centrality of the imagination in the Confucian texts. In so doing, we shall argue that the Aristotelian and Confucian views on the moral life are grounded in fundamentally different conceptions of what it means to become a person, a factor that will be important in distinguishing Confucian role ethics from the more contemporary nuanced versions of virtue ethics that we associate with the sentimentalist virtue ethics of Slote (2007), the care ethics of Noddings (2003), and the particularist ethics of Dancy (2006). It is not merely Aristotelian virtue ethics that we believe different from classical Confucianism, but contemporary variations of virtue ethics as well, keeping as they do the foundational role of the *individual*, and of *rationality* (for which terms there are no close lexical equivalents in classical Chinese). We would contend that the language of moral psychology familiar in virtue ethics past and present has little relevance for a Confucian tradition that makes no appeal to the notion of *psyche* as a mode of defining and individuating persons, or for *logos/ratio* as their essence. In this Confucian view of the moral life, we are not individuals in the discrete sense, but rather are transactional persons living – not "playing" – a multiplicity of roles that constitute who we are, and that allow us to pursue a unique distinctiveness and virtuosity in our conduct which combines our intellect and our emotions. We are, in other words, the sum of the roles we live in consonance with our fellows, cognitively and affectively.[4]

Taken on their own terms, the classical Confucian texts appeal to a relatively straightforward account of our actual life experience rather than abstract moral principles, and in so doing, provide a justification for reinstating the intimacy of family feeling as the concrete ground of an always emergent distinctively human order. There is a fundamental difference between the goal of Western ethical

4 The extent to which the contrasting understandings of person constitutes a fundamental disjunction is not lost on Sim (2007, 8, 13), or on Yu (2007, 23).

theories that are directed at enabling people to think and to talk about ethics more coherently, and that of the Confucians who not only want to provide a vocabulary for thinking through ethical issues, but who simultaneously seek to inspire people to become better persons. We refer to this Confucian vision as a *role ethics,* and we intend to advance it as a *vision* of human flourishing rather than as an alternative moral *theory*; it is a vision that seeks to integrate the social, political, economic, aesthetic, moral and the religious dimensions of our lives.

In the opening chapter of the *Classic of Family Reverence*, Confucius proclaims that family reverence (*xiào* 孝) is the "root of excellence (*dé* 德)" (Rosemont and Ames 2009). Of course, in our conduct we should love, respect, and honor our parents (and our ancestors as well) but how are these activities tied to developing qualities such as temperance, courage, and wisdom (to name only the three cardinal virtues first analyzed and discussed at length by Socrates in Plato's *Republic*, and then later by Aristotle)?[5] In this text, the familiar Confucian vocabulary – "consummate person or conduct (*rén* 仁)," "appropriateness (*yì* 義)," "ritual propriety (*lǐ* 禮)," and "wisdom (*zhì* 智)" – is muted by a sustained focus upon family reverence (*xiào*) and has relevance at the outset only within the context of the flourishing family. Simply put, when family reverence is functioning effectively within the home, all is well within the community, the polity, and indeed, the cosmos. Although it is not certain that the *Classic of Family Reverence* records the actual words of Confucius, based upon the received corpus, the centrality of the notion of family reverence in classical Confucianism cannot be disputed.

To make this point, we might turn to the most frequently referenced of Confucian "excellences" – *rén* 仁: which we render "consummate or authoritative conduct." Nothing is more defining of humanity for Confucius than the genuine concern of one human being for another, a feeling that typically has its origins within the life of the family. But significantly, *rén* does not precede practical employment; it is not a principle or standard that has some existence beyond the day-to-day, family-grounded lives of the people who realize it in their role relationships. *Rén* is admittedly more general than say, obedience, but it, too, can only be fostered in the deepening of role relations as one takes on the responsibilities and obligations of family, and then by extension, of communal living. *Rén* is thus a shared human flourishing. It is the achievement of the quality of relationships that, like the lines in fine calligraphy or sublime landscape painting, collaborate to maximum aesthetic effect.

When the quality of these human interactions is pursued broadly within the social and political forum, consummate conduct becomes exemplary for those in the community who would defer to it. Consummate conduct (*rén*) is thus per-

5 Who maintains the centrality of the three (1984, vol. 2, 1982/1250a).

ceived as a necessary condition for becoming exemplary as a person (*jūnzǐ* 君子) in the execution of their lived roles.[6] Becoming exemplary as a person, like becoming consummate, is thus irreducibly collaborative, dependent as it is upon a correlation with effective models rather than compliance with abstract principles:

> The Master remarked about Zǐjiàn 子賤, "He is truly an exemplary person (*jūnzǐ*). If the state of Lǔ 魯 had not other exemplary persons, where could he have gotten this from?" (5.3)[7]

Nowhere is such collaboration more obvious than in the playing of music. Four excellent musicians perform each in a distinctive way, yet what they produce as a string quartet is altogether distinct from the contribution of any one of the four artists, while each gives to the others and to the whole, significance and beauty – and often, in the case of religious music, a sense of the sacred.[8] The centrality of music in the Confucian tradition as providing a felicitous vocabulary for consummate human conduct should not go unnoticed.

Given that Confucianism is fundamentally an aestheticism, it is not surprising to find that it uses language such as the "beautiful (*měi* 美)" and the "unseemly, unrefined, crude, coarse (*è* 惡)" to denote modes of conduct (*Analects* 20:2). But *měi* in Chinese means "beautiful" by reference to how certain relations come together within a specific context; it is not nominalized and entified to mean "beauty-in-itself." So too human actions can only be seen as "virtuous" by reference to how they come together within a specific context rather than by being "virtues-in-themselves." Virtue, then, is nothing more or less than a practical and productive virtuosity.

What this means is that *rén* is not a specific virtue that can be named and analytically isolated as defining of one's character any more than what it means to behave in a consummately humane way can be stipulated and replicated without reference to specific roles and situation. *Rén* is generic as a cultivated virtuosity in role-specific dispositions that conduce to making any particular action optimally elegant and appropriate, and thus a source of significance (*yì* 義) for all concerned. Confucius gives alternative descriptions of *ren* conduct, suggesting a multivalence to the term denoting virtuosity in relations. *Rén* is not *a* "good" but an efficacious "good at, good in, good to, good for, good with" that describes a relational dexterity within the unfolding of social experience. *Rén* is "right" conduct only in so much as it is "right on" – whatever it takes to be timely

6 See, for example, *Analects* 4.5. All references to the *Analects* are based on Ames and Rosemont (1998).

7 See also 9.14, where Confucius claims that the model of an exemplary person living among barbarians would be for them transformative.

8 Rounds (1999) develops such themes in many original and incisive ways.

in strengthening relations that are appropriate to our shared purposes. It is "correct" behavior only in so much as it is a corrective – making those adjustments in relationships needed to maximize the shared possibilities available in the circumstances. It is not primarily a retrospective "what" but a prospective "how." By requiring that the quality of (inter)action be determined and evaluated relationally – that is, in asking after what persons do with their interdependence and mutuality both in terms of motivation and consequences – *rén* is the difference between efficacy and waste, between elegance and ugliness, between healthy relations and injurious ones.

Looking at our conventional ethical discourse from a Confucian perspective, the main problem in the way we have come to think about virtues is that we tend to "metaphysicalize" them and thus render them as one more iteration of what John Dewey has dubbed "*the* philosophical fallacy." In so doing, we take the fixed and final to come before experience (our appeal to moral principles), we mistakenly take kinds and categories as an adequate expression of what are complex, relationally defined social situations (our appeal to virtuous individuals), we think because we have abstract names we also have "things" that match up with them (our appeal to intangibles such as "courage" and "justice"). Certainly there are exceptions, important exceptions, to this generalization about the nature of Western moral philosophy past and present, but we want to establish what we consider an important difference between the Western theoretical preoccupation and the Confucian persuasion.

On our interpretation Confucian role ethics does not begin from an attempt to abstract from concrete living, to isolate, identify, and explain some causal factor in moral action, some originative principle or agency or faculty. Rather does Confucian role ethics begin by considering what is happening, and ends by trying to make what is happening happen better. In Confucian role ethics, moral excellence, like a work of art, is a specific expression of virtuosity and imagination assessed as a quantum of satisfaction, and only in that sense and against that measure, can it be judged in degree by applying the general terms of right or wrong, correct or incorrect. At the same time, far from entailing a strict application of some predetermined and self-sufficient moral principle or set thereof to difficult situations, *rén* accumulates as a reservoir of moral meaning that is embodied in people and that elevates and transforms the human experience, minimizing the emergence of morally problematic situations. Confucius is explicit (2.3) in identifying this achieved sense of belonging as the vital difference between a deference-patterned community with its self-regulating, non-coercive structure and an authoritarian society governed by the rule of law; *rén*'s function is to proactively forestall the emergence of morally deficient situations. It is a moral artistry that seeks to achieve a quality of life within the larger picture. Only occasionally and incidentally, when such inspiration fails to prevail, does a situation arise that requires the resolution of specific problems. As his ideal Confucius looks to a community that aspires to rise above an appeal to the rule of law in its pursuit of a self-regulating sufficiency:

> The Master said, "In hearing cases, I am the same as anyone. What we must strive to do is to rid the courts of cases altogether." (12.13)

We might extrapolate from this passage to infer that appeal to the application of moral rules or principles like appeal to law is in itself an admission of communal failure – too little too late. There is more justice to be found in creating a social fabric that precludes abusive situations than in punishing perpetrators of what is deemed unjust or evil actions. From a Confucian perspective, given the natural bonds of love, nurturance, loyalty, and respect between young and old, especially kin, any society that feels the need to enact laws threatening parents with incarceration as its means of dealing with child abuse is very probably in terminal decline.

Another seminal idea in the organically related vocabulary of classical Confucianism is *lǐ* 禮, or "ritual propriety" – an achieved sense of appropriateness (*yì* 義) in one's roles and relations. *Lǐ* is a communal grammar ultimately derived from family relations, which begins from making robust the roles that locate us within family.[9] As a grammar, it has the potential to engender the sublime through effective coordination and placement, allowing us to take a stand and to achieve a certain status. Put simply (if, again, oddly from a Western moral perspective), one does not simply do one's communal duty, but must do it in a certain way. One must act not only with elegance and dignity, but also in a way informed by the aesthetic and religious meaning dictated by custom and tradition. Propriety in one's roles and relations does not reduce to generic, formally prescribed "rites" and "rituals," performed at stipulated times to announce status and to punctuate the seasons of one's life, however much they may have functioned in that way before Confucius re-thought them. Certainly rituals played important political functions in China, but the *lǐ* of Confucius – the expression of propriety through one's roles and relations – are more, much more. They have a somatic dimension whereby body often communicates better than language the deference needed to communicate and strengthen the bonds among the participants in the various life forms. *Lǐ* have a profoundly affective aspect wherein feelings suffuse and fortify the relational activities, providing the communal fabric a tensile strength that resists rupture.

The performance of *lǐ* must be understood in light of the uniqueness of each participant and the profoundly aesthetic project of becoming a person. For Confucius, *lǐ* is a resolutely personal performance revealing one's worth to

9 In addition to our analysis here, readers might consult Li (2007).

oneself and to one's community. *Lǐ* is also a public discourse through which one constitutes and reveals oneself qualitatively as a unique human being, a whole person.

Importantly, there is no respite; *lǐ* requires the utmost attention in every detail of what one does at every moment that one is doing it, from the drama of the high court to the posture one assumes in going to sleep, from the reception of different guests to the proper way to comport oneself when alone, from how one behaves in formal dining situations to appropriate extemporaneous gestures.

If these Confucian demands seem excessive, and artificial, it is in significant measure due to the decline of standards in almost all areas of interpersonal human endeavor today. Insisting on some minimum standards of dress or decorum seems to smack of elitism; verbal language that in the past would have been frowned upon even in private ("Like, ya know, I can't get into reading; get what I mean?") is now tolerated in public speech; one of the few uses of body language that continue to be "meaningful" are intentional gestures of disrespect that are an immediate source of road rage.

The continuing reauthorization of our communal roles and institutions necessary for society to function well brings with it, at the same time, an opportunity for reconstruction and consummation. Some patterns of ritualized conduct are obligatory for minor no less than major interactions among people. Indeed, as we have already suggested, we find that for the early Confucians, there is no sharp distinction between politeness and morals. Where robust relationships are the source of appropriate conduct and felt worth, the kind of disintegrative actions that we associate with inconsiderate conduct and bad manners quite simply diminish the meaning invested in human relations, and in so doing, compromise and ultimately threaten the moral fabric of community. Confucius studies the accoutrements of ritual, not military affairs, because he believes rituals are more fundamental than law for regulating society properly.[10]

A central aim of Confucius in the *Analects*, perhaps *the* central aim, is to guide his students toward achieving the goal of becoming exemplary persons (*jūnzǐ*), requiring that they embody consummate conduct (*rén*) in all they do, and behave with propriety (that is, are *lǐ*-like) in all of their actions. Family reverence (*xiào*) permeates this instruction: "Revere the family at home and be deferential (*dì* 弟) in the community" is one admonition (1.6); "Do not act contrary to your parents' expectations" is another (2.5, 4.18); "Give your father and mother nothing to worry about except your physical well-being" is still another (2.6); "When your

10 See *Analects* 15.1: Duke Líng 靈 of Wèi 衛 asked Confucius about military formations. Confucius replied, "I have heard something about the use of ritual vessels, but have never studied military matters." On the following day, he left Wèi.

father and mother are alive, do not journey far, and when you do travel, be sure to have a specific destination" (4.19) is yet another.

While loyalty and obedience are necessary ingredients of family reverence, they are only part of it.[11]

> In serving your father and mother, remonstrate with them gently when they go astray. On seeing that they do not heed your instructions, remain respectful and do not act contrary. Although concerned, voice no resentment. (4.18)

This theme of "remonstrance" (*jiàn* 諫), enunciated even more forcefully in Chapter 15 of the *Classic of Family Reverence*, indicates clearly that loyalty and obedience, while necessary qualities of the *jūnzǐ*, are not sufficient; what is also needed is the desire to do at all times what is appropriate in the larger familial, moral, and spiritual context of accepted personal responsibilities.[12]

It is clear that for Confucius, merely "going through the motions" of meeting filial responsibilities, while perhaps necessary for social harmony, will nevertheless not conduce to one's development as an exemplary person. Something more is needed, and what that something more seems to be is a desire to do what it is right to do; we must not only perform our duties, we must *want* to perform them. This desire to serve one's parents, then, is the substance of the following passage:

> Zǐxià 子夏 asked about family reverence (*xiào*). The Master replied: "It all lies in showing the proper countenance. As for the young contributing their energies when there is work to be done, and deferring to their elders when there is wine and food to be had – how can merely doing this be considered family reverence?" (2.8)

Here we may call attention to the Confucian terms we have been analyzing in our sketch of familial-centered role ethics: *ren*, *yi*, *xiao*, *li*, *junzi*, none of which has a close counterpart in the vocabulary of Western moral theories past or present. The converse also holds: there is no close equivalent for "morals" in

11 For a psychological analysis of the relationship between loyalty and family reverence, see Hwang (1999).

12 *Analects* 2.24 and 14.22 are perhaps even clearer examples. The theme is also found in the *Mencius*, and even more in the *Xúnzǐ*, especially the chapters on the "Regulations of a King," "Human Nature is Unseemly," and "The Way of the Son." We use the term "accepted" here somewhat as Christine Korsgaard uses "autonomy". By "choosing" (her term) a "practical identity" (also her term) of being, say, a student majoring in a specific subject, she describes what in our terms would be described as accepting responsibility for all that goes with taking up a specific role. See Korsgaard (1996, 105–06), especially the discussion of her example of the math major. We are grateful to Yang Xiao for pointing out to us how apt Korsgaard's critique is for our account of role ethics (although that was certainly not her intent; Confucianism is nowhere mentioned in this or any other of her writings on ethics, and defending a Kantian orientation in her work, she would almost certainly not concur with our critique of the deontological position).

classical Chinese, nor for almost all of the other terms necessary today for having a discussion about "morals" in English today:" "freedom," "liberty," "rights," "autonomy," "dilemma," "individual," "choice," "rationality," "democracy," "supererogatory," "private," "normative," even "ought." We have argued the philosophical significance of these semantic facts elsewhere,[13] only noting here that they should not be taken as evidence of extreme philosophical naiveté on the part of Confucius or his followers.

Native speakers in every culture have vocabulary items for describing, analyzing, and evaluating human conduct, but their lexicon will be influenced strongly by a number of cultural factors, not least among them being the worldview of that culture in general, and the definition of what it is to be (or become) human within that worldview. Our medieval forebears used terms like "virtue," "honor," and "sin" very differently from the way these words are used today in describing and in evaluating human conduct, and other terms they employed – *soke, sake, varlet, chivalric, liegeful,* and so on – we do not use at all.

Similarly, the ancient Greek account of what it is to be a person has significantly influenced what contemporary Western philosophers have presupposed, but as Yu and Sim have themselves indicated, it too is distinct from ours in many respects. A number of the basic terms employed in contemporary moral discourse absent in the Confucian lexicon are not found in ancient Greek either, and a number of key Greek words used to describe, analyze and evaluate human conduct – *nous, akrasia, arête, eidos, logos, dikē, eudemonia, phronēsis,* and so on – have no precise lexical counterparts in contemporary English (or Chinese) and are difficult to translate without modifiers, circumlocutions, or a gloss.[14]

In order not to beg any important philosophical questions against the Confucians early on, then, we must understand how much our own moral vocabulary for describing, analyzing, and evaluating the conduct of our fellows rests on the concept of human beings being fundamentally autonomous individuals, the definition itself utilizing the vocabulary of contemporary moral discourse. This definition of the individual person permeates not only our moral thinking, but the institutions of government in developed capitalist societies which now dominate the world economically and politically, and therefore requires closer examination, for it is also the default foundation of the conceptual background Western readers are inclined to bring to Confucian philosophy. In wanting to

13 On the philosophical significance of the linguistic differences noted here and below, see Rosemont (1987) and the introduction to Ames and Rosemont (1998). See also fn. 4. Sim (2007, 6, and elsewhere), also acknowledges problems of translating moral terms cross-culturally.

14 Qian Mu, as cited in Dennerline 1988, is adamant that the Confucian concept-cluster (our expression) of Chinese terms has no counterpart in other languages.

highlight this conceptual background we want now to contrast Confucian role ethics with the two other ethical theories that are current in Western moral philosophy today (But most of our points will apply no less to the several strains of virtue ethics.)

For most of the past two-plus centuries – with a process of evolution that stretches back to antiquity – the basic conception of what it is to be a human being in Western civilization has been *individualism.*[15] That we are social creatures, strongly shaped by the others with whom we have interacted, has always been acknowledged on all sides, but has not been seen as of the essence of our humanity, or, at the more abstract level, of being of compelling value. Rather, what gives human beings their primary worth, their dignity, their integrity, their value, and what must command the respect of all, is their *autonomy,* or their capacity to become *autonomous* as a potential that applies to all individuals.[16]

With this basic view of human beings in place, certain other qualities must also inhere in them, or the notion of the autonomous individual would be incoherent. Individuals must be *rational* if they are autonomous; that is to say, they must be capable of going against instinct or conditioning, for creatures that can do neither are surely not autonomous. Further, human beings must enjoy *freedom*; if they were not free to rationally choose between alternative courses of action, and then act on the choice made, how could they be said to be autonomous? Finally, we must note that these qualities of individual human beings are taken as unalloyed goods in the ethical sense.

If we define human beings in this individualistic manner, it would follow that in thinking about how we ought to deal with our fellows, we should seek as general and as abstract a viewpoint as possible. If *everyone* has the (valued) qualities associated with individualism, then their gender, age, ethnic background, religious affiliation, skin color, and so on should play no significant role in our decisions about how to interact with them, apart from concern for (ethically irrelevant) detail. Thus, on this orientation, it is incumbent upon us to seek universal values and principles; else the hope of a world at peace, devoid of group conflicts, racism, sexism, and ethnocentrism, could never be realized. And the way to do this is obviously to do all we can to ignore and transcend our own spatiotemporal and cultural locations, and on the basis of pure reason, ascertain beliefs and principles that should be compelling to all other rational persons equally ignoring and transcending their specific backgrounds that differ from our own. Our differing heritages divide us, and generate conflict; our capacity to

15 Individualism has had too many philosophical and political champions to note ever since the Enlightenment began. Most of these advocates have not been overly critical of the concept – including Marx no less than apologists for capitalism – except at the margins, and to provide a needed corrective we highly recommend Macpherson (1964).

16 For a survey (and celebration) of the concept of autonomy, see Schneewind (1998).

reason unites us all, and hence offers a greater hope for a less violent human future than has been the case in the past, and at present. This emphasis on objectivity and impartiality has been a strong argument in favor of seeking universalism in ethics. Many people, and perhaps most Western philosophers, have been swayed by it, making any occasional challenges thereto seem either relativistic or authoritarian, or both.

Two such universalistic moral theories – both based on the concept of the individual we have outlined – have occupied Western philosophers since the Enlightenment: *deontological* ethics, focusing on the concept of one's duty, and *utilitarianism,* based on attending to the consequences of one's actions. Both claim universal scope, and both have been extremely influential as contributing to the conceptual grounding of the English, American, and French Revolutions. The former theory is associated with Immanuel Kant,[17] the latter with Jeremy Bentham and John Stuart Mill.[18] For Kant, logic reigns, and the focus is on compliance and consistency rather than consequences; for Bentham and Mill, the situation is more nearly – but not quite – reversed, since probabilities must weigh heavily in a moral agent's calculations about the consequences of one's actions.

Inadequate though this sketch is, it should suffice to make clear the stark contrast between the views of both Kantians and Utilitarians, on the one hand, and the early Confucians on the other, and the relevance of these differences for understanding the concept of family reverence, or *xiào.* That is, for the Confucian each situation requires the moral imagination necessary to put oneself in the place of the other (*shù* 恕), and then to invoke the conscientiousness to do one's utmost (*zhōng* 忠) to achieve what is optimally appropriate (*yì* 義) under the circumstances. Confucians do not seek the universal, but concentrate on the particular; they do not see abstract autonomous individuals, but rather concrete persons standing in a multiplicity of role relations with one another; they do not focus exclusively on either intentions or consequences (agents or their actions) but on the virtuosity and productivity of the dynamic relations themselves. In the Confucian sensibility the appeal is to these particular persons in this particular family, defined by these specific relations. Indeed, persons are what they mean for each other.

In discussing feelings for family and community members – those to whom, in ever widening circles, one stands in a role as now benefactor, later beneficiary – we do not mean to imply there are no cognitive dimensions in an account of role ethics. Quite the contrary. But *reasonableness,* not *rationality,* is the term we want to employ in explicating Confucian role ethics. There is a seat of thinking in early Confucianism (and other schools of Chinese thought), the *xīn* 心, originally a

17 The *locus classicus* is his *Critique of Practical Reason*; various editions.
18 Here the *locus classicus* is Mill's *Utilitarianism,* also in various editions.

picture of the aorta. But there's a catch: the *xīn* is also the seat of human feelings, which dooms in advance any effort to sharply distinguish the cognitive and the affective.[19]

One dimension of Confucian "family" that must not be overlooked is the role of friendship as an extension of family relations, and as a definite, often compensatory family value. In seeking out and developing our friendships we have a latitude and degree of freedom that is not characteristic of blood relatives, providing a porous border for the institution of family that allows for a more deliberate (reasonable) shaping of one's own personal relations, and hence, one's own person. These voluntary relations, although surrogate, often achieve a degree of feeling and commitment that goes beyond our more formal family bonds. Where one is necessarily amicable with a brother, one can be more critical and demanding with friends (*Analects* 13:28).

Confucians must take full cognizance of, analyze, and evaluate the specific relations that obtain among members of a family in a way that is difficult for followers of Kant, Bentham, or Mill. For these latter philosophers, if all autonomous individuals are seen in the abstract as requiring equal treatment, for example, then taking the special bonds that hold between parents and children (and other special relations) into account philosophically becomes impossible. This is, in our opinion, one of the main reasons, perhaps, why a role ethics grounded in familial relations has attracted relatively little attention in the Western philosophical narrative since medieval times. A major historian of familial moral thinking in the West, Jeffrey Blustein, notes this fact, but does not endeavor to explain it:

> After Hegel, philosophers did not stop talking about the normative aspects of parent-child relations altogether. What happened was that they no longer attempted to systematically apply their most dearly held moral and social values to the study of parenthood. The resolution of problems relating to the upbringing of children and to our expectations of them became a sideline, and the most profound issues affecting the lives of human beings in society were seen to lie elsewhere. (1982, 95)

In our political and legal thinking, both deontological and utilitarian ethical orientations play a major role, exerting a profound influence on legislatures and in the courts. But because both theories are rooted in the concept of a foundational individualism, developing adequate family laws and policies is difficult – another reason why the ethical studies of families has become a "sideline."

If our analyses of these positions and issues have merit, we can begin to see not only why questions of family *versus* state loyalties cannot be answered by these Western moral theories: They cannot even be asked. Indeed, *no* moral questions

19 The late Robert Solomon, beginning with his (1976), did much to overcome the Western prejudices that insisted on this invidious split.

concerning the family can even be framed for examination because, by definition, family members are not abstract, autonomous individuals, parts of the public, but are flesh and blood, highly specific young and old, male and female, fellow human beings related to ourselves in highly intimate ways. Thus all moral questions pertaining to family matters have been swept under the conceptual rug of a "private" realm that involves personal matters of taste and religious belief – a realm wherein moral and political philosophy do not enter.[20]

Only when we divest human beings of all qualities except their highly abstract individuality can we begin to think of developing a theory of moral principles that will hold in all instances. With respect to family, this is precisely what we cannot do if we are even to attempt to formulate the relevant moral questions about loyalties and obligations coherently. For as soon as we use the expression "my mother" in what it is not at all an abuse of language to call a "moral" situation, we are not dealing with an abstract, autonomous individual, but one who carried us, brought us into this world, nurtured and comforted us, giving of herself extraordinarily for our benefit.

Returning now to our main narrative of the contrast between role and virtue ethical orientations, uneasiness with some of the implications of the ethics of Kant and Mill – only a few of which have we touched on above – has led some Western philosophers to undertake a re-evaluation and reinterpretation of Aristotle's virtue ethics. Instead of asking, "What principles should guide my moral actions?" we should perhaps be asking "What kind of moral qualities should I endeavor to develop?" It is in the wake of these new directions in Western moral theory that many comparative philosophers have been given to characterizing Confucianism as a "virtue ethics."

Hopefully we have already shown how and why an Aristotelian virtue ethics is not the most appropriate model for understanding Confucian thought. Other, smaller but not inconsequential differences can also be noted. In the first place, Aristotle was writing largely for and about a warrior aristocracy, and the Confucians were anything but approving of warriors.[21] Confucius, on the other hand taught whoever came to him seeking to live a moral life. More importantly, Aristotle's virtue theory of ethics seems to require the postulate of universal character traits as a part of human nature,[22] and while the writings of the early

20 The work of the late Susan Moller Okin points up this weakness in the Western philosophical tradition. She criticizes Rawls (1970) on this score, but remains basically an individualist, for while she does want to retain a private realm, she wants to keep the family out of it in a separate "domestic" realm. See Okin (1989).

21 Sim (2007, 16) also sees this Aristotelian elitism as a limitation.

22 Wong (2007) explores this charge as raised by Gilbert Harman and John Doris (in separate works). He responds well to the challenge, but not in a way that would please any virtue ethicist committed to some form of foundational individualism.

Confucians certainly cohere, they are by no means in agreement on the constitution of human nature. They all presume that human beings – or in the Confucian case, perhaps "human becomings" – are open to and shaped by culturally generated patterns of behavior and taste, a position that is very different from presumed biological and metaphysical uniformities that we associate with Aristotle. That is, persons from their inchoate beginnings are to be understood as embedded in and nurtured by unique, transactional patterns of relations, rather than as discrete entities defined by common traits. The notion of *lǐ* 禮 locates what we refer to as "moral" conduct within a thick and richly textured pattern of relations and consequent interactions, with instruction largely effected through emulation.[23]

Another way that Aristotelian virtue ethics differs from Confucian role ethics is that while Aristotle does assume some *general* notion of community, the community is not in all cases *necessary* since many of the virtues may be cultivated in solitude. That is, the basic excellences he champions, as noted earlier – temperance, courage, and wisdom – *may* be cultivated in social situations, but they need not be: We can resist the temptation for third helpings of dessert when we are dining alone; test our courage by sky-diving, bull-fighting, or in many other ways defy death that do not require others; and of course we read, and usually reflect on things, by ourselves.[24]

Further, Aristotle's sense of the *polis* is a most *general* notion of community, with the basic roles being general: male/warrior/citizen; not the *specific* and *constitutive* set of roles as *this* son, *this* mother, *this* neighbor, and so on, that is required by the Confucian ethic. As we have argued earlier, there is a world of difference between the very low level of abstraction to be found in the notion of *roles* and the much higher levels found in the concepts of *virtues, principles*, or *laws* – or, most importantly, *individuals.* The basic Confucian excellences can only be acquired in the process of living one's roles appropriately with the others to whom one is related, kin and non-kin alike. As a corollary, it must follow from

23 See, for example, *Analects* 6.30.

24 Wan Junren (2004, 129) criticizes Alasdair MacIntyre and Aristotle on precisely this point. To the extent that communities matter for them, "these indispensable factors possess *only theoretical significance as part of the necessary explanatory context* for a given virtue ethic – they do not themselves *constitute the practice of virtue itself.*" MacIntyre (2004, 154) strongly denies that communities are in this way tangential for either Aristotle or himself, citing *Politics* I (1253a1–39), paraphrasing: "To be a member of a political society is to share with others a concept of the just and the unjust, the good and the bad, while to be outside political community is to be deprived of the possibility of developing the excellence specific to human beings. Only through the relationships of the household and the political community are human beings able to develop as human beings." Blum (1996), contra Aristotle and MacIntyre, argues for a stronger role for community in the production and practice of moral virtues than he thinks they would allow. (We thank Steve Angle for this reference.)

the Confucian role orientation that we need to look at the patient no less than the agent in ascertaining the extent to which the valued habits of conduct have been properly developed and exemplified. It is not action but interaction that is the focus of the Confucian.

There are, to be sure, a number of similarities between Aristotle and Confucius in the area of what we call moral thought. We do not dwell on those similarities herein because many other comparative philosophers have done so, and more importantly, because, as we have argued throughout, we believe the differences between them are far more significant. One way to show these differences and to sum up what has been said in comparing them thus far is simply to juxtapose their writings on a similar concept. Consider laws, for example. First, from the *Nichomachean Ethics:*

> But it is difficult to get from youth up a right training for excellence if one has not been brought up under the right laws; for to live temperately and hardily is not pleasant to most people, especially when they are young. For this reason their nurture and occupation should be fixed by law; for they will not be painful when they have become customary.[25]

And continuing:

> But it is surely not enough that when they are young they should get the right nurture and attention; since they must, even when they are grown up, practice and be habituated to them, we shall need laws for this as well, and generally speaking, to cover the whole of life; for most people obey necessity rather than argument, and punishments rather than what is noble. (1984, 1180a1–5)

From the *Analects:*

> The Master said: "Lead the people with administrative injunctions and keep them orderly with penal law, and they will avoid punishments but be without a sense of shame. Lead them with excellence and keep them orderly through observing ritual propriety and they will develop a sense of shame, and moreover, will order themselves. (2.3)

And again:

> The Master said: "If rulers are able to effect order in the state through the combination of observing ritual propriety and deferring to others, what more is needed? (4.3)

25 Commenting on this particular passage, Kupperman remarks, "[T]here is every reason to believe that Confucius would have been incredulous at Aristotle's suggestion that law should have an important role in the education of young children" (2004, 107). And in commenting on this and other insights of Kupperman – and others – MacIntyre notes, "But Confucianism involves not only a rejection of Western deontology and utilitarianism, but also, as Kupperman's comparison of Aristotelian and Confucian views makes clear, a rejection of the basic assumptions of most Western versions of an ethics of virtue" (2004, 2009).

Further, virtue ethics resonates with the deontic and utilitarian models outlined above (and differs from role ethics) in that all three of them are dependent upon rational calculation to determine moral conduct. Compliance with the moral law or the application of the principle of utility is fundamentally a deliberative, rational exercise, and the less emotive content to it, the better. While Aristotle's doctrine of the mean certainly entails *practical* reason with an "uncodifiability" that is resistant to rules, his understanding of the human being is still defined by appeal to reason and indeed, the higher aspects of the human being, by appeal to *theoria:*

> The actuality of God, which surpasses all of this in blessedness, must be contemplative; and of human activities, therefore, that which is most akin to this must be the most of the nature of happiness. (1984, 1178b20)

But for Confucius, one becomes distinguished as a person who behaves with family reverence just to the extent that one behaves with family reverence. One *xiào*s in order to be *xiào,* or perhaps better, one *xiào*s and is *xiào.* The Confucian excellences differ in form and content from the Aristotelian view in that for the latter, cultivating the proper emotion and attitude, largely through study, reflection, and disciplined training, is the means for generating approbationary behavior. For the followers of the Master, the doers and the deeds are coterminous and mutually entailing. Meet your obligations consistently, attentively, appropriately – and the requisite dispositions and emotions are omnipresent in those actions. And there are exemplars of such conduct to prove the validity of the teachings when and if one's commitment to following the proper way flags. Concrete models play a greater role in guiding moral conduct than appeal to abstracted principles.

Yet another way in which Confucian role ethics differs from all theories of virtue ethics with which we are familiar is that in the former, the ethical life is prerequisite for the spiritual, and for exemplary persons, is not distinct from it. Indeed, it is civility within the family and community that is the locus of human-centered Confucian religiousness, and it is inspired human living that is the source of spirituality. Ancestor reverence and sacrifice are important as reinforcing this more concrete and substantial human site of spiritual expression.[26]

Role ethics allows us to shave with Occam's razor a second time. Just as we might be skeptical of positing the existence of some ontological ground – God, substance, and so on as the "soul" of the totality – so too can we question whether we need to posit an individual self (nature, soul, person, character) behind the

26 See Ames (2003) for a characterization of this Confucian sense of religiousness. For a this-worldly analysis of *all* religious traditions, see Rosemont (2001).

many roles we live.[27] Role ethics emphasizes the continuity of particular behavioral interactions and the personal growth entailed by them without reifying and subordinating them to longer term, abstract dispositions. "Good with" and "good to" are more concrete than "good." Role ethics also focuses upon the aesthetic quality of our moral conduct – its intensity and appropriateness – and requires us to entertain the particular situations of our experience as they are actually felt and lived.

We would suggest that there is a tendency to make the same miscalculation in reflecting on virtues as we do in thinking about human nature. With human nature we are inclined to default to a retrospective causal or a teleological explanation of what it means to be a human *being* rather than providing a more holistic, prospective, and contextual account of what it means to *become* human – a *human becoming*, as it were. In so doing, we come to presuppose that human nature is either a ready-made potential to be actualized or some pre-existing ideal to be attained. It is believed by some scholars – Sim (2007, 13 and *passim)* being a good example – that agency and moral responsibility require the isolation of individuals from their relationships by positing such a definition of what it *is* to be human. In fact, on the contrary, such a ready-made definition of human *being* or a guiding teleological hand would on our reading compromise any robust existential notion of agency or responsibilities.

Similarly with Confucian "virtues," we are not referencing pre-existing metaphysical principles that by definition are causal, and that can ultimately stand as the objects of our contemplation. Nor are virtues some predetermined ideal that is to be actualized as personal character traits through the proper cultivation of human experience. Rather, "virtues," to use such language, are gerundive: "virtuing." They are an open-ended and always provisional virtuosity in our continuing patterns of relations. Such "virtues" are the activity of relating itself. And it is an activity that we are most often inclined to call "mothering" and "son-ing" and only then isolatable as abstractions such as "courage" or "justice." What we have with Confucian role ethics is a phenomenology of the concrete human experience lived within the relations of family and community as a basis for describing what it means to live life fully – morally and more than that.

Further, in ethics we usually assume that being moral has something to do with "complying with right and wrong" or as "being good" as though the notions of "right and wrong" and "good" are available to us by appeal to some pre-existing

27 William James, in his essay "Some Metaphysical Problems Pragmatically Considered," goes after this same problem of "substance" – that is, "the phenomenal properties of things … *ad*here, or *co*here, rather, *with each other*, and the notion of substance inaccessible to us, which we think accounts for such cohesion by supporting it, as cement might support pieces of mosaic, must be abandoned. The fact of bare cohesion itself is all that the notion of the substance signifies. Behind that fact is nothing" (2000, 42).

standard: a pre-existing principle (causal) or some pre-existing ideal defined in the language of virtues (teleological). From the Confucian perspective, what we need instead is a phenomenology of experience as a basis for describing what it means to act in such a way as to enhance our relations. That is, we have to ask: What makes this situation comprising these particular relations better, and what makes it worse? We take the substance of morality to be nothing more or less than positive growth in the constitutive relations of any particular situation.

Within the context of cross-cultural accommodation, role ethics avoids intractable moral conflict by abjuring any appeal to universals and assuming that appropriate conduct is always a matter of continuing, collateral or multilateral negotiation within the complexity of particular circumstances. Indeed, the collaborative nature of moral conduct requires that it be mutual and accommodating.

In sum, while Confucian role ethics surely bears more of a resemblance to Aristotle than to Kantian or Utilitarian ethics, we do not believe virtue ethics, past or present, conceptually grounded in individuals, rationality and freedom, and with little attention paid philosophically to the family, is an appropriate description of the views on the cultivated moral sensibilities of the Master and his followers. Nor do we believe that such a virtue ethics with its exaggerated emphasis on rationality as method can serve as a morality for the culturally diverse and rich world of today.

Having said this, we want to make it clear that while we are persuaded we have much to learn from Confucian role ethics, we do not believe our current understanding of role ethics to be an ultimate and self-sufficient vision of the moral life. In fact, it is Aristotle's sustained and often unsuccessful struggle to balance and coordinate the conflicting demands of impartiality and partiality, of first philosophy and particular context, that serves as an object lesson and shows a way forward for us. At the same time, we believe that Confucian role ethics provides a basis for further reflection and expansion on how to achieve a quality of human flourishing that at once respects bottomless particularity and the indeterminacy such particularity entails, and at the same time, allows for the development of a more robust sense of regulative ideals that do not require the excesses of first philosophy.

We are convinced there is much to be learned from Confucian role ethics as it was and is, and we are equally convinced that much must be done to develop it further – especially in re-defining a number of roles, and hence the family – if it is to be a viable candidate as a vision of a global yet culturally specific moral life appropriate for the twenty-first century. But we believe it can indeed be such a candidate – there are parents, children, grandparents, neighbors, friends and more in every culture – in a way that the ethics of Aristotle, Kant, or Bentham and Mill cannot.[28]

References

Ames R., and H. Rosemont, Jr. 1998. *The Analects of Confucius: a philosophical translation.* New York: Ballantine.

Ames, R. 2003. *Li* 禮 and the A-theistic religiousness of classical Confucianism. In *Confucian Spirituality,* ed. W. Tu and M. Tucker. New York: Crossroads Press, pp. 165–182.

Aristotle. 1984. *The Collected Works of Aristotle,* 2 vols. Ed. J. Barnes. Princeton: Princeton University Press.

Blum, L. Community and virtue. In *How Should One Live? Essays on the Virtues,* ed. R. Crisp. New York: Oxford University Press.

Blustein, J. 1982. *Parents and children: the ethics of the family.* New York: Oxford University Press.

Carrithers, M., S. Collins, and S. Lukes, eds. 1985. *The category of person.* Cambridge: Cambridge University Press.

Ching, J. 1978. Chinese Ethics and Kant. *Philosophy East and West* 28 (2): pp. 161–172.

Dancy, J. 2006. *Ethics without principles.* New York: Oxford University Press.

Dennerline, J. 1988. *Qian Mu and the world of seven mansions.* New Haven: Yale University Press.

Hwang, K. 1999. Filial piety and loyalty: two types of social identification in Confucianism. *Asian Journal of Social Psychology* (2), pp. 161–183.

Ivanhoe, P. 2006. Filial piety as a virtue. In *Working virtue,* ed. P. Ivanhoe and R. Walker. Pp. 297–312. New York: Oxford University Press.

Kant, I. 1959. *Foundations of the metaphysics of morals.* Indianapolis: Library of Liberal Arts, Bobbs-Merrill Co.

Korsgaard, C. 1996. *Sources of Normativity.* Cambridge: Cambridge University Press.

Kupperman, J. 2004. Tradition and community in the formation of character and self. In *Confucian Ethics,* ed. K. Shun and D. Wong, pp. 103–123. Cambridge: Cambridge University Press.

Li, C. 2007. *Li* as Cultural Grammar. *Philosophy East and West,* 57 (3), pp. 311–329.

MacIntyre, A. 2004a. Once more on Confucian and Aristotelian conceptions of the virtues: a response to Professor Wan. In *Chinese philosophy in an era of globalization,* ed. R. Wang, tr. E. Slingerland. Pp. 151–162. Albany: State University of New York Press.

—.2004b. Questions for Confucians. In *Confucian Ethics,* ed. K. Shun and D. Wong, pp. 203–218. Cambridge: Cambridge University Press.

Macpherson, C. 1964. *The political theory of possessive individualism: Hobbes to Locke.* New York: Oxford University Press.

Noddings, N. 2003. *Caring,* 2nd ed. Berkeley: University of California Press.

Okin, S. 1989. *Justice, Gender and the Family.* New York: Basic Books.

28 The subject of our current collaboration, tentatively titled *Confucian Role Ethics: A Moral Vision for the 21st Century.*

Rawls, J. *Theory of justice.* Cambridge: Harvard University Press.

Rosemont, H. Jr. and R. Ames. 2009. *The Chinese classic of family reverence: a philosophical translation of the* Xiaojing. Honolulu: University of Hawai'i Press.

Rosemont, H., Jr. 1976. Notes from a Confucian perspective: which human acts are moral acts? *International Philosophical Quarterly*, 16 (1), pp. 49–61.

—.1987. Against Relativism. In *Interpreting across boundaries,* ed. G. Larson and E. Deutsch, pp. 36–70. Princeton: Princeton University Press.

—.2001. *Rationality & Religious Experience.* Chicago & LaSalle IL: Open Court.

Rounds, D., with the Lafayette String Quartet. 1999. *The four and the one: in praise of string quartet.* Fort Bragg, CA: Lost Coast Press.

Schneewind, J. 1998. *The invention of autonomy: a history of modern moral philosophy.* Cambridge: Cambridge University Press.

Shun, K. 2008. Some methodological reflections on comparative ethics. Unpublished manuscript.

Sim, M. 2007. *Remastering morals with Aristotle and Confucius.* Cambridge: Cambridge University Press.

Slote, M. 2007. *The ethics of care and empathy.* London: Routledge.

Solomon, R. 1976. *The passions.* New York: Doubleday.

Wilson, S. 2002. Conformity, individuality, and the nature of virtue: A classical Confucian contribution to contemporary ethical reflection. In *Confucius and the Analects,* ed. B. Van Norden, pp. 94–115. New York: Oxford University Press.

Wan, J. 2004. Contrasting Confucian virtue ethics and MacIntyre's Aristotelian virtue theory. In *Chinese philosophy in an era of globalization,* ed. R. Wang, tr. E. Slingerland. Pp. 123–149. Albany: State University of New York Press.

Wong, D. 2007. If we are not by ourselves, if we are not strangers. In *Polishing the Chinese mirror: essays in honor of Henry Rosemont, Jr.,* ed. M. Chandler and R. Littlejohn, pp. 331–351. LaSalle: Open Court.

Yearley, L. 2003. Virtues and religious virtues in the Confucian tradition. In *Confucian Spirituality,* ed. W. Tu and M. Tucker, pp. 134–162. New York: Crossroads Press.

Yu, J. 2005. Confucius' relational self and Aristotle's political animal. *History of Philosophy Quarterly,* 22 (4): pp. 281–300.

—.2007. *The ethics of Confucius and Aristotle: mirrors of virtue.* New York: Routledge.

Roger T. Ames / Henry Rosemont, Jr.

From Kupperman's Character Ethics to Confucian Role Ethics: Putting Humpty Dumpty Together Again

Abstract

The institution of family has not received much attention from contemporary philosophers and theologians. Two contemporary exceptions to this generalization about the neglect of family and familial relations in Western moral philosophy are the late Susan Miller Okin and Joel Kupperman, both of whom have given long and careful attention to the role of this institution in their detailed treatments of justice and character respectively. The focus of our interest in these two philosophers has to do with their understanding of the relationship between person and family in achieving justice and in developing personal character respectively. We find that Okin provides us with a clear statement of the problem that the current inequitable institution of family poses for achieving a just society, and that Kupperman's character ethics points us in the right direction for appreciating the role that family has in developing moral competence. In this article we will assay these two positions as we have come to understand them, and then turn to a consideration of the importance of family in our real experience to make the argument that Confucian role ethics in taking family relations as the entry point for developing moral competence has much to offer contemporary conversations in moral philosophy. Finally, returning to Confucian role ethics, we will invoke the *Great Learning* (*daxue* 大學) as the first of the *Four Books* that lays out the Confucian project of personal cultivation within family, community, and tradition.

Reinstating Family in Moral Philosophy

With a few oblique exceptions (such as Aristotle, Rousseau, and Hegel), the family, and the relations among and between family members, have not received much detailed attention from Western philosophers and theologians. And much of what notice family has received has been in a more negative than positive light with respect to the capacities of this social institution to enable full human development. Plato, for example, strictly forbade all forms of family life for the guardians of his Republic as corrupting of their abilities to govern and protect the citizens.[1] A few Christian savants have made tolerable remarks about the institution of marriage and the family, but to most of them married life, being profane, is decidedly inferior to the loftier existence of the monk or nun, who, because of their abstinence from worldly desires and pursuits, are – or should be – closer to God.[2]

But humans are social beings, and the socialization process begins and develops in the family. Thus, if morality is the form and content of our social relations, then thinking about morality must include thinking about the family, and to the extent that the family is neglected in thinking about morality, to just that extent will morality be broken, like Humpty Dumpty. Herein we would like to try to piece him together again.

Two contemporary exceptions to our generalization about the neglect of family and familial relations in Western moral philosophy are the late Susan Miller Okin and Joel Kupperman, both of whom have given long and careful attention to the role of this institution in their detailed treatments of justice and character respectively. The focus of our interest in these two philosophers has to do with their understanding of the relationship between person and family in achieving justice and in developing personal character respectively. We find that Okin provides us with a clear statement of the problem that the current inequitable institution of family poses for achieving a just society, and that Kupperman's character ethics points us in the right direction for appreciating the role that family has in developing moral competence. In this article we will assay these two positions as we have come to understand them, and then turn to a consideration of the importance of family in our real experience to make the argument that Confucian role ethics in taking family relations as the entry point for developing moral competence has much to offer contemporary conversations in moral philosophy. Finally, returning to Confucian role ethics, we will invoke the *Great Learning* (*daxue* 大學) as the first of the *Four Books* that lays out the

1 *Republic* 5.465 c – e. See also the beginning of Book 8: "We are agreed, then, Glaucon, that the state which is to achieve the height of good government must have community of wives and children and all education …" Plato 1961. Aristotle criticizes Plato's "community of wives and children" in Book II of the *Politics*, 1260b – 1266a, but nowhere comments on the equality of women that flows from the Platonic ideal. His own view of the nature of the family, however – as described in Books VIII and IX of the *Nicomachean Ethics* – while nearer to our modern view, is nevertheless justified, in the end, by religion, and conducted on the basis of reason, with misogyny, chauvinism and slavery somehow becoming "reasonable" to him if not to us. Aristotle 1984.

2 Beginning with Paul, who says in 1 Corinthians 7:38, "[H]e who marries his betrothed does well, and he who refrains from marriage will do better."

Confucian project of personal cultivation within family, community, and tradition.

Okin and the Importance of Family in Formulating a Theory of Justice

Okin, while somewhat critical of John Rawls, is still building on his influential theory of justice. She makes the argument that developing a sense of justice in our adult political life cannot take place unless justice is first learned and practiced in the family. Indeed, in her influential work *Justice, Gender, and the Family* Okin reserves a key place for the family, and is sharply critical of those moral theorists who think that they can ignore it.

We offer our critique of Okin here to make clear how the Confucian formulation of justice would begin from family life itself rather than from the abstractions of either principles or discrete and autonomous individuals. Rather than starting from a reflection on justice in the life of the family itself, and then extending a familial conception of actualized justice into the public sphere, Okin instead chooses to draw upon an abstract, public definition of justice – that is, an equality of opportunity for all – to restructure the institution of family. Her assessment of family inequities is persuasive. But her thin Rawlsian solution of constructing ideal institutions and policies that can then be applied to achieve a quantifiable justice defined largely in terms of equal distribution of work and compensation among generic individuals is much less satisfying.

Okin offers a compelling argument that the institution of family as it is presently constituted by a hierarchical structure of roles saturated by a pervasive gender bias is fundamentally unjust. And given the crucial importance of family as the veritable "school of justice" in the moral development and education of children, the assumption that we can construct a just society on such a tenuous foundation is, as she properly claims, untenable. This being the case, it is both undeniably true and at the same time deplorable that most scholars who would offer us a theory of justice have chosen to do so while ignoring the family altogether (for example, Bruce Ackerman, Ronald Dworkin, and Robert Nozick).[3] The alternative to those thinkers who would neglect the institution of family is another group of theorists who, in using a false gender neutrality, are able to skip over the issue of gender discrimination within the family and community by pretending it does not exist (for example, Alasdair MacIntyre and Derek Phillips).[4] And then there are those few scholars late and soon who actually take the family into account, but who would exempt it from the demands of justice by

3 Ackerman 1980, Dworkin 1977, Nozick 1974.
4 MacIntyre 1981 and 1984, Phillips 1986.

claiming that the norms governing their idealized conception of family such as love, fidelity and trust are of a higher order than simply respect for what is just and fair (for example, Jean-Jacque Rousseau, David Hume, Michael Sandel and Roberto Unger).[5]

Okin frames the problem well, but her solution is disappointing. While she does seek to rectify the family as a patently unjust institution upon which so much of social justice is built, and on which justice ultimately depends, she offers a Rawlsian-inspired attempt to apply the principle of justice to a family of autonomous individuals in order to establish equal opportunity among them. Okin's ostensive solution is in fact an integral part of the problem itself, requiring as it does the retention of a foundational individualism as central to the definition of what it is to be a human being while relying exclusively upon a principled understanding of justice as the instrument for effecting a just world. Her underlying assumption is that an abstract principle of justice can be mechanically applied to abstract individuals who are conjoined by extrinsic, causal relations. As such, she ignores both the intimacy, mutuality, and particularity that is invariably defining of relations in real families, and the always particular context from which putative principles ultimately derive and to which they are to be applied. This reductionism with respect to the subject of justice is targeted quite sharply (although almost surely unintentionally) by feminist philosophers Martha Minow and Mary Lyndon Shanley in the introduction to a special issue of *Hypatia* they edited on the family when they note as "a paradoxical characteristic of family life" the fact that "the individual must be seen simultaneously as a distinct individual and as a person fundamentally involved in relationships of dependence, care, and responsibility."[6] They are correct on this point: if we presuppose that human beings should be seen as fundamentally discrete, autonomous individuals then family life does indeed become paradoxical.

With respect to the inequities that are pervasive in the institution of family, the greatest source of injustice for Okin is gender discrimination and its implications for work and pay. And she would solve these ubiquitous inequalities that attend gender by terminating the distinction of gender altogether. But how do we do this, and would erasing gender solve the problem even if we were able to do so? Whatever attempt we might make to reconceive the human experience in a non-gendered way, we must begin from the fact of gender as a sexual and a historical difference, and then ask: Is it desirable to construct a society free of gender discrimination in which the seemingly distinctive practices of "mothering" and "fathering," "sistering" and "brothering," are made obsolete terms? Said another way, it might be thin justice for women that is premised upon them becoming

5 Rousseau (1959–1969), Hume 1975, Sandel 1982, Unger 1975.
6 Minow and Shanley 1996.

ungendered persons rather than remaining women, and thin justice for family members as well by reducing them to generic individuals rather than allowing them to be the unique persons they are within their thick familial bonds.

Does not the appreciation of real differences – those of gender, generation, and most importantly, personal differences – give the lie to the idea that justice is to be achieved by treating all people the same? Like Okin, we are keenly aware of the profound influence that family has on moral development, and we certainly agree with her that family should serve as the "school of justice" for our children, but not in a way that eliminates any interesting notion of family by making it into a committee of fungible equals. Should we not instead strive for a society in which gender differences like all other real differences are an integral part of a much more robust conception of justice?

A Confucian Critique of Okin's Theory of Justice

Viewed from a Confucian point of view, if Okin's book were to reflect the process we *ought* to follow in formulating a practicable conception of justice, it would have to be retitled *The Family, Gender, and Justice.* That is, a Confucian critique of Okin would begin by arguing that consideration for the wholeness of experience would require that we start with life in the lived family within which not only sex and gender but also ubiquitous patterns of hierarchy have been familiar distinctions, and try to reconstruct a vision of all relations, gender included, that would best serve the interests of the many diverse and constantly shifting roles lived by each member of the family. The goal would not be to enforce a simple equality among the family's distinctive members, but rather to achieve a parity that saves productive differences as much as possible, while precluding coercion in all of the relational transactions that are defining of family life, keeping in mind at all times that family relations are always changing to a certain extent as the family members all grow older.

Since we basically agree with Okin that gender is largely a social product rather than a distinction determined by human biology, we can and must strive to redefine gender difference in a way that replaces an oppressive inequality with a complementary and productive parity. Ironically, a heavy-handed conception of distributive justice that, in imposing a quantifiable standard of equity on family, fails to respect the processual, phasal, and resolutely hierarchical nature of family life, is itself reductive and violent, becoming a procedural strategy for enforcing conformity at the unacceptable expense of excising real differences and their creative possibilities. In failing to accommodate family roles lived through richly textured and constantly changing patterns of both natural and socially constructed differences, such a theory is an anathema to the optimizing of the family experience for all of its members. After all, it must be this aspiration to optimize the family experience that is surely the ultimate goal of any conception of real, actualized justice. To our minds, Okin does not "do justice" to the particularities of persons in families or to the correlative nature of relations, and as a consequence fails to do justice to the notion of justice itself.

Kupperman and the Role of Family in Early Character Development

Against this background, we now turn to Joel Kupperman's contribution to this discussion of the relationship between persons and family. In the field of ethics over the past generation we have witnessed a sustained dissatisfaction with narrow rule-based approaches to ethics, and have seen developments in different quarters that are seeking to reinstate different dimensions of the human experience that have been excluded from consideration. The revival of virtue ethics, the rise of sentimentalism, of particularism, and of care ethics, and a sustained professional reflection on the role of emotions and somaticity in the moral life are all attempts to understand ethics in a more holistic way.

Kupperman's work is an important contribution to this sea change in ethics. His main argument is that ethical philosophy should be structured around the development of character as it begins in family relations and is further developed within the context of community and tradition. In his earlier work – especially in his seminal monograph *Character* – Kupperman has formulated a doctrine of "character ethics" that he posits as a robust alternative to familiar versions of virtue ethics. And he sees in the Confucian emphasis on personal cultivation a close analogue to his long-term concern with character development. With his formulation of this doctrine of character ethics, he is glad to break ranks with those who would advocate virtue ethics, and is further prepared to argue that Confucius himself should be included as a fellow character-ethicist.[7]

In seeking to replace virtue ethics with character ethics, Kupperman is doing his best to put the humpty-dumpty of ethical philosophy back together again. That is, he challenges what he calls the "snapshot" view of ethical decision-making in virtue ethics, and equally the "big moment" ethics we associate with Kant and Bentham and Mill.[8] This fragmenting approach to our understanding of ethics has introduced a plethora of fractures and fault lines into what he takes to be the relatively seamless process of developing the qualities of character that enable us to express a moral competence in our daily conduct. Such compartmentalizing, while acknowledging relevant issues in ethics, seems at the same

7 Kupperman 1991, 108–109.
8 "Big moment" is Kupperman's own term. See Kupperman (1971).

time to isolate and decontextualize them. While virtues, for example, are generally classified and treated separately and simply, Kupperman's appeal to character development requires that we appreciate the interpenetration among personal qualities and accommodate their true complexity, and further that we take the aggregate of both positive and negative qualities into consideration at the same time. For Kupperman, "selves are constructed during a life rather than being present at birth."[9] That is, he attempts to restore process and duration to the notion of human development, to respect the interpenetration of virtues in time, and to abandon any severe distinction between what one does and what is done to one.

> Anyone's character is likely to be affected, at any point in life, by social norms, a person's social class and family relations, how that person spends most of her or his time, and so on; as these factor change, a change in character will be the natural (although not inevitable) result.[10]

Kupperman is adamant that character development is importantly dependent upon the contexts of community and tradition:

> To the extent that a person can be viewed as creating a character, this self-creation does not take place in a void: It occurs against the background of types of people in a community and in relation to social roles and options that are available. It is impossible not to be, in some sense, a person of one's time, however many prevailing opinions and attitudes one rejects ... Tradition and a network of more or less common understandings thus underlie the development of individual character.[11]

Kupperman's robust conception of character is more personal and particular than virtue traits, and has an active, continuous, and particularizing role that both unifies and stabilizes lives through time. Consistent with the continuities and context recovered with this processual understanding of the development of character, Kupperman challenges any atomistic view of choice that would reduce it to serial discrete, impersonal decisions, by seeing choice itself as a process in which a continuing current of commitment and responsibility serves to unify ostensive judgements:

> The decision-procedure is oriented toward single decisions, viewed as disconnected from other decisions, in a way which ignores or slights the moral importance of continuity of commitment. ... Many of the most crucial "choices" in our lives turn out to be clusters of an indeterminate number of choices, most or all of which point in the same direction, which are such that many are not reflective or explicit. Any model of choice in human life must take account of this.[12]

9 Kupperman 1991, 37.
10 Kupperman 1991, 56.
11 Kupperman 1991, 111.
12 Kupperman 1991, 70, 74.

In the various dimensions of character development, Kupperman wants to understand moral conduct in a vital and more holistic sense by reinstating in significant degree the processive nature, the always specific context, the particularity, and the growth that are all characteristic of moral conduct. But even though Kupperman has taken us in the right direction by restoring some of the continuities in human conduct that have been underrepresented in virtue ethics, we would contend that he does not go far enough. We are able to identify several remaining disjunctions and dichotomies in his own theory of character ethics that prevent him, like all of the king's men, from reinstating the wholeness and the capaciousness of our actual moral experience.

First, Kupperman insists on retaining the default concept of a discrete, separate, and reified "self" as the emergent product of character development:

> Normally, a human organism will regard herself or himself as having a single self, with the life of the organism as its outer boundaries, and this will coincide with the view of outside observers. … A normal human being begins life with a protoself, and a self begins to appear in the course of early childhood. It is constructed within the protoself, typically not by conscious decisions but rather by the formation of habits and attitudes and the emergence of characteristic ways of thinking and behaving.[13]

For Kupperman, "character approximates the nature of self" where "character is to the major matters of life as the nature of self is to all of life."[14] That is, there is for Kupperman a definite individuality to the self that serves as the ground and locus of one's character development that becomes manifest in its more important undertakings.[15]

And when we ask the question: What then is the relationship between this self, its character, and its conduct? Kupperman would retain a clear distinction between the self and the character it has accrued that "flows" from this self into its actions:

> Character certainly has a causal role in behavior: In many cases, part of the explanation of why someone behaved in such and such a manner must be that he or she is such and such a person. But another part of a causal explanation of behavior will be features of the situation.[16]

In Kupperman's more recent work, and specifically, in the two versions of his "Tradition and Community in the Formation of Character and Self",[17] he presents a view of the role of the family in personal development that is certainly more

13 Kupperman 1991, 38, 43–44.
14 Kupperman 1991, 47.
15 Kupperman 1991, 19.
16 Kupperman 1991, 59.
17 There are two versions of this essay, with the later one included in Kupperman 2004, and the earlier one in Kupperman (1999).

robust than Okin's, but that still retains this reified conception of a unified and discrete self. In this essay, Kupperman does insist upon the importance of family, community, and tradition in the formative process of creating the foundation for a moral self in the following terms:

> Tradition is, in Confucius' presentation of the development of a good self, not only a source of inspiration and advice but also (more importantly) a source of modeling. The right kind of parent-child relation, in his view, has this character. One develops a self that of course is separate but is not entirely separate: there will be elements reminiscent of parents, who in turn had developed selves that included elements reminiscent of their parents, and so on.[18]

Kupperman's notion of the self as a "self-as-collage" includes "elements derived from outside sources" that have both a causal and a constitutive status and "layers that represent the absorption (or sometimes, rejection) of various influences at various stages of life, going back to early childhood."[19] Although he often references and seems to appreciate the relational nature of the Confucian person, he is still consistent in maintaining that an individual can be accurately described, analyzed, and evaluated independently of other human beings. With this assumption of an individual and discrete self, he interprets persons in families in an importantly different way than we do from a role ethics perspective.

We maintain that the familiar dualisms such as subject/object, agent/action, mind/body, nature/nurture, and so on, that arise from substance ontology have little relevance for the notion of relationally constituted persons integral to Confucian role ethics. Indeed, this Confucian conception of person makes no appeal to superordinate, substantive categories such as "soul," "self," "will," "faculties," "nature," "mind," "character," and so on, but instead locates "person" gerundively as the embodied, social activity of thinking and feeling within the manifold of relations that constitutes family, community, and the natural environment. Person thus understood is a complex event rather than a discrete "thing," a process of "becoming" rather than an essential "being," an on-going "doing" rather than an autonomous "is," a configuration of concrete, dynamic, and constitutive relations rather than an individuated substance defined by some subsisting agency.

Herbert Fingarette made this point elegantly some time ago, when he said: "For Confucius, unless there are at least two human beings, there are no human beings."[20] In any moral (or political) sense, role ethics is the claim that we can neither be well described, analyzed, or evaluated as persons apart from the other persons with whom we interact, and that persons are best described, analyzed

18 Kupperman 2004, 115.
19 Kupperman 2004, 117.
20 See Fingarette (1983).

and evaluated morally (and politically) in terms of the specific roles that guide their actions with specific others.

A Confucian Critique of Kupperman's Character Ethics

We would argue that Confucian role ethics in several important ways offers a basis for a more capacious vision of justice than Okin does, and a more holistic vision of the moral life than Kupperman's character ethics does. First, consistent with the spirit of Kupperman's attempt to restore wholeness to experience, Confucian role ethics would insist on the primacy of relationships, and would preclude any notion of final individuality. Personal discreteness is a conceptual abstraction and strict autonomy a misleading fiction; association is a fact. And the roles we live are simply the way in which this fact of association is further stipulated and specified.

We hasten to make the point that giving up the notion of a superordinate "self" far from surrendering one's personal uniqueness, in fact, enhances it. That is, the "natural kinds" talk that usually stands behind claims about a shared human nature and a concomitant essential self mitigates the degree of difference we find in a Confucian notion of person where person is constituted by a dynamic manifold of always specific relations.

Secondly, Confucian role ethics would resist the uncritical substance ontology underlying Kupperman's conception of agency that requires a separation between the agent of conduct and the conduct itself. The notion of *ren* 仁 that is central to Confucian role ethics entails no such agency/action dichotomy. *Ren* requires a narrative rather than an analytic understanding of person. And *ren* is cultivated by correlating one's own conduct with those models close at hand rather than by acting in concert with some abstract moral principles.[21] It is for this reason that it is often unclear whether *ren* denotes a consummate person or the conduct of such a person, or like its cognate *ren* 人, whether the referent is singular or plural. *Ren* is an open-ended generalization made off of particular historical accomplishments of consummate conduct rather than referencing some innate and essential element that is characteristic of all members of the set called human "beings." Indeed, *ren* is a gerundive notion – a verbal noun – that is descriptive of consummate "person-ing."

Thirdly, Confucian role ethicists would fault Kupperman for failing to appreciate the dramatic role that body has as integral to achieving personal identity and consummate conduct. He appeals to the familiar language of "a psychological field which is present in a newborn infant and which continues

21 *Analects* 6.30.

throughout that infant's life,"[22] but has little to say about the body as the root through which human conduct, being nourished and grown, becomes refulgent. It is no coincidence that the simplified graph for body 體 is 体 – that is, quite literally, the graphic denotation of the root of a person. The body – always a collaboration between person and world, between organism and environment – is at once carnal and vital, seen and lived, receptive and responsive. Not only does the world shape the body, but through our bodily sensorium we structure, conceptualize, and theorize our world of experience.[23] Indeed, it is because the body is the medium through which our ancestors and their culture live on in us that keeping one's body intact has been the first among the several precepts of family reverence (*xiao* 孝).[24]

Fourthly, while Kupperman appeals to a language of process to express character formation and the choices that are made to effect this transformation, he again has little to say about the vital role that the process of moral imagination plays in consummate thinking and living. In Confucian role ethics, it is our educated imagination that, drawing upon all of our human resources, defers action until we can conjure forth the full range of possibilities that allows for optimal growth in our relationships. And said plainly, it is this growth in relationships that is the very substance of morality.

Fifthly, Confucian role ethics does not compete with virtue ethics or any other ethical *theory* but is rather a vision of the moral life that resists the theoretical/practical divide. When we read Kupperman's monograph *Character*, the expectation is that we learn from it a conceptual vocabulary that enables us to think about personal moral development in a more cogent and nuanced way. When we read the Confucian canons, however, the aspiration is higher. The expectation is that while we certainly can appropriate a cluster of terms that enable a critical reflection on our conduct, we ought, more fundamentally, to be inspired by the exhortations and the models of the cultural heroes to become better people.

And finally, despite the incisive, sensitive, and nuanced reading Kupperman always gives the *Analects*, and in spite of what he has to say about the importance of family in that text, we believe that Confucian role ethics requires that much more be said about this institution. And it is to this task that we now turn.

22 Kupperman 1991, 43.
23 See Ames 2011, especially 102–114.
24 See Rosemont and Ames 2008, 105.

A Meditation on the Importance of Family in Ordinary Experience

Kupperman surely believes, as do we, that it is of great importance worldwide to bring the family center stage in thinking about how to address the Herculean economic, social, political and environmental tasks we face today. Surely a great many families can be characterized as sexist, oppressive, or just generally dysfunctional. But many more of them are not, and families are not going to disappear as an institution no matter what some people might wish. Moreover, admitting that "family values" has regularly been employed conceptually in the service of arch-conservative social and political orientations, reinforcing patriarchy, sexism, homophobia and worse, family values can nevertheless quite straightforwardly be modified along much more progressive social, political and economic lines; or so we want to claim in advancing an ethic of roles that is grounded in family.

But if our efforts are to receive serious consideration, the concept of individualism as it has been advocated for in liberal thinking must be challenged at its core. We believe that an ethics of roles inspired by our own reading of the classical Confucian texts offers a real alternative to a foundational individualism that can constitute one such line of engagement. The challenge of role ethics, however, will not be worth much unless accounts of human interactions can be given in non-individualistic moral terms that do not fly in the face of our experiences in and of family life, and our intuitions about them. Thus we want to take the opportunity of this celebration of the Kupperman oeuvre to invite him to comment on how well, or how poorly, the following sketch of some distinctive elements of family life from a role perspective meshes with his sympathetic, but still seemingly individualistic interpretation of persons, especially as he believes his account better captures more basic intuitions about human interactions by employing the concept of individual character and creativity as they apply to human beings.

Apart from Okin, Kupperman, and a few other feminist philosophers, the neglect of the family in modern Western philosophy has continued through the 20th century. The reason for the neglect is easy enough to discern on (at least) two counts. First, family matters have long been considered to be *private* matters, whereas morality is concerned with one's *public* persona.[25] In part this distinction has come about as an implication of increasing sympathy for the idea of

25 This private/public distinction was not drawn by the early Confucians with respect to males, although a "inner-outer" (*neiwai* 内外) variation on it was at the basis of Confucian gender discrimination. The Confucians did draw a distinction between the family and the government, but in many respects the latter was simply a radial extension as the family writ large. There were a number of dimensions of the Confucian family that we would consider "public" today, notable among them being the performance of many rituals.

the separation of church and state, with the church left to dictate duties and obligations that are mandatory only so long as the person involved accepts the creed of a specific church. That is to say, such obligations are in the *personal* or private sphere, and would cease being binding if one forswore the creed. In the *public* sphere, however, moral duties and obligations are seen to be mandatory in the society in which one lives, full stop; the only alternative is exile.

An even more important reason, we believe, for not examining potential moral concerns pertaining to the family is that the dominant Western moral theories are largely grounded in the concept of human beings as fundamentally rational, free, and autonomous individuals (who are also usually self-interested). Whether this idea (presupposition, actually) is taken descriptively or prescriptively is not important in their advocacy that must treat all other human beings as free, rational and autonomous individuals.

But we do not see or treat our parents, grandparents and children in this way. Family relations, especially the most basic of them – namely, those between parents and children – cannot be described, analyzed, or evaluated on the basis of free and rational autonomous individuals interacting with one another, for parents are implicated in the lives of their children, and children in the lives of their parents. That is to say, a significant element in how both parents and children define who they are, is in terms of the other.[26] Herein lies a part of the paradoxical nature of family life when viewed from an individualistic perspective, as noted earlier.

In other work we chose to translate *xiao* as "family reverence" rather than the more common "filial piety."[27] There are several reasons why we abandoned the standard translation, beginning with the Christian flavor that "piety" tends to evoke that is altogether out of place in the Confucian context. An even more important reason is that it is the family that is the locus of one's spiritual development in Confucianism. A person is engaged in a fully secular family, but it is at the same time engaging in what we see as an authentic religious discipline that one undergoes in fulfilling familial roles, sacralizing them and then extending them outward to non-kin. This being so, it would perhaps be appropriate to begin thinking a bit more *reverently* about families – our own first, and others too, as the Confucians seem to have done.[28]

---

26 We will claim that *all* interpersonal relations and interactions can be fruitfully described, analyzed, and evaluated on the model of parents and children, benefactor and beneficiary – even the interrelations between friends, neighbors, colleagues and others. Nothing of ethical significance, we are arguing, will be lost by abandoning a foundational individualism.

27 Rosemont and Ames 2008.

28 It might well be objected that the overall view of the family portrayed herein is so wildly idealistic as to not be worth taking seriously. Two quick replies: 1) The picture suggested here might be more realistic than a number of accounts of the family – East and West – have been.

Roles in Marriage, Family, and Parenting

To quickly sketch this different perspective from which to see persons, think of how different we become, in a very real sense, when we marry. We remain part of the family whence we came, but our roles within them are altered as we are now forming another family of our own, and we also enter into the family of the spouse we have chosen. All of these relationships change us in significant ways, as every married person knows well.

We are changed even more when our first child is born, followed by that child's siblings, all of whom contribute much to the definition of who we have been, who we are now, and who we will be, just as we too have contributed significantly to who they have become. Hence, when it is "my daughter" or "my son" that must be used in the description of a supposedly moral situation involving a mother or father, the adequacy of formulating and acting upon some abstract principle vanishes. If we as parents do not have the requisite cognitive and affective resources within us to ascertain the most appropriate means of dealing with our own children in any given situation, Kant can no more assist us than can Bentham or Mill, or any other universalist moral philosopher, for that matter. We do not look for a rule that will apply to all abstract individuals all of the time, but rather are genuinely concerned about what it is most appropriate to do with *this* son or daughter, *right now.*

Role ethics has a bottom-up rather than top-down orientation, in that it is based on and develops out of immediate human experience, grounded in family life, and not based on the rational development of universal principles to be employed by abstract unencumbered individuals whose obligations are always altogether general. Of course parents do not live solely in the immediate present when living their roles with their children; they must remember their past interactions, and contemplate future ones as well. But these, too, are ongoing elements of our daily experience, as every parent, we believe, will attest.

We must take time into account when discussing the responsibilities of parents to and for their children, and the children's responsibilities toward their parents. Consider for a moment a situation that is deeply moral in role ethics, but

---

Individualism is supposed to have been a characteristic only of the family in the West. Until the 19th century children were seen largely in economic terms. The nuclearization of the family in the West contributed greatly to the rise of capitalism, and many more stereotypes of the history of the family, whether compiled by sociologists (Western families), anthropologists (non-Western families), or by historians, comparative or otherwise, are deserving of careful scrutiny. In *The East in the West* Jack Goody 1996, 2 challenges these stereotypes, as well as the disciplinary methodologies that have generated them. His analyses, and his citations should be read by everyone interested in the structure(s) of families – East and West. "There is nothing wrong with building castles in the sky," said Thoreau; "That is where they belong. Now put the foundations under them."

might well be invisible from other, universal moral perspectives. The situation is from the standpoint of a son. Should I place my aged mother in a nursing home, or keep her in mine? Well, that might well depend on how old I am when I ask the question. If I'm 35, I might well believe I will maximize utility for my wife, children and co-workers by moving her to a nursing home. And I can formulate a universalizable maxim for doing so, believing strongly that I would not want to be a burden to my children, and following the same maxim, would want them to institutionalize me. At 60, however, I might answer the question differently. Understanding how even the best of such institutions diminishes human flourishing, and given my ever-declining vigor, I might well not be able to formulate a maxim about institutionalizing my parents that I would want my own children to follow, nor can I intelligently calculate benefits for all concerned.

Returning to the parental role, time enters equally into all deliberations we make in the discharge of our responsibilities to and for our children, deliberations not totally circumscribed by the ages of any of us, for each of us must think, and act in accordance with details of the past, the present, and the future in ascertaining how to fulfill our role as father or mother.[29] We must, in the first instance, think about the *present* when attending to that dimension of our paternal role as responsible *caretakers*, seeing, that is, to the needs of our children for food, shelter, clothing, books, security, love, and more. In addition to *caring* for them, however – meeting their physical, mental and emotional needs – we are also aware of our responsibility for *raising them* to become adults, and now we must attend no less carefully to the *future* than to the present. This is to say that as parents, we must not only attend to our children as they are right now but also as we believe it would be best for them to become in the future. There are certain ways we should like our children to be when they grow up, and certain ways we do not want them to be, the details of which will be largely dependent on our children's mental, physical and psychological makeup. The details will, however, be equally dependent on our own family history, our ethnicity, citizenship, and other social factors that have largely determined the hopes, fears, dreams and goals we have not only for ourselves, but altogether naturally have for our children as well. Without such factors we would not be who we are, nor would we be a family in any meaningful sense of the word.

In raising children our stated concern is not solely, or perhaps even mainly, to seek to maximize the possibility of their later becoming fully autonomous and free individuals, rationally choosing their own futures, as moralities grounded in

29 In proffering this analysis of the several dimensions of parental roles we have profited much from a paper by William Ruddick 1988. Although his concerns were bioethical in nature – conflicts between doctors and parents vis-à-vis the treatment of children – his insights, especially his distinction between caring for and raising children, are no less appropriate for the issues we deal with herein.

individualism would demand. (*Teachers* might conceivably hold this or a similar goal for *students*, but the case with *parents* and their *children* is radically different). But that demand is in our view not only impossible to meet, it is an undesirable one; to a brief consideration of which we now turn, again with a focus on temporality.[30]

Family and the Ordering of Values

We attempt to live in accordance with an order and pattern of values that influences importantly who we are and what we do. We have these values because we believe them to be good ones, and we endeavor to exemplify them in our conduct with our offspring no less than with others. Needless to say we will endeavor to instill our value ordering in our children, for a major part of our parental responsibility is to have them become value-oriented, and if we do not orient them toward our own ordering, which others might we use? How could we conceivably choose among them?[31] This is not to say we do not re-order our values at times, for many people do. Some who place patriotism above an aversion to killing may volunteer for military service, and then combat, but later become pacificists. Others leave, or join a church. Still others come to have more, or less sympathy for the plight of the poor. Our opposition to capital punishment may wither if one of our own children is brutally murdered, and so on.

Presumably, however, we alter our values in a reasoned way. We can explain why we no longer accept violence as a means of settling disputes, or come to see the evasiveness of "blame the victim" arguments with respect to poverty, and we can explain these changes in discussions with our children (and with parents as well). But at any given moment, we believe our value orderings are pretty good ones, we attempt to reflect them in our actions, we look forward to discussions with our children about them, and we want our children to embrace them and

30 Even here a caveat should perhaps be entered: If one of our former ethics students were to defend the autogenocide of the Khmer Rouge in Cambodia, for example, we would surely believe we had failed, at least to some extent, as teachers.

31 We emphasize the prioritization of values to make it clear that we do not believe it is possible to "take on a new set of values" as most people would be inclined to say. One cannot logically take on a whole new set of values, but only re-order the values they (and everyone else except sociopaths) already have. How, for example, could one ever get you to change your mind about the worth of a particular value except by appealing to a more basic value you both share? Everyone values security, everyone values freedom; but different people order those values differently. And if members of one camp convince some members of another to change their minds, these latter have not "taken on a whole new set of values," but have simply re-ordered the values they have long held, sometimes, but not always, permanently. In situation X, freedom trumps security, but in Y the opposite ordering might obtain.

model them. *Caretakers* may not have to do these things with respect to the young, but *parents* must, and it would be decidedly unfilial for the children not to take them seriously.

A Non-exemplary Son: Immoral as Well?

Consider a person whose chosen career has been that of a union organizer. He has enjoyed his work overall, and been extremely proud and happy when another labor unit, through his efforts, votes in a union to represent their interests in negotiations with the corporate hierarchy. His career has not made him rich, but has provided the wherewithal to send his son to college, and to law school thereafter, a goal the boy has embraced since his high school sophomore year. Now, after passing the bar exam the son announces that the best job offer he has had came from the largest union-busting firm in the state, and he has accepted it.

It seems to us that any pride and joy the father might take at this turn of events – the son has a good job, and clearly chosen it independently – would almost immediately be replaced by depression, perhaps severe. And this would not simply be because of the choice the son has made, but because of the way the father now had to view his own role as a father in a very different, much more negative manner, namely as largely a failure. It is not merely that the father secretly might have wished for the son to choose to become a labor lawyer; had the son chosen real estate law, criminal law, or become an assistant district attorney, the father might or might not have been a bit disappointed, yet no more than that. But for the son to embark on a career that was the antithesis of the values of solidarity and social justice his father has lived for and attempted to embody, would be proof positive to him that his fathering had been radically deficient in some vital respects.

It might be tempting to think here that the father is just being self-centered in some way or another, either by wanting to live vicariously through his son's work, or by being a dogmatist, or simply not thinking of how the son might take pride in the knowledge of his independence and ability to make up his own mind. But if we shift attention directly to the son himself as he begins a career devoted to undoing his father's life work and dreams: What would we think of him? Notice that so long as we merely see him as an individual who has made a rational choice, we will probably just shrug our shoulders and say "So what?" Our strong sense, however, is that if we focus on him as a *son* of *this* father we would not think much of him, very probably seeing him as unfeeling, or worse. We would certainly characterize him as *self-centered* for being so unmindful of the significance of this decision for his father, who, because of his son's decision, has become a much-altered person, and not merely because of his sadness. We would hold the son in low regard because of his lack of gratitude, and also because of his *irreverence* toward his family, with untoward consequences for the others with whom his life has been intertwined.[32]

Parents must, of course, balance their guiding conduct toward their children with an appreciation of the uniqueness of each one of them. The desired goal would be to have them take on these values not merely because they are the values of their parents, but because the children believe such values are *good* values, and want to commit themselves to them for this reason. And it seems that this goal can only be achieved on the basis of the *love* of the parents for their children, and not because of an abstract moral *rule* or *principle.* Returning to the union-organizing father, how could he possibly assign a higher place in his values to the categorical imperative or the utility principle than to the priorities that have given his life meaning, purpose, and satisfaction?

The Dysfunctional Family Objection

It might be objected here that all of this is well and good, but what do we do with fathers who don't love their children very much, and are rigid dogmatists to boot? How can we be reverent toward such a family? Don't we need some more general moral principles applicable to these situations? If love can bring the parental behavior into accord with the requisite moral principles without invoking the principles upon reflection, fine, this objection might continue, but how do we handle the unloving or uncaring parents – of which, obviously and unfortunately, there are a great many today – without more general moral principles?

Such an objection is very probably the most common to be made about the particularistic nature of Confucianism.[33] In reply, first, it may be irreverent, but

32 Aristotle would not agree with us at all, for he held that despite the fact that his seemingly "unfriendly doctrine" on this score was "opposed to the opinions men hold," he nevertheless claimed that "... [T] he fortunes of descendants and of all a man's friends should not affect his happiness ... ." Aristotle 1984, Book I, 1101a–b.

33 Usually couched as a conflict arising from the fact that good Confucians are supposed to serve in government when called upon, on the one hand, and the fact that the ruler you are now serving is a thoroughgoing rotter; what to do? What rule or principle will Confucius follow? If we are correct in our interpretation, however, there are no such rules or principles to be found in the early texts. But we may nevertheless resolve the conflict easily. Rather than searching for an abstract principle, we must ask, as one who is serving in government, whether *this* ruler, here now; is he reformable? If the answer is affirmative, we must ask a second highly specific question: Do we have the qualities and skills to reform him? If the answer to this question is also affirmative, King Wen becomes our model exemplar, and we continue to serve, remonstrating all the while. If the answer to the first question is "yes," but is "no" to the second, Confucius himself becomes our model, as we return to family and community, and "serve

not irrelevant to turn the question around. In cases of wretched fathers, why would we have any reason to believe they will see the light and become good Kantians or Utilitarians? Almost surely almost all such fathers will not have read any of the works of these philosophers, and how will we make them do so? At any level even remotely resembling the practical, how can this kind of objection be seen to have more force against Confucius than Kant, Bentham or Mill?

More importantly, the question underlying the objection cannot be answered as stated, because it is requesting a rule or a principle to follow, and, we are arguing that there are no such rules or principles to be gleaned from the texts of early Confucianism; it is particularistic to the core. But this does not mean there is no answer to the question, for there always is one, only framed differently.

If I see that my father is unduly indoctrinating my younger siblings, and seems to show indifference to them, I must first ask why he is this way, and attempt to correct the cause of the problem if possible. If the first question cannot be answered, my next question is whether or not I have the capacity to change his behavior in order for my siblings to flourish. If the answer is "Yes," I do so. If my answer is "No," I must then ask whether I can help my mother change him. Or ask my uncles and aunts (his brothers and sisters), or his parents (my grandparents) to get him to change his ways. And if all else fails, I can then simply do my best to shelter my siblings from my father as best I can whenever he is being overbearing or abusive. In an extreme case, I may have to ask for outside assistance from a public agency, or in a desperate situation, from the police. In sum, what I do is dependent on who *I* am, who *my* father is, and the specific personalities and capacities of other members of *my* family. But there is always an answer to the question that we obtain upon reflection at times, but without invoking universal rules or principles.

The Primacy of Family in Confucian Role Ethics

The moral of the story thus far should be clear: When dealing with relationships between parents and children we cannot see any of the participants as free, autonomous individuals, for they are too intimately bound up with one another not only in their interactions, but in their sense of who they are, have been and will become as well; in all cases, bonded by love. What it means, in large part, to be a father or a mother is to be sensitive to the personalities, abilities and feelings of

government" from there, as *Lunyu* 2.21 makes clear, and 7.16 and 8.13 reinforce. And if we answer the first question "No, we don't believe he is reformable," then we must raise the flag of rebellion, with King Wu as our hero and precedent-setter. In sum, no conflicts; there is always a decision procedure. It is always highly particularistic – but none the worse for that, it would seem.

their children at all times, taking these into account both when caring for them *now*, and raising them with an eye to the *future*. And what it means to be a son or daughter, is to be sensitive to the beliefs and feelings of one's parents before electing and following any significant goal in their lives, a sensitivity that must be maintained throughout their parents' lives, as a matter of loyalty. This loyalty does not preclude remonstrating with parents, of course (or others in authority) as all the texts of classical Confucianism make clear.

How much of each behavior and attendant attitude parents should seek to instill in their children depends in part on their own value ordering, but depends even more on the specific personalities of the children. For Confucians, challenging authority is not to be taken lightly; but neither is loyalty or obedience if these qualities are not exhibited outwardly without a proper inward orientation. For them, these qualities were reciprocal, and every parent and teacher had to be aware of when and how best to inculcate the appropriate feelings to accompany appropriate behavior. In the first book of the *Analects*, for example, we find "It is a rare thing for someone who has a sense of familial and fraternal responsibility (孝弟) to have a taste for defying authority." (1.2) But at the same time, "As for young people contributing their energies when there is work to be done, and deferring to their elders when there is wine and food to be had – how can merely doing these things be considered as being familially reverent?" (2.8). Somehow true family reverence would provide insight into when authority might be defied, for Confucius equally noted that "To see what it is appropriate to do, and not do it, is cowardice." (2.24).

The textual evidence suggests that the early Confucians didn't think too long or hard about the institution of the family *qua* family either, but for very different reasons than their Western counterparts: the family is seen as so basic for human flourishing as to be self-evident, and hence not in need of detailed analysis or justification. For the Confucians, the question is not *whether* the family is necessary for human beings to develop and flourish, for it is obvious that it is, and without it, it is assumed that one does not have the means to become human.[34] The question is rather *which* behavior models are most appropriate in a family in order for its members to develop and flourish.[35]

The early Confucian texts are certainly not simply child-rearing manuals, but they *are* child-rearing manuals in part, and read with care and sensitivity still

34 David Hall and Roger Ames have argued for the family being the most foundational of all metaphors in Chinese thought. See their *Anticipating China*, SUNY Press, 1995, esp. pp. 271–77; see also their references there to the sociological work of Ambrose King.

35 This would explain why "family reverence" (*xiao* 孝) appears relatively infrequently in the *Analects* in comparison to the other terms of ethical import for Confucius. Only later is *xiao* treated at length in its own right in the *Xiaojing*. See our translation of this text, Rosemont and Ames 2009. Our Introduction to the text takes up some of the themes elaborated upon herein.

have much to teach parents (and teachers) today about how to nurture the young in the present, and raise them with an eye to the future. Conversely, what it means to be a son or daughter is in part to be sensitive to the beliefs and feelings of one's parents before electing and following any significant goal in their own lives, a sensitivity that must be maintained throughout their parents' lives, as a matter of loyalty. And perhaps after their deaths as well.

A Thought Experiment: On Reviving Family Reverence

There is a third factor of time that parents must take into account in meeting their responsibilities both to care for and raise their children. In addition to the present and the future, parents must attend to the past. Here, it seems to us, the early Confucians have much to say to everyone today, with their detailed concern for rituals, especially those involving ancestor veneration. Perhaps it is with respect to our dead forebearers that the concept of *xiao* as family reverence can be seen most vividly, most religiously, and most importantly, as a strategy for strengthening the roles of those still alive.

Much of who and what we are may be traced fairly directly to our ancestors, from our appearance to our native tongue, from our ethnicity to the specifics of the socialization processes we have undergone. Most of our tastes in food, music, dress, avocations, and more can usually be traced directly to our parents and grandparents, and their grandparents in turn. (In a number of cases we can also trace our antipathy to certain of these tastes, or others, directly to them, too.) The odds are that each of us bears a strong physical resemblance to one or more of our grandparents or great grandparents. Like it or not, we belong to a family, and moreover, a family with a history (and perhaps more than one). It follows from this that the more we know of our familial past, and the more we stay in touch with it, the better we can know who we are now, and envisage possibilities of who we might, or should become.

This point is obvious to the families of the rich and the powerful. Probably each member of the Rockefeller, Kennedy, Bush, and Vanderbilt families has a strong sense of who they are, and a sense of belonging to a special group, with a special history. All of them can very probably name not only their four grandparents, but most of their eight great-grandparents as well. Most ordinary Americans can't do this, but the point still applies equally to all families. Each of us almost surely has a hero or heroine or two in the family tree, and very probably an occasional villain as well. Each of us has eight great-grandparents. Their fame or infamy may have been great or local, but the histories of all families should be seen as special to the members thereof. Yet in order to obtain that sense of *belonging* to a family with a history (which every family has), you must know about that history, especially the lives of the ancestors who have made that history. It behooves all of us, then, to learn of our family's history, to listen carefully to the stories told to us by our grandparents and their siblings, to look at old photographs, and/or do a bit of genealogical detective work. Knowing where we have come from provides major clues as to who we are, and might become, as we continue developing the history of our family – and contributing to it.

Learning our family's history is not merely in pursuit of justifying a coat of arms on the silverware; genealogy and heraldry are very distinct enterprises. And we shouldn't engage in studying where we came from just in order to brag about some past hero to whom we're related. Great granduncle Tom may have been a fine sheriff in a Western frontier town; but on the other hand he might have been a horse thief properly hanged by a fine sheriff in a Western frontier town.

To our mind there is no better way to obtain this sense of belonging, of feeling the continuity of a family line, than by a ritual honoring of the ancestors on occasion, especially for parents and grandparents. It should thus be a significant dimension of our role as parents to instill in our children this sense of coming from, and belonging to a family with a history. And we must demonstrate our responsibilities to our own parents and their parents in turn, teaching them that these responsibilities do not cease at their deaths. It is our responsibility to our forebears to see that their memory is not entirely erased by time.

Hence, in order to be appropriate models for our children we should periodically engage in a ritual that honors our ancestors, a ritual that might be widespread throughout our culture, or more locally, or it might be a ritual unique to our own family's heritage, or we may well have to initiate a ritual on our own to pass on to our children. We each enrich the lives of our children by continuing to discharge our responsibilities toward our parents and grandparents after they have died by remembering them via a ritual of remembrance.

It may sound strange to say that we can owe a debt to the dead, but it is not. Even atheists can understand the obligatory nature of keeping a deathbed promise.[36] And doesn't every son and daughter raised in a loving home "promise," even if only implicitly, not to forget their parents, nor to let our own children forget them? Rituals, especially family rituals, have tended to occupy the thoughts of most Western philosophers no more than the family has, but rituals can form a basic bond for families, and significantly affect our self-identification, as well as our sense of worth.[37]

36 See Nagel 1979, 6.

37 Aristotle would be in opposition again for he focused only on the ontological status of the dead. He did not believe we should think or act on behalf of them, or when considering or justifying our actions, "For it seems … that even if anything whether good or evil penetrates to [the dead], it must be something weak and negligible, either in itself or for them, or if not, at

To see this point another way, consider the fact that a great many people invariably 'talk' to the tombstone when they visit a cemetery to pay respects to a deceased relative, teacher, or friend. There is nothing surprising about this, as it is altogether human. We *know* the deceased cannot hear us, but we speak anyway "as if they were present."[38]

As members of families then, and especially as we become parents, our roles take on religious no less than moral, social, and political significance. In meeting our manifold responsibilities to our children, and our parents, we are obliged to attend carefully to the present, to the future, and to the past, and thereby we become enabled to see, and feel ourselves linked closely to what has gone before, what is now, and what will come tomorrow; a small, but not inconsequential brush with immortality – here, now, in *this* world.[39]

For this insight if for no other all of us owe a continuing debt to the early Confucians. In the past, ritual practices honoring ancestors undoubtedly stemmed from the almost universal belief in ghosts and spirits, benign and malevolent, in keeping with the theologies of the world's religions. This occurred in China too, of course, and here is where the peculiar genius of the early Confucians is of such great relevance today, over and above the social, political and economic insights they can provide us as we undertake the task of seriously rethinking the family. The Confucians also show us how these rituals and customs can continue to be moving, satisfying and sustaining even for the increasing number of us the world over who give no credence to the idea of ghosts and spirits. Even in the absence of such entities, or deities, we may indeed be reverent – especially toward our families.

In conclusion, it seems that our lives have been, and always will be lived through roles that have encumbered us since earliest childhood, interacting with others to contribute to their flourishing as they contribute to ours, making it all but impossible to ascertain what I might be as an individual self in any meaningful sense. Rather do we seem to be the sum of the roles we live, roles that we first learned how to live and practice in family, and roles that we continue to live and practice in family today.

All of these perspectives – personal, social, moral and spiritual – on the lived family are visible from the vantage point of a role ethics centered on persons as constituted by the others with whom they interact; they are much more difficult to see, or appreciate, from the standpoint of any other ethical system built on the fiction of human beings as free, autonomous, and isolable individuals like the

least it must be such in degree and kind as not to make happy those who are not happy nor to take away their blessedness from those who are." Aristotle 1984, Book I, 1101b.

38 *Analects* 3.12, and see also 11.12. For further discussion of the psychological dimensions of engaging in mourning rituals, see Rosemont 2007.

39 For more on the spiritual sense of time and non-physical immortality, see Rosemont (2001).

person in A.E. Housman's poem: "I, a stranger and afraid // In a world I never made."[40]

Confucian Role Ethics in the Confucian Project

Descending from our meditation on the importance of family in ordinary life, we return to the *Great Learning* 大學 that sets out to define the Confucian project, taking family feeling as the entry point for developing moral competence. The central message of this terse yet comprehensive document is that while personal, familial, social, political, and indeed cosmic cultivation is ultimately coterminous and mutually entailing, it must always begin from a commitment to personal cultivation within the roles and relations of family and community. Said another way, personal cultivation for the relationally constituted person is irreducibly social, with its locus of cultivation being the roles and relations that begin radially with family itself. In the language of the *Great Learning:*

> There is the important and the incidental in things and a beginning and an end in what we do. It is in realizing what should have priority that one approaches the proper way (*dao*). .. Once they saw how things fit together most productively, their wisdom reached its heights; once their wisdom reached its heights, their thoughts were sincere; once their thoughts were sincere, their heartminds knew what is proper; once their heartminds knew what is proper, their persons were cultivated; once their persons were cultivated, their families were set right; once their families were set right, their state was properly ordered; and once their states were properly ordered, there was peace in the world. [41]

Each person stands as a unique perspective on family, community, polity, and cosmos, and through a dedication to deliberate growth and articulation, everyone has the possibility of bringing the resolution of the relationships that locate and constitute them within family and community into clearer and more meaningful focus. The "learning" (*xue* 學) of the *Great Learning* is the cultivation of productive, transpersonal habits of conduct that radiate out through family, community, and polity to ultimately transform the cosmos. The meaning of the family is implicated in and dependent upon the productive cultivation of each of its members, and by extension, the meaning of the entire cosmos is implicated in and dependent upon the productive cultivation of each person within family and community. Personal worth is the source of human culture, and human culture

40 Housman 1922.

41 Zhu Xi (1969 reprint): *Daxue* 1a–2a: 物有本末，事有終始，知所先後，則近道矣。。。物格而後知至，知至而後意誠，意誠而後心正，心正而後身修，身修而後家齊，家齊而後國治，國治而後天下平。

in turn is the aggregating resource that provides a context and a resource for each person's cultivation.

While certainly having important theoretical implications, the enduring power of this Confucian project as it is given shape in the *Great Learning* is that it proceeds from a relatively straightforward account of the actual human experience. Confucianism is a pragmatic naturalism in the sense that, rather than relying upon metaphysical presuppositions or supernatural speculations, it focuses instead on the possibilities for enhancing personal worth available to us here and now through enchanting the ordinary affairs of the day. A grandmother's love for her grandchild is at once the most ordinary of things, and the most extraordinary of things.

Confucius, by developing his insights around the most basic and enduring aspects of the ordinary human experience – family reverence, deference to others, friendship, a cultivated sense of shame, the centrality of education, the politics of community and country, intergenerational responsibility and respect, and so on – has guaranteed the continuing relevance of Confucian role ethics, and not for the Chinese alone.

References

Ackerman, Bruce (1980). *Social Justice in the Liberal State.* New Haven: Yale University Press.

Ames, Roger T. (2011). *Confucian Role Ethics: A Vocabulary.* Hong Kong and Honolulu: The Chinese University of Hong Kong Press and University of Hawai'i Press.

Aristotle (1984). *The Complete Works of Aristotle.* Edited by Jonathan Barnes. Princeton: Princeton University Press.

Dworkin, Ronald (1977). *Taking Rights Seriously.* Cambridge: Harvard University Press.

Fingarette, Herbert (1983). "The Music of Humanity in the Conversations of Confucius." *Journal of Chinese Philosophy,* volume 10.

Goody, Jack (1996). *The East in the West.* Cambridge: Cambridge University Press.

Housman, A.E. (1922). *Last Poems,* Poem XII. New York: Henry Holt & Co.

Hume, David (1975). *Enquiry Concerning the Principles of Morals.* Oxford: Oxford University Press.

Kupperman, Joel J. (2004). "Tradition and Community in the Formation of Character and Self." *Confucian Ethics: A Comparative Study of Self, Autonomy, and Community.* Edited by Kwong-loi Shun and David B. Wong. Cambridge: Cambridge University Press.

— (1999). *Learning from Asian Philosophy.* New York: Oxford University Press.

— (1991). *Character.* New York and Oxford: Oxford University Press.

— (1971). "Confucius and the Nature of Religious Ethics," in *Philosophy East & West,* volume 21, 1971.

MacIntyre, Alasdair (1981). *After Virtue.* Notre Dame: University of Notre Dame Press.

— (1984) *Whose Justice? Which Rationality?* Notre Dame: University of Notre Dame Press.

Minow, Martha and Mary Lyndon Shanley (1996). "Introduction to a Special Issue on the Family and Feminist Theory." *Hypatia* 11 no. 1.

Nagel (1979). "Death." *Mortal Questions.* Cambridge: Cambridge University Press.

Nozick, Robert (1974). *Anarchy, State, and Utopia.* New York: Basic Books, 1974.

Phillips, Derek L. (1986). *Toward a Just Social Order.* Princeton: Princeton University Press.

Plato (1961). *The Collected Dialogues of Plato.* Edited by Edith Hamilton and Huntington Cairns. New York: Pantheon Books.

Rosemont, Henry Jr. (2007). "On the Non-Finality of Physical Death in Classical Confucianism." *Acta Orientalia Vilnensia,* Volume 8, no. 2.

— (2001). *Rationality and Religious Experience: The Continuing Relevance of the World's Spiritual Traditions.* Chicago: Open Court.

Rosemont, Henry Jr. and Roger T. Ames (2008), *The Chinese Classic of Family Reverence: A Philosophical Translation of the* Xiaojing. Honolulu: University of Hawai'i Press.

Rousseau, Jean-Jacque (1959–1969). *Discourse on Political Economy* in *Oeuvres Completes* Paris: Pleiade, Volume 3.

Ruddick, William (1988). "Parenthood: Three Concepts and a Principle." *Family Values.* Edited by Laurence Houlgate. Florence, KY: Wadsworth Publishing Co.

Sandel, Michael (1982). *Liberalism and the Limits of Justice.* Cambridge: Cambridge University Press.

Unger, Roberto (1975). *Knowedge and Politics.* New York: The Free Press.

Roger T. Ames

Travelling Together with *Gravitas*: The Intergenerational Transmission of Confucian Culture

Henry Rosemont and I are contributing jointly-written essays for this volume as an object lesson in how we have come to understand the narrative nature of philosophizing within traditional Confucian philosophy and culture.[1] We will argue that *dao* 道 – that is, 'forging our way together in the world,' or what we might elaborate upon as 'travelling through a shared physical, social, and cultural landscape' – is *the* metaphor that governs the central project of the *Analects of Confucius* and continues in the Chinese philosophical tradition to become one of its defining terms of art. As Confucius himself declares, each generation inherits the guiding moral compass of 'this culture of ours' (*siwen* 斯文) (*Analects* 9.5) from those who have come before. It is then incumbent on them to embody this culture, to apply it effectively to resolve the pressing issues of their day, and in that process, to reauthorize it for their own time and place. Throughout their lives, they model the cultural practices for the generations that succeed them, and in so doing, recommend to their progeny that they do the same for those generations yet to come. Indeed, says Confucius, 'It is human beings that extend the way, not the way that extends human beings' (*Analects* 15.29).[2] Confucianism as a living culture thus not only has 'legs,' but indeed is more roundly genealogical as it is embodied, revitalized, and then passed on by each succeeding generation.

In this essay I will first try to develop a more nuanced understanding of what is meant by '*dao*-ing' in the Confucian tradition – that is, 'travelling together through a shared cultural landscape.' Next I will turn to the expression *xiao* 孝 or *xiaodao* 孝道 that Rosemont and I have translated as 'the way of family reverence' to explore the process of cultural transmission within living family

1 Contemporary Western philosophers such as Charles Taylor are taking the conception of person in this narrative direction. Taylor (1989, p. 35) argues that 'One is a self only among other selves. A self can never be described without reference to those who surround it.' 'But this is to state another basic condition of making sense of ourselves, that we grasp our lives in a *narrative*. … In order to have a sense of who we are, we have to have a notion of how we have become, and of where we are going.' (p. 47)

2 All translations are from Ames and Rosemont (1998).

lineages.[3] The third term I will invoke is *ru* 儒 or 'literati culture' (now conventionally translated unfortunately as 'Confucianism') to register the dynamics of an always changing yet persistent elite cultural landscape as it has been both conserved and constantly reconfigured across the centuries. I will then conclude by appealing to lineages of landscape painters from the Tang (618–907) through to the early Qing (1644–1911) dynasties as an illustrative case of both familial *xiao* and literati *ru* transmission.

In Rosemont's best effort to allow the Confucian tradition to speak for itself, he has begun our account of 'travelling through a shared cultural landscape' with his attempt to identify some of our own philosophical presuppositions that might willy-nilly be projected onto and thus overwrite very different sensibilities in the continuing construction of a shared familial and communal Confucian identity. The first among these uncommon assumptions is an uncritical foundational individualism that is most often defined in terms of autonomy, equality, freedom, rationality, and usually self-interest. This liberal notion of individualism has such deep roots in our tradition and is so entrenched as a cultural commonsense that it has become a default ideology that has only rarely and fairly recently been challenged by erstwhile alternatives.[4] The problem with assuming that persons can be accurately described, analyzed, and evaluated as individuals – psychologically, politically, and morally – in isolation from other human beings, however, is that where it was once a benign fiction, it has now become pernicious as a moral justification for a trenchant, self-interested libertarianism. Such an individualism not only fails to provide us access to a sufficiently robust understanding of shared life in family and community, but further stands in tension with the empirical fact of associated living. Indeed, such a fictive individualism ignores the intimacy, mutuality, and particularity that is invariably defining of relations in real families. In failing to accommodate family roles lived through richly textured and constantly changing patterns of both natural and socially constructed differences, abstract individualism itself becomes reductive and violent by enforcing conformity at the unacceptable expense of excising real diversity and its creative possibilities.

In his discussion of the central importance of lived family roles and relations, Rosemont draws upon what we have come to advocate as a *sui generis* regimen of 'Confucian role ethics' to argue that lives lived in our evolving roles as children and parents, as beneficiaries and benefactors, are too intimately bound up with

3 See Rosemont and Ames (2009), pp. 1, 34–36 and 105–116 for an argument for this interpretation and translation of *xiao*.

4 A.T. Nuyen (2012), 'Confucian Role Ethics'. *Comparative and Continental Philosophy* 4.1, 141–150 offers Charles Taylor (1989), Dorothy Emmett (1966), Marion Smiley (1992), and Larry May (1992) as some examples of recent Western ethical theorists who offer a relational and role-based conception of person.

one another to allow for the divisive and fragmenting assumptions that ground liberal individualism. We live associated lives, and are irreducibly social not only in the transactions that constitute our unique narratives, but in our most basic, role-informed sense of personal identity. The omnipresent responsibilities of family life not only direct our attention to the pressing current and future concerns of the day, but they also provide us with a historical and narrative sense of where we have come from, and in important degree, tell us who we are.

Within the interpretive framework of Confucian philosophy, associated, interpersonal living is taken to be an uncontested, empirical fact. Every person lives and every event takes place within a vital natural, social, and cultural context. Association being a fact, our different roles lived within family and society are nothing more than the stipulation of specific modes of associated living: mothers and grandsons, teachers and neighbors. But while we must take associated living as a simple fact, the consummate conduct that comes to inspire and to produce virtuosity in these stipulated roles lived in family, community, and the cultural narrative broadly – that is, Confucian role ethics – is an achievement; it is what we are able with imagination to make of the fact of association.

Let me build on Rosemont's reflections on the tensions he registers between ethical theories grounded in individualism and the vision of the moral life espoused as Confucian role ethics by turning to a fuller and more specific discussion of the dynamics of interpersonal and intergenerational transmission within Confucian culture. It seems appropriate to frame this discussion with a memorable passage from an essay by Ralph Waldo Emerson, a thinker out of Rosemont's and my own past to whom we as Americans owe a profound debt in the shaping of our own national and cultural identity. Emerson appeals to a rather simple image of a carpenter hewing wood to make a rather profound statement about the march of continuing civilization and the morality that must necessarily inform it. Emerson draws an intriguing contrast between the ineffectiveness of 'going it alone' in this world, and the indomitable felicity of squaring civilization behind our shoulders and living lives that are propelled by the moral and cultural *gravitas* that such a shared purchase and momentum provides:

> Civilization depends on morality. Everything good in man leans on what is higher. This rule holds in small as in great. Thus, all our strength and success in the work of our hands depend on our borrowing the aid of the elements. You have seen a carpenter on a ladder with a broad-axe chopping upward chips and slivers from a beam. How awkward! at what disadvantage he works! But see him on the ground, dressing his timber under him. Now, not his feeble muscles, but the force of gravity brings down the axe; that is to say, the planet itself splits his stick.[5]

5 'American Civilization' in *Atlantic Monthly* 1862.

Emerson's image of lives empowered by the weight of a common civilization recalls the key philosophical notion of 'a forging of our way together in the world' (*dao*). How then are we to understand this important Confucian metaphor for the journey that we all join at birth in our families and communities?

We must begin by exploring Confucianism's own vocabulary and, in thus allowing the tradition to speak for itself, establish an interpretive context for reading the tradition. *Dao*, conventionally translated as 'the Way,' is probably the most pervasive and widely recognized idea in Chinese philosophy. The specific character of Chinese philosophy arises because a dominant cultural factor in the tradition, now and then, has been the primacy of vital relationality and its many implications. To understand the ongoing process of cosmic transformation then, we must acknowledge the inseparability of any 'thing' and its relations with an always changing context. Corollary to this 'event' (rather than substance) ontology is the priority of process and change over form and stasis. This processual cosmology locates the human sojourn within the framework of an emergent, prospective sense of cosmic order wherein form itself is expressed as the cadence or rhythm of life. Of course this vital process cosmology stands in a rather stark contrast with a tradition of classical Greek ontology and metaphysics defined as it is in terms of antecedent and unchanging first principles from which cosmic order is derived.

In this Chinese process cosmology, the notion of *dao* speaks to both the unbounded wholeness and the openendedness of human experience as it unfolds among the presencing of the myriad things (*wanwu* 萬物 or *wanyou* 萬有) of which the human being has pride of place. Indeed, on both the bronzes and in the recently recovered bamboo strips, the character for *dao* itself is not simply a road, but includes graphically a representation of the itinerant human being encountering a crossroad:  and 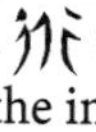 respectively. And its dyadic correlate, *de* 德, references the commitment to the insistent, unique particularity of these myriad things within this continuing process. Said another way, the doctrine of internal relations in this process cosmology that would construe 'things' as being constituted by their vital relations guarantees the uniqueness of particulars as evolving matrixes of always distinct relationships.

It is because experience is always entertained and engaged from one particular perspective or another that the totality of experience, *dao*, and the myriad things as the content of experience, *de*, are simply two nonanalytic ways of looking at the same phenomenon, with the former emphasizing the continuity of experience and the latter the multiplicity of its content. And as we will see below, when in Confucian role ethics we focus on the relationship of particular persons and their various environments, the binomial expression *daode* is not simply descriptive of persons and their contexts; indeed, it becomes a normative term that speaks to the virtuosity that is achieved in and expressed through productive relations.

Taking the gerundive, processional, and dynamic sense of *dao* as primary, its several derived meanings emerge rather naturally: 'to lead forth' requires the 'explaining' of a 'method, art, teaching, or doctrine' that then produces a 'way, path, or road' that allows us to make our way forward. Thus, at its most fundamental level, *dao* denotes the active project of 'moving ahead in the world,' of 'forging a way forward,' of 'road building.' It is to register the dynamic implications of *dao* that we have on occasion used the neologism 'way-making' as a translation (Ames and Hall, 2003, *passim*). By extension and derivative of this active sense, *dao* comes to connote a pathway that has been made, and hence that can be travelled.

The parts of speech that order our European languages – nouns, verbs, adjectives and adverbs – encourage us to divide up the world in a culturally specific manner. Under the influence of these grammatical determinants, we are inclined to separate things from actions, attributes from modalities, 'where' from 'when,' and 'how' from 'what.' However, given the fluidity between space, time, and matter assumed in this classical Chinese process cosmology, these familiar categories do not govern the way in which the holistic Chinese world is parsed and divided up. Time, space, and matter are simply explanatory categories used to describe different aspects of the same transforming and transformative experience. Thus, language such as *dao* that is used to define a Chinese world must be seen as crossing the borders of time, space, and matter. *Dao* as both '*what* is' (things and their various attributes) and '*how* things are' (their actions and various modalities) serves as a perfect example of this dynamic holism. To say 'I know' – literally, 'I know *dao*' (*wo zhidao* 我知道) – has as much to do with the subjects of knowing and their quality of understanding as it does with the objects of knowledge and their attributes. Thus, there is no clear line between what we might take to be putative things and events: A 'thing' is a distinctive, dynamic focus located within an unbounded field of experience that is holographically implicated within this focus, requiring a focus-field rather than a part-whole language to give it expression. Each note as it is played in Beethoven's Ninth has implicated within it, and can only be evaluated, by appeal to the symphony as a whole.

Turning to the human world and to the human *dao*, this process cosmology is expressed through the centrality of personal cultivation as the generative source of meaningful relations that bring us together on our particular pathways through the world. Human beings are not only travellers; they must also be road builders because the continuing human culture – the human *dao* – is always provisional and ever under construction. Again, the primacy of vital relationality means that the locus of this personal cultivation lies embedded within those evolving roles and relationships that constitute each of us in the narratives of our lives. The particular and yet continuous and vital character of the human culture is captured in a passage in which the protégée of Confucius, Zigong, is questioned about Confucius's academic lineage. Zigong replies:

> The way (*dao*) of the early Zhou dynasty Kings Wen and Wu has not collapsed, but still lives on in the people. Since those of superior character realize the greater part of it, and those of lesser quality realize some of it, everyone has something of Wen and Wu's way in them. Who then does the Master not learn from? And again, how could there be a single constant teacher for him? (*Analects* 19.22)

Of immediate import in this passage is the choice of King Wen – literally, King 'Culture' – as the source of Confucius's education, and the claim that this living culture is embodied and realized in different degrees in the people themselves. The cultural narrative – the *dao* – unfolds in the ineluctable transmission of civilization in the broadest sense from one generation to the next.

Surveying and parsing the range of meaning invested in this polysemic term *dao* – 'travelling through a shared physical, social, and cultural landscape' – we can identify at least three overlapping and mutually entailing semantic dimensions that have relevance to the image of travelling together with *gravitas.*

First, there is the primary 'momentum' sense of *dao* as an unfolding cultural disposition. There is a palpable glacial weight to *dao* as the continuing propensity of experience that provides us with identity and historical context as we inch ahead together. It is this sense of *dao* that justifies its familiar translation as 'the Way.' If we look for approximations for *dao* in our own language, it can be understood as a generic idea such as 'culture' or 'civilization' or 'life' that resists resolution into familiar, exclusive dualisms such as 'subject/object,' 'form/function,' 'agency/action,' 'fact/value,' and so on. *Dao* in this sense is the confluence of lived experience as our narratives converge into a shared cultural identity, with all of the cadence, continuities, transitions, and disjunctions that are characteristic of the stream of human experience.

Secondly, we must underscore the fact that *dao* is normative rather than simply descriptive because human beings have a proactive, creative role in making our way forward in the world. There is certainly an ineluctable force of circumstances at play in our lived experience that accounts for the persistence and regularity of our daily lives. But this unfolding process is underdetermined, allowing for our own unique and creative influence upon its course. Indeed, the indeterminate aspect that honeycombs what is determinate and intelligible in life provides a range of creative possibilities, and allows for the spontaneous emergence of novelty within each moment of experience. Making our way forward is participatory, allowing for an educated responsiveness to the more fluid and indeterminate opportunities that this experience presents. And our capacity to respond to these novel opportunities in an optimal way is itself dependent upon the richness and depth of our own past experience. Indeed, it is the educated palate that can anticipate and most fully enjoy the new culinary experiences that become available to us.

Thirdly, the human being, far from being perceived as a minor player, has a major, even religious role as a cosmic collaborator. Personal cultivation is the ultimate source of meaning, and in this process, it is the achieved intensity and extensiveness of one's roles and relations that determines the degree of one's influence on the natural, social, and cultural world. The human being through a regimen of personal cultivation has both the opportunity and the responsibility to become co-creator with the heavens and the earth. It is in this sense that the sage (*shengren* 聖人) as the most accomplished among human beings is elevated to a truly cosmic plane that allows humanity to be properly described as 'the heartmind of the cosmos' (*tiandi zhi xin* 天地之心).

The most familiar yet derivative understanding of *dao* is a post hoc combination of these more primary meanings: the objectified use of *dao* that is expressed in the familiar demonstrative translation as 'the Way.' To nominalize and thus overdetermine *dao* can betray its fluidity, reflexivity, and openness to the future, and when given priority, is often the first step to inadvertently overwriting a prospective, process sensibility with retrospective, substance assumptions. On the other hand, such a reading respects the aggregating weight of the tradition and the sacredness with which it becomes imbued. But even when we reflect on a temporally prior 'way' that is invested with the weight and authority of the tradition – the way of Confucius, for example – we must allow that our own present vantage point involves us reflexively in our interpretation and reauthorization of it, making 'Confucius' dynamic and corporate rather than simply referential and antiquarian.

We now turn from this perhaps overly abstract reflection on the more generic and cosmological sense of *dao* – 'travelling through a shared physical, social, and cultural landscape' – to a consideration of the more concrete *xiaodao* 孝道 – that is, 'the way of family reverence.' With *xiaodao* then, we encounter what is a literally a more familiar 'way' of understanding this seminal idea, *dao*, in the sense that the words 'familiy' and 'familiar' share the same root.

But before we turn to *xiao* itself, we must first clarify the nature and the significance of the institution of family within this Confucian context. The distinguished sociologist Fei Xiaotong draws a contrast between the nuclear 'family' that for anthropologists takes its major significance from being the site of reproduction, and the dominant historical pattern of premodern Chinese families as lineages of persons with the same surname (*shizu* 氏族), and by extension, as clans (*jiazu* 家族) made up of several lineages who share the same surname. While these lineages certainly have the function of reproduction, Fei insists that within the Chinese experience they serve as 'a medium through which all activities are organized' (Fei, 1992, p. 84). That is, in addition to the perpetuation of the family, lineages have complex political, economic, and religious functions that are expressed along the vertical and hierarchical axes of the father-son and mother-daughter-in-law relationships. Lineage relations are again reinforced socially and religiously through the institutions of ancestor reverence, a continuing practice that archaeology tells us dates back at least to the Neolithic Age (Keightley, 1998).

The contemporary anthropologist Yiqun Zhou marshals scholarly consensus behind her claim that premodern Chinese society was 'for several thousand years largely a polity organized by kinship principles' (Zhou, 2010, p. 19). In weighing the extent to which social order was derived from and dependent upon family relations, Zhou insists that, in contrast with the Greeks, 'the Chinese state was never conceived as a political community that equaled the sum of its citizens', and that 'the relationship between the rulers and the ruled was considered analogous to the relationship between parents and children' (Zhou, 2010, pp. 17–18n51). She cites the late Qing scholar Yan Fu who claims that imperial China from its beginnings was 'seventy percent a lineage organization and thirty percent an empire' (Zhou, 2010, p. 19n55). It is this persistent family-based socio-political organization of Chinese society that has within this antique culture, late and soon, elevated the specific family values and obligations circumscribed by the term *xiao* to serve as the governing moral imperative.

Early in the tradition, the *Analects* is explicit in registering the foundational importance of family feeling as providing the entry point and the trajectory for the Confucian project of becoming consummate human beings through personal cultivation. Indeed, *xiao* is taken metaphorically as the 'root' from which *dao* as the vision of the moral life draws its energy and takes its form:

> Exemplary persons (*junzi* 君子) concentrate their efforts on the root, for the root having set, one's vision of the moral life (*dao* 道) will emerge therefrom. As for family reverence (*xiao* 孝) and fraternal deference (*ti* 弟), these are, I suspect, the root of becoming consummate in one's conduct (*ren* 仁). (*Analects* 1.2)

The profound influence of family on personal development begins from the utter dependency of the infant upon the family relations into which it is born. It is thus important to understand that an infant is not perceived as a discrete life form, but is rather inclusive of and constituted by these same family relations. And if infancy teaches us anything, and it teaches us much, its first lesson should be the inescapably interdependent nature of human beings for their very survival. The family is conceived as the center of all personal, social, political, and ultimately, cosmic order. All meaning ripples out in concentric circles that begin from a regimen of personal cultivation within the moral space of increasingly meaningful family roles and relations. These circles extend outward through community to the most distant ends of the cosmos, and then with value added return again to inform and nourish the family as its primary source.

In the *Chinese Classic of Family Reverence*, Confucius elevates this 'way of family reverence' and declares it to be the very substance of morality and education: 'It is family reverence (*xiao*) that is the root of moral virtuosity, and whence education (*jiao*) itself is born.'[6] (Rosemont and Ames, 2009, p. 105) The opening chapter of the *Chinese Classic of Family Reverence* provides us with the familiar radial progression from a primary center that we saw above and find consistently in the Confucian literature, beginning from concern for one's own physical person as what is closest at hand, extending to care for one's family and kin, and then culminating in service to the ruler and to posterity. In this passage, King 'Culture' (*wen*) is once again singled out as the source from which the current generation draws its inspiration and to whom it makes return with the cultural dividends it has accrued.

> Your physical person with its hair and skin are received from your parents. Vigilance in not allowing anything to do injury to your person is where family reverence begins; distinguishing yourself and walking the proper way (*dao*) in the world; raising your name high for posterity and thereby bringing esteem to your father and mother – it is in these things that family reverence finds its consummation. This family reverence then begins in service to your parents, continues in service to your lord, and culminates in distinguishing yourself in the world. In the 'Greater Odes' section of the *Book of Songs* it says: 'How can you not remember your ancestor, King Wen? You must cultivate yourself and extend his excellence.'[7] (Rosemont and Ames, 2009, p. 105)

The charge in this passage to keep the body intact certainly refers to one's own physicality, but it also lends itself to a broader reading: That is, each generation has the responsibility of keeping the corpus of culture that it comes to embody whole and alive. One way of understanding the dynamics of 'family reverence' (*xiao*) as intergenerational transmission through this process of embodiment is to appeal to two cognate characters that are integral to the continuities of the family lineage: *ti* 體 ('body,' 'embodying,' 'forming and shaping') and *li* 禮 ('achieving propriety in one's roles and relations,' 'ritual') (Ames, 2011, pp. 102–14). Without the formal dimension provided in human experience by embodied

---

6 We must resist any simplistic equation between filial deference and obedience. *Xiao* that is focused on the bottom-up deference children owe their elders must be distinguished clearly from *paterfamilias*, the top-down power and privilege of the father. At times being truly filial within the family, like being a loyal minister within the court, requires courageous remonstrance (*jian* 諫) rather than automatic compliance. Such remonstrance is not perceived as merely an option, but as a sacred obligation. In the *Chinese Classic of Family Reverence* 15, Confucius responds impatiently a question by Zengzi that would reduce filial deference to simple obedience, making the case that such automatic compliance often produces immorality in conduct that is the opposite of what is intended.

7 *Songs* 235. Cf. Legge (1960):431 and Karlgren (1950b):187.

living and by the social grammar of meaningful roles and relations, there is a very real question as to whether the significant refinement achieved in and through our life forms would even be possible. As we have seen, 'the lived body' through its 'embodied living' is the site of growth in and a conveyance of the cultural corpus of knowledge – linguistic facility and proficiency, religious rituals and mythologies, the aesthetics of cooking, song, and dance, the modeling of mores and values, instruction and apprenticeship in cognitive technologies, and so on – as a continuing, intergenerational process through which a living civilization itself is perpetuated.

'Family reverence' (*xiao*) serves as the primary cultural imperative, and makes every life significant as a conduit of the living culture – the way of becoming human (*rendao* 人道). As we have seen above, even 'those of lesser quality realize some of it.' Still, the culmination of *xiao* lies with those who are able to raise their name high for posterity and in so doing bring esteem to their family lineage. It is these exemplars who in every age and who over the eons have enabled us to transcend our animality and intensify the human experience with the elegance and refinement of culture in its highest sense. And it is to the role of this elite class of consummatory literati or *ru* 儒 in perpetuating the persistent yet transforming orthodoxy of this cultural corridor – what is called the *daotong* 道統 – that we now turn.

The philosopher and teacher, Kongfuzi 孔夫子, latinized as 'Confucius,' lends his name to the English (but not the Chinese) expression of this tradition called 'Confucianism.'[8] Confucius was certainly a flesh-and-blood historical person who lived, taught, and died some twenty-five centuries ago, consolidating in his own time a formidable legacy of wisdom that has been passed down and applied through the ages to shape the character of an entire culture. In and of itself, the profoundly personal model of Confucius remembered by his protégés through those intimate snapshots of his life collected in the middle chapters of the *Analects* has its own value and meaning. But then, as Confucius reportedly said of himself, most of what he had to offer had ancient roots, and he was one who was inclined to follow the established path rather than strike out in new directions (*Analects* 7.1). Indeed it is perhaps for this reason that in the Chinese language itself the tradition is not identified specifically with the person Confucius as 'Confucianism,' but rather with the ongoing *ru* 儒 literati class who over the centuries has provided the cultural tradition with its evolving 'literati learning' (*ruxue* 儒學).

8 Tim Barrett (2005, p. 518) has identified Sir John Francis Davis (1795–1890) as the first person on record to have used the word 'Confucianism' (Davis, 1836, p. 45). See Standaert (1999, pp. 115–32) for a detailed discussion of the *ru* tradition and its interpretation as 'Confucianism' that absolves the Jesuits of this problematic equation.

The earliest occurrence of the term *ru* in the extant corpus is found in a single passage of the *Analects:*

> The Master remarked to Zixia, 'You want to become the kind of *ru* literatus who is exemplary in conduct, not the kind that is a petty person.' (*Analects* 6.13)

These *ru* are in fact, as suggested by the etymology of the character, a class of 'gentle' people that dates back at least sixty generations before Confucius to the Shang dynasty (1600–1046 BCE) and includes some eighty generations of scholars and intellectuals after Confucius's death.[9] This gentry class of intellectuals has across the ages and in different ways in different times contributed its own best thoughts to this 'literati learning' as a continuous, living tradition. In the Shang, the *ru* began in earnest to aestheticize urban life with the elaborate practices of a bronze culture that has become emblematic of an emerging Chinese culture in museums around the world. Consistent with Confucius's own premises, this scholarly legacy called *ruxue* – the always-porous core of an aggregating Chinese culture – is both vital and corporate, and what we now have come to call 'Confucianism' is in fact a shared culture that has been appropriated, commented upon, reinterpreted, elaborated further, and reauthorized in each generation. And the *ru*, far from being doctrinaire advocates of some specific dogma, at different times across the centuries reflect different values and embrace an ever evolving range of ideas and cultural practices.

I want to conclude this essay by appealing to a few of the masters of the landscape painting lineage who lived during the millennium from the Tang dynasty through to the Qing as one specific example of how *ruxue* culture has persisted while at the same time, has changed to express the evolving values of each age.

In briefly surveying the story of a truly complex genealogy of *ru*, we might begin from the oldest and best known of the Four Masters of the Yuan dynasty (1271–1368), Huang Gongwang (1269–1354) who is preeminent in the long history of Chinese painting. Huang was a highly respected intellectual whose construction of the Temple of the Three Doctrines (*sanjiaotang*) reflects an ecumenical philosophical attitude that accommodates Confucianism, Daoism, and Buddhism. Huang in his brushwork is much influenced by and builds upon the Dong-Ju school of the Tang dynasty that includes works by Dong Yuan (ca. 900–962) and his student Juran (fl. 975–993). Indeed, one of his most famous paintings is entitled 'Summer Mountains after Dong Yuan'.

But Huang Gongwang not only inherits, reauthorizes, and passes on the style of painting from the generations that came before him, he in turn inspires the ages that follow. The great, late Ming dynasty (1368–1644) painter and theorist

9 The character *ru* 儒 is cognate with *ru* 需 'supple', 臑 'pliant, soft', 孺 'child, weak, mild'.

Dong Qichong (1555–1636), for example, is a prominent advocate of the expressive literati style of the Yuan Masters with works such as 'Landscape After Huang Gongwang' (Eichman, 2011, p. 63). But Dong is not only indebted to Huang Gongwang in his painting, but also remembers in his work the Tang and Song dynasty precursors of Huang with 'Landscape After Dong Yuan and Fan Kuan' (Eichman, 2011, p. 65).

Not unexpectedly, Dong Qichong's students follow their teacher in their admiration of Huang Gongwang with Wang Shimin (1592–1680), one of the Four Wangs of the Qing dynasty (1644–1911), painting his 'Landscape in the Style of Huang Gongwang', and a second Wang Yuanqi (1642–1715) painting his 'Landscape in the Manner of Ni Zan (1301–1374, another Yuan Master and a close friend of Huang) and Huang Gongwang,' with Wang Shimin's 'Landscape After Ni Zan' (Eichman, 2011, p. 79) continuing the lineage. And then there is the third Wang Jian's (1598–1677) 'After Huang Gongwang's "Secret Forest"' (Eichman, 2011, p. 91).

But then as the teacher of the Four Wangs, as Dong Qichong himself rises to real prominence, he too becomes included as a source of this aggregating influence with Wang Yuanqi's 'Color Landscape after Dong Qichong's Interpretation of Huang Gongwang 1710'. As is clear from this remarkable genealogy, the living tradition is transmitted in the body of work produced by each generation, allowing for those who have come before to live on in the new oeuvre and to continue to inspire those yet to come.

And we must ask: What was the meaning and function of these works of art in a world that for the most part included amateurs (in both senses) rather than professionals, and that did not have galleries or museums for public display? These works are narrative paintings and handscrolls that take us on an episodic, interactive, cultural journey as we walk through the paintings themselves. And at another level, these works recall the eventful lives of the literati artists who belonged to a particular place and to their own lineage of artists, friends, and colleagues. But as these works were passed on from hand to hand in their transmission, they were always available to later generations of connoisseurs not only to be remarked upon and enjoyed, but to be further enhanced by adding their own chops, poems, calligraphy, and colophons that conduced to refinement and 're-creation' for their own time and place.

References

Ames, R.T. (2011), *Confucian Role Ethics: A Vocabulary.* Hong Kong and Honolulu: Chinese University Press and University of Hawai'i Press.

Ames, R.T. and Rosemont, H. Jr. (trans.) (1998), *The Analects of Confucius: A Philosophical Translation.* New York: Ballantine.

Ames, R.T. and Hall, D.L. (trans.) (2003), *Daodejing: 'Making This Life Significant' – A Philosophical Translation.* New York: Ballantine.

Barrett, T. (2005), 'Chinese Religion in English Guise: The History of an Illusion'. *Modern Asian Studies*, 39.3, 509–33.

Davis, Sir James F. (1836), *The Chinese: A General Description of the Empire of China and its Inhabitants*, Volume II. London: Charles Knight & Co.

Eichman, Shawn, et al. (2011). *Masterpieces of Landscape Painting from the Forbidden City.* Honolulu: Honolulu Academy of Arts.

Emerson, R.W. (1862), 'American Civilization'. *Atlantic Monthly*, 9, 502–11.

Emmet, D. (1966), *Rules, Roles and Relations.* London: Macmillan.

Fei, Xiaotong. (1992), *From the Soil: The Foundations of Chinese Society.* A translation of *Xiangtu Zhongguo* 鄉土中國 by Gary G. Hamilton and Wang Zheng. Berkeley: University of California Press.

Keightley, David N. (1998), 'Shamanism, Death, and the Ancestors: Religious Mediation in Neolithic and Shang China, ca. 5000–1000 B.C.' *Asiatische Studien*, 52, 763–828.

May, L. (1992), *Sharing Responsibility.* Chicago: University of Chicago Press.

Rosemont, H. Jr., and Ames, R.T. (trans.) (2009), *The Chinese Classic of Family Reverence: A Philosophical Translation of the Xiaojing.* Honolulu: University of Hawai'i Press.

Smiley, M. (1992). *Moral Responsibility and the Boundaries of Community.* Chicago: University of Chicago Press.

Standaert, N. (1999). 'The Jesuits did NOT Manufacture "Confucianism"'. *East Asian Science, Technology and Medicine*, 16, 115–32.

Taylor, C. (1989), *Sources of the Self: The Making of the Modern Identity.* Cambridge: Harvard University Press.

Zhou, Yiqun. (2010), *Festival, Feasts, and Gender Relations in Ancient China and Greece.* New York: Cambridge University Press.

Epilogue

It is the best of times and it is the worst of times. In the beginning decades of the twenty-first century, exponential scientific and technological innovations have given human beings the opportunity to live lives of extraordinary duration, comfort and convenience. At least for most people in the developed world, we live longer and we live better than ever before, and it gets even better with every passing day. As a species, we now have the science to clean the water and produce the food so that no child on the planet need go to bed sick or hungry. If only we had the social intelligence and the political will, we could in our time be embarking upon an epoch of increasing peace and prosperity.

At the same time, we are living in a moment of increasing urgency. The darkness of a perfect storm of global proportions is gathering on the horizon that will immanently threaten our familiar ways of living if not ultimately the very survival of humanity as a species. Ours is a world beset by climate change, by extreme weather events, by an ever accelerating increase in population, by gross income inequities, by food and water shortages, by environmental degradation, by looming pandemics, by energy shortage, by international terrorism, by nuclear proliferation, by consumer waste, and by growing legions of the hopeless poor and dispossessed. Perhaps the most disturbing element in the overall picture is the nearly vertical trajectory in the galloping pace of precipitous negative change as it approaches a tipping point that takes us past any possibility of return.

We are facing a largely human-precipitated predicament that can only be engaged wholesale by a world community acting in concert. This increasingly dire situation can only be addressed and arrested by effecting a global-scale radical change in human intentions, values, and practices. And to our shame perhaps our best hope is it will be necessity itself rather than any enlightened awareness on the part of the human community that will serve as the imperative for change.

While this perfect storm has been gathering both globally and locally, over just one generation, the rise of Asia, and particularly of China, has precipitated a sea change in the prevailing economic and political order. Development generally and the global impact of China's own growth more specifically, are producing a range of changing economic and political patterns that are relatively easy to track. But what about cultural change? What difference does this dramatic reconfiguration of economic and political dominance make for an elite world cultural order that has long been dominated by a powerful liberalism? And what will be the role of traditional Chinese customs and values in the evolution of a newly emerging cultural order?

Within China, we have over the past decades witnessed a dramatic rise of "Schools of Canonical Learning" across college campuses. And internationally at the best institutions of higher learning across America and the globe we have seen the proliferation of now more than four hundred and fifty Chinese government-funded "Confucius Institutes" that are committed to promoting literacy on traditional Chinese culture. It is clear that Chinese culture is being actively promoted both domestically and internationally by a collaboration of academic and political forces within China itself. What does Chinese culture have on offer for a changing world cultural order?

This is the question that has motivated much of our work. And our answer has been that it offers a different vision, and thus answer, to the question of what it means to be human. *What* is a human "being"? This was a perennial Greek question asked in Plato's *Phaedo* and Aristotle's *De Anima*. And perhaps the most persistent answer from the time of Pythagoras was an ontological one: The "being" of a human being is a permanent, ready-made, and self-sufficient soul. And "know thyself" – the signature exhortation of Socrates – is to know this soul. Each of us *is* a person, and from conception, has the integrity of *being* a person.

In what way does a person as a human "becoming" *become* consummately human? This then was the perennial Confucian question asked explicitly in all of the *Four Books:* in *the Great Learning*, in the *Analects of Confucius*, in the *Mencius*, and again in the *Zhongyong*. And the answer from the time of Confucius was a moral, aesthetic, and ultimately religious one. One *becomes* human by cultivating those thick, intrinsic roles and relations that constitute one's initial conditions and that locate the trajectory of one's life force within family, community, and cosmos. "Cultivate your person" – the signature exhortation of the Confucian canons – is the ground of the Confucian project of becoming consummate as a person. In this Confucian tradition, we need each other. If there is only one person, there are no persons.

That we are all social creatures, strongly influenced by the others with whom we interact, has been acknowledged broadly by philosophers and many others on all sides. But within our classical and modern discourses, there are reasons why this social dimension has been marginalized and rarely seen as being of the essence of our humanity at the moral and political (and ontological) level. On this view, our social selves cannot be of compelling worth because our concrete circumstances are in an important sense accidental in that we have exercised no control over them – that is, we are not responsible for who our parents are, the native languages we speak, our ethnicity, and so forth. Consequently, what does give human beings their primary worth, their dignity, their integrity and their value – and what must command the respect of all – is their ability to act purposively and to exercise their capacity for self-determination, that is, their *autonomy.* And of course, in order for human beings to be truly autonomous, they must neither be coerced nor governed by instinct or passion. That is, they must be *free* and *rational* in the choices that they make.

Confucianism has a "focus-field," narrative conception of person that provides a robust alternative to this liberal individualism. Confucian role ethics has a holistic vision of the moral life grounded in and responsible to our empirical experience. The starting point is simple. In Confucian role ethics, association is a fact. We do not live our lives inside our skins. Everything we do – physically, psychologically, socially – is resolutely transactional and collaborative. Within the interpretive framework of Confucian philosophy, associated, interpersonal living is taken to be an uncontested, empirical fact. Every person lives and every event takes place within a vital natural, social, and cultural context. Confucian role ethics appeals to specific roles for stipulating the specific forms that association take within lives lived in family and community – that is, the various roles we live as sons and teachers, grandmothers and neighbors. For Confucianism, not only are these roles descriptive of our associations, but they are also prescriptive in the sense that roles in family and community are themselves normative, guiding us in the direction of appropriate conduct. Whereas mere association is a given, flourishing families and communities are what we are able to make of this condition as the highest human achievement.

While certainly having important theoretical implications (see below), the enduring power of this Confucian project is that it proceeds from a relatively straightforward account of the actual human experience. It is a pragmatic naturalism in the sense that, rather than relying upon metaphysical presuppositions or supernatural speculations, it focuses instead on the possibilities for enhancing personal worth available to us here and now through enchanting the ordinary affairs of the day. A grandmother's love for her grandchild is at once the most ordinary of things, and the most extraordinary of things.

When we look for the cultural resources necessary to respond to the global and national predicament described above as a perfect storm, we might anticipate the need for a shift in values, intentions, and practices that takes us from the preponderance of conflicts among self-interested, single actors – who view the "social contract" only narrowly and legalistically – to a pattern of collaboration achieved through the strengthening of relationships within families, communities, corporations, and polities necessary to overcome what are the shared problems of our day.

Many of the ideas discussed in these essays have been developed further in the two volumes we have written separately: Ames's *Confucian Roles Ethics: A Vocabulary*, and Rosemont's *Against Individualism: A Confucian Rethinking of the Foundations of Morality, Politics, Family & Religion.* In those works and these essays that precede them, we believe we have made at least an initial case for 1) early Confucianism being best interpreted as a morality grounded in roles, 2) the ongoing relevance of this role ethics in thinking about solutions to many of today's problems, and 3) seeing the Confucian persuasion in religious and spiritual terms as a human-centered rather than God-centered religiousness.

But we have only begun to explore the manifold of implications of moving from a vision of human beings as autonomous individuals with some identifiable and unchanging essence, to seeing ourselves as well as our fellows as relationally constituted. Indeed, when all of the others with whom we interact in our role relationships have been uniquely identified, so have we. Said another way, apart from the "we" of our role relations, there is no essential "I" to be seen in isolation. This latter "seeing" involves making a gestalt shift that requires us to shift much else in our thinking and living as well. And we hope that our fellow philosophers and others with some sympathy for our claims will begin exploring these implications. Seeing humans more as "becoming" then "being" – that is, always changing and altogether interrelated, for example – must needs require rethinking many of the dichotomies it have become almost second nature for us in describing and evaluating ourselves and our fellow humans: mind/matter; appearance/reality; subject/object; cognitive/affective; essential/contingent, agent/action, mind/body, inner/outer, and so on.

More directly with respect to the three areas on which we have focused herein and have developed in our monographs, even if our arguments can be sustained there still remains a great deal of work yet to be done. On the first issue of whether role ethics is the best reading of Confucius, for example, there are numerous problems and questions we have yet to address:. Can Mencius or Xunzi or Zisi be said to embrace role ethics more fully than the Master? With respect to hierarchy, is benefactor and beneficiary the least misleading of the possible renderings of *shangxia* 上下? Can there be genuinely conflicting situations involving roles in the *Lunyu?* Given the shared process cosmology, what would it mean to invoke a Daoist role ethics? To what extent is a role ethics orientation a possible interpretation for Song and Ming Neo-Confucian texts? And many more.

On the second issue of relevance to pressing issues of the day, a family-based culture will surely call for a somewhat different political dynamic than one grounded in the discrete individual. Indeed, Ian Sullivan in his further development of Confucian role ethics in rejecting the familiar public/private dichotomy is extending the language of "role ethics" to "role politics." How might a family orientation incline us to move from a largely representative to a more direct form of democracy? How would the responsibilities and functions of governance be different? How might we accommodate larger, intergenerational families in the ineluctible growth of mega-cities? What changes would be needed to insure adequate production and distribution of goods? And again, much more.

An equal number of interesting and important concerns, ripe for investigation, are linked to the third issue we have taken up, but with much remaining work to be done: that is, the religious and spiritual dimension of Confucian role ethics: Might atheists achieve genuine religious experiences in the sense of being different from but not less than the types of experience frequently reported by the faithful? Would a religiously oriented Confucianism suggests a model of authentic religiousness that could be of signal importance today because it would not require any "theological" or supernatural beliefs that offend against good science?

We are continuing to address such issues ourselves, and look forward to having others join us in exploring the possibilities of the paradigm shift in moral philosophy toward an ethics of roles that was first suggested, we believe, some twenty-five centuries ago, and far away.

Acknowledgments

We would like to acknowledge the kind permission of the editors and publishers of the following essays to reprint them in the present volume:

1. Henry Rosemont, Jr. (1991). "Rights-bearing Individuals and Role-bearing Persons." In *Rules, Rituals, and Responsibility: Essays Dedicated to Herbert Fingarette*. Edited by Mary I. Bockover. La Salle, IL: Open Court.
2. "Family Reverence (*xiao* 孝) in the *Analects:* Confucian Role Ethics and the Dynamics of Intergenerational Transmission" (2014). *Dao Companion to the Analects*. Edited by Amy Olberding. Springer Publishing.
3. "From Kupperman's Character Ethics to Confucian Role Ethics: Putting Humpty Together Again" (2014). In *Moral Cultivation and Confucian Character: Engaging Joel J. Kupperman*. Edited by Li Chenyang and Ni Peimin. Albany: State University of New York Press.
4. "Were the Early Confucians Virtuous?" (2011). In *Ethics in Early China: An Anthology*. Edited by C. Fraser, D. Robbins, and T. O'Leary. Hong Kong: Hong Kong University Press.
5. "Interpretation and Translation" (2010). In *Eastwards: Western Views on East Asian Culture*. Kraushaar, Frank (ed.) Bern: Peter Lang.
6. "Family Reverence (*xiao*) as the Source of Consummatory Conduct (*ren*)" (Spring 2008). *Dao: A Journal of Comparative Philosophy* Vol VII No 1.
7. Rosemont. "Travelling through Time with Family and Culture: Confucian Meditations" In *Landscape and Travelling East and West: A Philosophical Journey*. Edited by Hans-Georg Moeller and Andrew Whitehead. Bloomsbury Academic (formerly Continuum).
8. Ames. "Travelling Together with *Gravitas:* The Intergenerational Transmission of Confucian Culture" (2014). In *Landscape and Travelling East and West: A Philosophical Journey*. Edited by Hans-Georg Moeller and Andrew Whitehead. Bloomsbury Academic (formerly Continuum).